Archaeology and Anthropology

RH

ASA Monographs

ISSN 0066-9679

The Relevance of Models for Social Anthropology, ed M. Banton
Political Systems and the Distribution of Power, ed M. Banton
Anthropological Approaches to the Study of Religion, ed M. Banton
The Social Anthropology of Complex Societies, ed M. Banton
The Structural Study of Myth and Totemism, ed E R. Leach
Themes in Economic Anthropology, ed R. Firth
History and Social Anthropology, ed I M. Lewis
Socialization: The Approach from Social Anthropology, ed P. Mayer
Witchcraft Confessions and Accusations, ed M. Douglas
Social Anthropology and Language, ed E. Ardener
Rethinking Kinship and Marriage, ed R. Needham
Urban Ethnicity, ed A. Cohen
Social Anthropology and Medicine, ed J B. Loudon
Social Anthropology and Law, ed I. Hamnett
The Anthropology of the Body, ed J. Blacking
Regional Cults, ed R P. Werbner
Sex and Age as Principles of Social Differentiation, ed J. La Fontaine
Social and Ecological Systems, ed P C Burnham and R F. Ellen
Social Anthropology of Work, ed S. Wallman
The Structure of Folk Models, ed L. Holy and L. Stuchlik
Religious Organization and Religious Experience, ed J. Davis
Semantic Anthropology, ed D. Parkin
Social Anthropology and Development Policy, ed R. Grillo and A. Rew
Reason and Morality, ed J. Overing
Anthropology at Home, ed A. Jackson
Migrants, Workers, and the Social Order, ed J S. Eades
History and Ethnicity, ed E. Tonkin, M. McDonald and M. Chapman
Anthropology and the Riddle of the Sphinx: Paradox and Change in the Life Course, ed P. Spencer
Anthropology and Autobiography, ed J. Okely and H. Callaway
Contemporary Futures: Perspectives from Social Anthropology, ed S. Wallman
Socialism: Ideals, Ideologies and Local Practice, ed C M. Hann
Environmentalism: The View from Anthropology, ed K. Milton
Questions of Consciousness, eds A P. Cohen and N. Rapport
After Writing Culture: Epistemology and Praxis in Contemporary Anthropology, eds A. James, A. Dawson and J. Hockey
Ritual, Performance, Media, ed F. Hughes-Freeland
The Anthropology of Power, ed A. Cheater
An Anthropology of Indirect Communication, ed J. Hendry and C W. Watson
Elite Cultures, ed C. Shore and S. Nugent
Participating in Development, ed P. Sillitoe, A. Bicker and J. Pottier
Human Rights in Global Perspective, ed R A. Wilson and J P. Mitchell
The Qualities of Time, ed W. James and D. Mills
Locating the Field: Space, Place and Context in Anthropology, ed S. Coleman and P. Collins
Anthropology and Science: Epistemologies in Practice, ed J. Edwards, P. Harvey and P. Wade
Creativity and Cultural Improvisation, ed E. Hallam and T. Ingold
Anthropology and the New Cosmopolitanism: Rooted, Feminist and Vernacular Perspectives, ed P. Werbner
Thinking Through Tourism, ed J. Scott and T. Selwyn
Ownership and Appropriation, ed V. Strang and M. Busse

Archaeology and Anthropology
Past, Present and Future

Edited by
David Shankland

B L O O M S B U R Y
LONDON • NEW DELHI • NEW YORK • SYDNEY

Bloomsbury Academic
An imprint of Bloomsbury Publishing Plc

50 Bedford Square
London

1385 Broadway
New York
NY 10018
USA

www.bloomsbury.com

First published in 2012 by Berg
Reprinted by Bloomsbury Academic 2013

British Library Cataloguing-in-Publication Data
A catalogue record for this book is available from the British Library.

ISBN: HB: 978-1-8478-8966-9
PB: 978-1-8478-8965-2

Library of Congress Cataloging-in-Publication Data
A catalog record for this book is available from the Library of Congress.

Archaeology and anthropology: past, present and future/edited by
David Shankland.
p. cm. – (ASA monographs)
Includes bibliographical references and index.
ISBN 978-0-8578-5419-3 (alk. paper) – ISBN 978-1-8478-8965-2 (alk. paper) –
ISBN 978-1-8478-8967-6 (alk. paper) – ISBN 978-1-8478-8966-9 (alk. paper)
1. Ethnoarchaeology. 2. Social archaeology. 3. Anthropology.
I. Shankland, David.
CC79.E85A748 2012
301–dc23   2012005580

Typeset by Apex CoVantage, LLC, Madison, WI, USA
Printed and bound in Great Britain

To my son, Robert Shankland

Contents

Acknowledgments

The conference from which this volume is derived took place at the University of Bristol, April 6–9, 2009. I would like to thank the vice-chancellor, Professor Eric Thomas, and the dean of arts, Professor Charles Martindale, for their kindness in facilitating this event. I should like to thank also the Wenner-Gren Foundation for their generous sponsorship. The Wenner-Gren's continuing funding of anthropology across the world is as admirable as it is indispensable. The conference was ably assisted by NomadIT, who maintain the conference's full program on the Association of Social Anthropologists' (ASA) website at http://www.theasa.org/conferences/asa09/. Finally, I would like to thank my colleagues in the Department of Archaeology and Anthropology, whose cordial assistance made the conference a delightful three days.

List of Figures

Notes on Contributors

Paola Filippucci is Lecturer in Social Anthropology at Murray Edwards College, Cambridge. Her research interests include war remembrance, social memory, and the cultural construction of the past. She is currently working on a monograph, provisionally entitled *Au Pays des Ruines: War, space and place in eastern France*.

Joost Fontein is Lecturer in Social Anthropology at Edinburgh University. His various research projects explore the political materialities of memory, landscape, water, and human remains in Zimbabwe. His first book *The silence of great Zimbabwe: Contested landscapes and the power of heritage*, was published by UCL Press in 2006.

Nick Hanks is currently researching the use of space in different modes of ritual, and is a member of the Contemporary Paganism and Alternative Spiritualities in Europe (CPASE) research group. He works for English Heritage, and studied Historical Archaeology at Bristol University and Theatre Studies at Warwick University.

Chris Hann is a founding director and head of the department "Resilience and Transformation in Eurasia" at the Max Planck Institute for Social Anthropology, Halle (Saale). His main interests are in economic and political anthropology, with particular reference to socialism and the long-term history of Eurasia. Recent publications include *Economic anthropology: History, ethnography, critique* (Polity Press, 2011, with Keith Hart).

John Harries is a teaching fellow with Social Anthropology and Health in Social Science, at Edinburgh University. His research interests include landscape, materiality, memory, and the presence of the past. He has recently finished researching a monograph, *Beothuk ghosts*, on remembering the Beothuk, an extinct native people.

Michael Herzfeld is Professor of Anthropology at Harvard University, and has authored ten books, including *A place in history* (1991), *Cultural intimacy* (1997), *The body impolitic* (2004), and *Evicted from eternity* (2009), and has produced two ethnographic films about Rome. His research in Greece, Italy, and Thailand addresses heritage and gentrification, nationalism, and the ethnography of knowledge.

Ian Hodder was trained at the Institute of Archaeology, UCL and at Cambridge University. After briefly teaching at Leeds, he returned to Cambridge where he became Professor of Archaeology and a Fellow of the British Academy. In 1999 he moved to Stanford University as Dunlevie Family Professor in the Anthropology Department.

Tim Ingold is Professor of Social Anthropology at Aberdeen University. He has carried out ethnographic fieldwork in Lapland, and has written widely, including on the circumpolar North, on evolutionary theory, human–animal relations, language and tool use, and environmental perception and skilled practice. His latest book, *Being alive*, was published in 2011.

Richard D. G. Irvine lectures in the Division of Social Anthropology, University of Cambridge, where he received his PhD for a study of contemporary Catholic English Benedictine monasticism. His research focuses on the anthropology of Britain, with a particular interest in the role of religion in social life. He is currently exploring the moral dimensions of land use and environmental change in East Anglia.

Rosemary A. Joyce, Professor of Anthropology at the University of California, Berkeley, has conducted archaeological fieldwork in Honduras since 1977. She currently is writing about origins of museum collecting. Her books include *Gender and power in pre-Hispanic Mesoamerica*; *The languages of archaeology*; *Embodied lives*; and *Ancient bodies, ancient lives*.

Cara Krmpotich is Assistant Professor of Museum Studies, University of Toronto. Her research interests include repatriation, memory and material culture, and museum and source community relations. She is currently working on two books and has published in the *Journal of Material Culture and Mortality* and *Museum Management and Curatorship*.

Lynn Meskell was educated at Sydney University, then at Cambridge. She is Professor of Anthropology at Stanford University (United States). Her fieldwork has been conducted in South Africa, Egypt, Turkey, Sicily, Cyprus, Greece, Australia, and the Pacific. Her most recent book is entitled *The nature of heritage: The new South Africa* (Blackwells, 2011).

David Shankland is Director of the Royal Anthropological Institute, and Reader in Anthropology at the University of Bristol. He is a former Assistant/Acting Director of the British Institute of Archaeology at Ankara.

Paul Sillitoe is Professor of Anthropology at Durham University and Shell Chair of Sustainable Development at Qatar University. His current research interests focus on tribal political economies and local natural resource management strategies. His most recent book is *From land to mouth: The agricultural "economy" of the Wola of the New Guinea Highlands*.

Stella Souvatzi is an adjunct lecturer, Open Universities of Cyprus and Greece. Her research is concerned with the Neolithic of Greece and the eastern Mediterranean, and with the theory of archaeology and anthropology. She is the author of *A social archaeology of households in Neolithic Greece, an anthropological approach*.

Julian Thomas is Professor of Archaeology at Manchester University. His research is concerned with the Neolithic of Britain and Europe, the theory and philosophy of archaeology, and the relationship between archaeology and anthropology. His publications include *Time, culture and identity* (1996), *Understanding the Neolithic* (1999), and *Archaeology and modernity* (2004).

Candace Weddle received her PhD from the University of Southern California and now works as an independent art historian and archaeologist. She has carried out research in Italy, Romania, and Turkey, including a season as a member of the Austrian Archaeological Institute's team excavating the "Temple of Domitian" in Ephesos. Her current primary research interest is the sensory experience of Greco-Roman sacrifice.

Introduction: Archaeology and Anthropology: Divorce and Partial Reconciliation

David Shankland

Once upon a time, social anthropology and archaeology in the United Kingdom divorced. It is commonly remarked that these days archaeology has begun to welcome social anthropology back into the fold. This is true, as the remarkable essays in *Ethnographies of Archaeological Practice*, among many others, illustrate (Edgeworth 2006). However, in spite of the partial reconciliation, there is still a rift. This may be seen in a number of ways. The respective methodologies employed by social anthropology and archaeology, their approaches to data, teaching, and dissemination, are all markedly different. The disciplines still maintain their professional and associational existences largely, though not entirely, in isolation from one another.

It is important to stress the difference at the outset. Any attempt to say that the separation is *only* based on prejudice is quite mistaken. Of course stereotyping may play a part in all human interaction, and relations between archaeology and anthropology are no exception to this rule. I have heard unnecessarily strong skepticism expressed by practitioners of both disciplines about each other. I have myself experienced caustic responses occasionally, particularly when planning modest attempts to look at the fields in tandem. Nevertheless, the divorce is not simply the product of a negative emotional reaction between two otherwise similar parties. The study of how they may differ helps us to understand the intellectual foundations of both subjects and highlights in what way bringing them together again may spark off a creative response. Gosden, for example, has published a thoughtful monograph on this theme (1999), while Hodder has long written on this topic (1982) and in this volume, too, explores key aspects of overlap that may be particularly stimulating to examine in the light of recent developments.

If there is, then, a separation based on genuine differences (however creative these may be) and not only mutual prejudice, when did these come about? Some level of fusion under the general name "anthropology" looks entirely normal at the end of the nineteenth century, when it was routine for those interested in archaeology to be interested in ethnography, and vice versa. One could, for instance, draw on the archaeologists and classicists in the Balkans working from the British School at

Athens. Wace, though an archaeologist, wrote with Thompson a work on the Vlachs that is still of importance (Wace and Thompson 1914). Hasluck, whom we look at in more detail later on, wrote extensively on the overlap between Christianity and Islam and on the Bektashis (Hasluck 1929). Anthropologists in their turn were often at home with archaeology. Just before the Great War, the Oxford anthropologist Marett, now unfairly neglected, simply conceived no difference at all between any field of anthropology, writing a beautifully coherent account of a four-field approach in his book entitled *Anthropology*, published in 1911 and frequently reprinted thereafter.

Yet by the second half of the twentieth century, it was equally usual that a text-book in social anthropology made no mention of archaeology at all. Lienhardt's erudite *Social Anthropology* (1964), for instance, which replaces Marett's, has excised the subject almost entirely. The excellent *Social Anthropology in Perspective* by I. M. Lewis (1976), rightly deserving its high reputation and perhaps in retrospect written at the apogee of social anthropology, is entirely bereft of archaeology. I say this not at all to belittle works from which I have gained great profit and pleasure: it is simply the case that archaeology did not strike the authors or publishers as being relevant at that time. Likewise, by the end of the twentieth century, social anthropology curricula typically made no attempt to teach archaeology. Even at Cambridge, where undergraduates have until now been taught together in the "Arch and Anth" Faculty in their first year, they appear to separate as quickly as possible into their constituent disciplines thereafter.

Between these two points, when and how did the breakup come about? Was it gradual or sudden? Hann in this volume rightly cautions against using the word *revolution*, noting that it may obscure as much as it may illuminate. To take the title of the Goody (1995) work on the Malinowskian epoch, *Expansive Moment* is perhaps a reasonable substitute, permitting us to see what may have coalesced from any earlier anticipatory movements but without denying them. Indeed, something does appear to have crystallized through that Malinowskian moment. After it, skepticism as to the importance of archaeology to anthropology can be found explicitly. Before it, debate appears to be subordinate to those who would prefer unity between fields, as examination of the archives helps to show (Kuklick 1991; see also Stocking 1999).

Of the different Malinowskian impulses that came to shape social anthropology and contribute toward the separation, one of the clearest is the contrast between a single person and a team. There is no overriding reason why the lone fieldworker model should have become an idée fixe of the social anthropology movement. That it became so is indisputable, but it did not *have* to. The Haddon expedition to the Torres Straits, with its multiple fields of interest and team researchers, was widely held to be a success at the time (Herle and Rouse 1998). It could easily have been replicated, and improved on, regularly throughout the subsequent century. As a matter of course, expeditions of social anthropology could have been devised with specialists, team leaders, data gatherers, data recorders, and analysts. It is true that there may have been, and no doubt still are today, certain circumstances wherein a team could work only with the greatest of difficulty, but the vast proportion of research, if planned and executed properly, could, I suggest, be team based. It is a different kind of field project, one that has its own dynamic and culture, and indeed its own problems and challenges, but there is absolutely nothing that would prevent by definition teamwork from becoming a standard for the discipline, and prevent it from looking at a host of diverse intellectual questions appropriate to social anthropology. There are certain obvious times, the Great Depression, for example, or the period of the economic recession in the early 1990s in Britain, when it would have looked difficult to raise the funding for many such or very large teams, but archaeologists suffer from precisely the same economic cycles and have learned to expand and contract with them.

Single-researcher anthropological fieldwork did, however, become the norm, and arguably helped the discipline's romantic image at that time, a romance that is still not entirely dissipated. It reflected, too, a philosophical change. Moving toward the single-researcher model facilitated an epistemological transformation that implied that the source of human knowledge comes from the person, not from books. This meant that acquisition of the local language could lead to the fount of knowledge through direct communication with people. Contrariwise, it was no longer necessary to achieve fluency in the high culture of that society: its written records or work written about it, its bureaucracy and administration, its politely arrayed ranks, its architecture, drawing rooms, diplomats, and international statesmen. At a stroke, the whole of the apparatus of centuries of learning about other societies could be put to one side with relief: it simply was no longer necessary to be traditionally learned in order to qualify as an intellectual. Thus, without necessarily doing so consciously, this model of social anthropology had rediscovered the old contrast in monotheistic religions between the lone mystic reaching into the heart of the person to find true knowledge and the teams of scholars agonizing over their superficial rules and texts. Their great feat is that they brought this mystical method, suitably refashioned, into academia and gained acceptance with it.

The orientation of the two disciplines toward time is a third great difference between them, and though in some ways the best known (e.g., Gellner 1995), it nevertheless needs to be rehearsed, because it is so absolutely key to the diverse paths that they have taken. A useful way to conceive this difference is in terms of the causal relationship between the present and the past, for they are precisely opposed. To begin with social anthropology, in the aftermath of the Malinowskian moment (even if his own individual input into this may be debated), an idea coalesced within social anthropology that the past no longer held a causal hold over the future: that, rather, the past could be continuously reinterpreted, rewritten, and reimposed by those who held sway at any given time. It may be said immediately that this idea is neither completely original nor confined to anthropology: George Orwell's *1984* sketched out precisely how this might be done, after all. What was so remarkable was that an idea that may have occurred independently to several thinkers became ensconced absolutely at the heart of a whole movement. Individual anthropologists might have varied in the way that they interpreted or even needed to articulate this approach, but so long as this emphasis on the present was maintained, even if unwritten, this did not necessarily matter. For example, the prescription "the social must be explained by the social" borrowed from Durkheim sometimes was used as a device in the teaching of social anthropology. This at once had the effect of excluding other approaches (e.g., those that sought a psychological explanation for social behavior as Seligman might have) and also impeded any attempt by history, chronology, or indeed geographical determinism to creep in. The present, with its endless recreating of the social "now," became the context through which all needed to be approached. This helps to explain the use of the phrase *ethnographic present* when writing or discussing fieldwork; more than just a tic, as has sometimes been claimed, it actually neatly encapsulated a whole epistemology.

Archaeology, over a slightly longer time frame, moved in exactly the opposite direction (for a good introduction, see Trigger 2006). For just as anthropology was perfecting the idea that ethnography gathered by a single proponent was the ideal way to gather information about this shifting "now," archaeology was beginning to fine-tune its methodology through the instigation of stratigraphic excavation, which at once facilitated and legitimized the meticulous sifting of data in its temporal context. This inculcation of endless pains in placing all conceivable material evidence in exact relation to all other evidence within a chronological sequence fitted within an archaeological movement that already saw its prime task as to identify the unfolding of human civilizations or societies over time. It facilitated, in turn, the identification of whole cultures with one aspect of their technical attributes, the consequences of which Joyce discusses in this volume. It also demanded an almost infinite expansion of archaeological teams at excavations, because the better the excavation, the more data; the more data, the more they can be analyzed and the more people are necessary to sift, assemble, preserve, and ultimately write about it. In each case, the epistemology suits the practice: social anthropology, regarding the lone researcher as the fount of all knowledge, concentrated ever more intensely on the individual experience of fieldwork; archaeology, exteriorizing the process of discovery, became ever more practiced at handling huge amounts of data.

Archaeology and anthropology, then, did not just divorce. They separated into different lifestyles, which were epistemologically, methodologically, and practically separate. Though both were, in theory, interested in the world's peoples in global perspective, they even divided geographically. The great archaeological excavations in the classical heartlands of Greece, Anatolia, and the southern Mediterranean continued almost unabated throughout the twentieth century, stopping only for war. This has resulted in some projects lasting almost unbroken for 100 years or more, generations of excavators succeeding each other in turn. In contrast, anthropology—even if it has notable subspecialisms in Oceania and India—could hardly be conceived without a thorough knowledge of sub-Saharan Africa, so that generations of social anthropologists who had not been to that country nevertheless developed what felt like an intimate knowledge of its societies. The early work of Herzfeld in Greece (1987), who in this volume outlines his equally fascinating later researches in Thailand and Rome, famously helped to draw attention to this dichotomy.

It is not surprising, then, that the two sides largely ceased to work with one another. Leach, who enjoyed stating things as clearly as possible, wrote the following as an afterword to an early effort by Spriggs (1977) to bring both sides together (one that included younger academics who were later to become distinguished in their respective fields, including Robert Chapman, Ian Hodder, Roy Ellen, and John Gledhill):

> The conference purported to be concerned with the relations between archaeology and social anthropology. In their different ways the various authors all end up by saying that not only does no such relationship exist but that they find it very difficult to envisage how any practically useful cross-examination might develop in the future. Platitudes apart, the implications seem to be wholly negative. (Leach 1977, 161)

Leach's public declaration of mutual antipathy was hardly helpful, as Thomas discusses in more detail in his most insightful contribution to this volume (see also Garrow and Yarrow 2010). Yet I would argue that there was in addition a process of *internal* dialogue that helped the two sides to remain distinct and, as it were, pure of each other. Thus, Leach's pouring cold water on those tentative efforts to bring the two sides together was only the most public, and prominent, form of dissent. In social anthropology, we can see this in the Association of Social Anthropologists (ASA), whose very founding was aimed at distinguishing its members from the earlier, more universal approaches that were current until then. It is striking that even the 2003–2004 *Directory of Members* of the ASA contains *not a single* full member whose self-categorization includes any mention of interest in archaeology (ASA 2003, 1–125). The word *archaeology* is simply banished: not by any formal ruling but by a kind of informal self-cleansing of the recent past from the collective self-representation. It is perhaps this, as much as anything else, that prompted Ingold's regretful comment in *Man*: "The history of anthropology in the twentieth century has been one in which these components of the discipline, once combined in nineteenth-century evolutionism, have drifted ever further apart" (1992, 694), ideas that he returns to in his chapter here.

Archaeology in turn, though, did not always find it easy to empathize with the aims of social anthropology. Where what might be called "proto-Malinowski" ideas did emerge from within archaeology, they appear not to have taken root. In other words, diverging approaches or conclusions by individual researchers did not necessarily alter established disciplinary practices. This strikingly Kuhnian pattern, whereby anomalies are carefully ignored as long as possible, makes one realize just how Malinowski was facilitated by coming from outside. In doing so, he was restrained by no long-standing social ties and hardly respectful of those to whom he might have felt obligated. Innovators from within, by contrast, have to be unscrupulous twice over to succeed: they have to overcome the prevailing intellectual ethos and at the same time avoid appearing as troublemakers to those who have helped them take their initial steps in the field. Yet without brutal political maneuvering their innovation is far less likely to find its own stable institutional niche.

In order to demonstrate this through a case study, we may turn to archaeology's classical heartland, to the British School at Athens, to a life that is immensely revealing in helping us to understand how these social pressures might work. The chief protagonist is Frederick William Hasluck (1878–1920), a Cambridge man of unquestioned brilliance in one of the university's greatest periods: the time of Moore, Russell, Forster, and Keynes. After a double first in classics, during which time he was influenced by Ridgeway's varied interests as well as the intellectual life more broadly at King's (Salmeri 2004), Hasluck went with a vice-chancellor's studentship to the British School at Athens in 1901. He quickly became the librarian, assistant director, and then in 1910 acting director. Then, equally rapidly, his fortunes changed. He developed tuberculosis, was sacked from his post, and died in obscurity in Switzerland (Shankland 2004b, 2009). What happened to destroy such a promising career?

Almost by accident, Hasluck had found himself fighting an intellectual battle that has remarkable parallels with that publicly debated by Malinowski a decade later with Elliot Smith (1928). The way that this came about is as follows. Ramsay, an epigrapher and classicist, had in the 1880s and 1890s conducted a number of surface surveys of Anatolia, which resulted in publications of the greatest interest (among them Ramsay 1890, 1895). Ramsay had a deep knowledge of late antiquity and a commitment to the historical truth of the scriptures, particularly the New Testament (1907). His researches can be read with profit and pleasure by anyone interested in the region today. An early example of a globe-trotting academic, he achieved a major reputation, became a best-selling author, and received a knighthood.

The theoretical framework that he used, however, was based on survivalism and profoundly unsatisfactory. His problem was that the material that he wished to use to write about the past was often incorporated into present-day Anatolia, in Muslim villages, whether as part of their folklore, varied religious customs, or material culture in the form of reuse in mosques, graves, or houses. Unable to develop a complex understanding of this variety, Ramsay simply declared anything to do with the mosque Islamic, and all else a residue of the pagan or late Christian past. This meant that customs such as worshipping at streams, or trees, or the very common Anatolian habit of making vows or sacrifices at tombs, were relics of a previous time and could give the researcher direct access to it.

This astonishingly frozen approach to the way that the present may be related to the past was exactly one of those things that the post-Malinowski social anthropologists were so good at dealing with. Hasluck, with an intimate knowledge of Modern Greek and of the territories of the Balkans more generally, anticipated their arguments beautifully. He pointed out, for instance, in an essay on the monasteries at Athos that the histories of the individual institutions varied according to which of the Orthodox patriarchs claimed national sovereignty over them, and reflected present-day political concerns rather than being purely a product of chronology (Hasluck 1924). He wrote elegantly and skeptically on the tombs of Arab warriors in Anatolia, pointing out that "any chance combination of circumstances may give a religious colour to commonplace discovery, and anything remotely resembling a tomb presupposes a buried saint" (1929, 716). In a number of essays on transference and shared religious traditions that are still of importance today, he was able to demonstrate the enormous variety with which religious traditions could be combined and recombined. More precisely, aiming particularly at Ramsay, in a carefully worked essay published as the long first chapter in his posthumous *Christianity and Islam under the Sultans* (1929), he adopted a position that was quite clear in its anticipatory presentism. The following are its closing lines:

> The inference is that changes in political and social conditions, especially changes of population, of which Asia Minor has seen so much, can and do obliterate the most ancient local religious traditions, and, consequently, that our pretensions to accuracy in delineating local religious history must largely depend on our knowledge of these changes. Without this knowledge, which we seldom or never have, the assumption too often made on the ground of some accidental similarity that one half-known cult has supplanted another is picturesque but unprofitable guesswork. (p. 118)

This intellectual engagement had taken Hasluck so far from a traditional conception of archaeology that he eventually became a pioneering ethnographer of the Alevi/Bektashis in the Balkans, researches that were interrupted by the Great War and his illness. By the time he was dying in Switzerland, he had clearly begun to realize that the key to understanding the religious culture of the Alevis is a structural relationship between follower and holy man that is governed by patrilineal descent. Indeed, toward the end of his life, he was writing and researching in a way that is almost indistinguishable from the social anthropology that came a decade later. His detailed notes resulted in a posthumous article in the *Journal of the Royal Anthropological Institute* (1921) and form a substantial part of his published remains (1929, 121–295, 475–89, 500–551, *passim*). It was fully seventy years later that the next major study of the rural Alevis appeared, that by Altan Gokalp in 1980.

Hasluck was by all accounts a charming man, with a host of friends. He was not particularly good at institutional politics. Though a prolific writer, he did not, once published, wish particularly to proselytize for his point of view, relying on the quiet, even laconic arguments of his pen. After his successful start at the British School, this quiescence led to his downfall (Shankland 2009). Outmaneuvered by Wace for the directorship, his work was looked upon with some amusement as having to do with folklore and customs rather than serious excavation; seriously in bad dudgeon for having married Margaret Hardie, a student at the school, a lady who was forceful and smacked to the London Committee of suffragetism, he found himself suddenly at the wrong end of institutional politics. Wace, by then director in Athens, persuaded the London Committee that Hasluck should be removed from a permanent contract to one that was to be renewed annually, then wrote to London asking them to dismiss him. Albeit reluctantly, the committee agreed. Already in poor health, Hasluck was forced to live in central Athens away from the school. Eventually after a period of war work, Hasluck and his wife migrated to Switzerland, where he died in obscurity, lamented by his spouse and his close friend the folklorist Dawkins, the former director.

The British School at Athens had lost its most original scholar among some very bright talent indeed. It carried on with anthropology in the sense of being interested in other cultures but never with the internal shift that characterized the Malinowski movement and that Hasluck had anticipated. Though well-known among specialists of the Balkans (e.g., Duijzings 1999), Hasluck is not usually mentioned among general anthropological works, even very much among those who write today about the anthropology of Greece, an irony given his well-nigh perfect fluency in colloquial Modern Greek and his decade of living intimately within the country.

I explain this story in depth, because it illustrates so beautifully the point at issue. Archaeology and social anthropology, though they can be and were long taught together successfully, may also metamorphose into differing intellectual paths, which may or may not result in separation. In Hasluck's case, the experiment in diversity sparked no answering chord, and he was firmly eclipsed. Malinowski, coming from outside, was both less inhibited than Hasluck and less bound by convention. Looking at the sad story of Hasluck's life, and contrasting it with Malinowski's fruitfulness, one might even say that it was necessary for someone like Malinowski to start a countermovement from outside, simply because it would be so difficult to flourish from within.

Weighing the Balance

This separation having taken place, what are its pros and cons? From the point of view of archaeology, concentrating on digging enabled the discipline to achieve a technical mastery of excavation that still marks out British projects to this day. It is not just the very best projects that exhibit this high standard of empirical work; somehow the discipline has succeeded in routinizing the immensely complex procedure of putting together a team to work in the field, obtaining the material, and storing and archiving it, so that the same standards are expected from the smallest to the most renowned of excavations. I should be astonished if there is any other nation that has the same consistently high standards, at the same time as successfully passing them down from generation to generation to ensure that they renew themselves as the elders retire.

Such outstanding control over data is one factor in ensuring that Britain has in turn been one of the leading nations in the revolution that is occurring in archaeology globally. The impulse to understand, sort, label, and identify the material remains of the past leads directly to ever greater demands on the science of microanalysis. The last two or three decades of archaeometry have begun to answer these, so that there are a host of new techniques in analysis that are now becoming commonplace, among them advances in radiocarbon dating, dendrochronology, thermolumines-cence, mass spectrometry, electron microscopy, and isotope analysis. Taken cumu-latively, they appear at least to give a level of precision that may even become the envy of social anthropologists, even though they have the advantage of being able to talk with their subjects.

This advance in scientific archaeology has occurred alongside, even slightly fol-lowing, the discipline's partial reconciliation with social anthropology. It is perhaps invidious to impute any specific date to this, as there have been a number of sus-tained attempts from within archaeology, such as those by Gordon Childe (discussed by Hann in his chapter) and Orme (1992), and the more complex initiative by Hodder broadly known as postprocessualism. In all this, one significant point is certainly the break in British archaeology from the European tradition that gave rise to the creation of the World Archaeology Congress (WAC). Stimulated by the late Peter Ucko, himself originally an anthropologist, but supported by a formidable array of leading archaeologists including Renfrew and Hodder, the Congress resulted in an increased awareness of a whole host of issues that still appear modern today, such as the place of the indigenous peoples in the excavation process, the political role of archaeology in nationalism, the creation of knowledge from the excavation, and so on (Ucko 1987). This admirable creative burst was sustained both by Ucko him-self, who insisted that a large number of publications emerge from the first large conference, and by the World Archaeology Congress itself, which has subsequently flourished so markedly. It has continued in the *Journal of Social Archaeology*, of which Meskell was a founding editor; she continues the debate in her contribution to this volume and in the coruscating variety of her *Companion to Social Archaeology* (Meskell and Preucel 2006).

However stimulating (and Souvatzi in her chapter shows most interestingly how anthropology and social archaeology may be brought together), a potential disad-vantage of this approach is that it occasionally leads to a curious type of immodesty among archaeologists, who, having spent decades attempting to understand the mi-croshifts in their particular period, suddenly become experts in the contemporary country where they have happened to work. As they do not always speak the lan-guage well, and even more rarely have studied the modern period, it can trigger precisely that superficiality that social anthropologists have always claimed to be avoiding by undertaking fieldwork. In archaeologists' defense, it is hardly possi-ble to avoid negotiating with contemporary issues. A recent example of this can be found in Britain concerning the Druidic movements, a romantic impulse that Sillitoe discusses in this volume. Such is their success that a person can claim to be a Druid and thereby possess legal rights over the remains of the past that are denied to non-Druids, into which latter category archaeologists also usually fall.

However necessary, when translated into a foreign context, this lack of self-consciousness when moving between fields and eras is worrying. It may be able to be resolved by ensuring that there are local anthropologists working with the team, though there is the obvious danger that then the excavation may become overreliant on a particular source of information. Though expressed in modern guise, these questions are older than they look, having occurred in Ramsay's time, when he began to write on the Young Turk revolution without learning Turkish first (indeed, he absurdly assumed that his own incomprehension meant that Turkish villagers were unable to speak Turkish), and before that in Crete, when Arthur Evans became interested in contemporary affairs. There is no panacea, though it clearly is a desideratum that archaeologists become grammatically correct in the vernacular, as well as the earlier languages, of the countries where they work.

It is also not at all clear how the two different streams of thought represented broadly by the scientific and social archaeology movements can be reconciled. A skeptic could argue that, though the introduction of a sense of social complexity in the study of the remains of the past has made the practice of archaeology much more immediate, and even much more human, in the end the crucial point is whether the microanalysis on any particular artifact does what it claims to do accurately. In one notable case, the large excavations at Çatalhöyük appear to have worked with this creative tension superbly, whatever the debate that must be present in any group of persons working together at any one time. I must immediately declare an interest, in that the team extremely graciously allowed me to work with them for several seasons in the 1990s (Shankland 1996), but it does seem to provide a concrete instance that can be studied with great profit, even though its very size and complexity might mean that it is difficult to emulate frequently in the future (for a comment on this see, for instance, Campbell 2008; see also Hodder 2005 for comparative reflections on this theme). In the end, leaving any one project to one side, it is perhaps most relevant to note the scale of the change. Only twenty years ago, it was unusual for social anthropologists to work with archaeologists at excavations. Now, it is becoming unsurprising, even normal, resulting in a wave of diverse approaches that show no signs of running out of momentum.

Pros and Cons for Anthropology

The pros and cons for social anthropology are more complex and tricky to assess, partly because it is not yet normal for anthropologists to invite archaeologists to work with them in the field. I can now think immediately how this would have helped me with regard to my most intense period of fieldwork in a mountain Alevi village in Anatolia (Shankland 2003). Only much later did I realize, for example, that the large houses that the villagers had built out of wood, which most families were living in during my time there, were themselves fairly new and probably reflected a recent period of prosperity. To have conducted a house survey (not of the people only but also of the fabric and sequence of each building) would have been immensely revealing as to the recent chronology of the settlement and its socioeconomic activities during the twentieth century. It incidentally would have revealed the extent of the relations between the Anatolian Greek (Rum) and Armenian population in the late Ottoman Empire, because many of these interchanges occurred through the providing of specialist services, such as wall construction. Irvine, Hanks, and Weddle explore this question further beautifully in their contribution to this volume, while Filippucci, Harries, Fontein, and Krmpotich offer an equally interesting alternative possibility in their discussion of bones. It is entirely possible that a vast proportion of anthropological work conducted in the field today would equally benefit from having archaeologists on board, in ways that are not always predictable.

Yet in order for this sort of mutual intellectual exploration to happen with any regularity, it is clear that social anthropologists will have to be more ready to work in teams than before. To share material with archaeologists, by definition, means that it must be recorded in such a way that it can be accessed jointly. In order to share, in turn, there need to be agreed research protocols (at least between the team members) in a way that is not usual within anthropology field projects, even today. There is an increasing number of publications on fieldwork, as well as more recently the emergence of database programs written especially for fieldwork. Nevertheless, the integration of huge amounts of shared data in archaeological projects is far in advance of anything that I know anthropologically, precisely because it is through this material that their projects must be judged. To say that social anthropological fieldwork does not need this level of contextualization of data because of its access to living communities would be greatly debatable: The rapidity of social change is such that even after a very short time fieldwork sites are changing enormously. Very soon after a period in the field is concluded, we too may have no more than our data to fall back on. Though there are remarkably fine ethnographers still today, it is highly unlikely that social anthropological fieldwork routinely comes up to the standards of contemporary archaeological recording.

Leaving aside, though, the methodological points, a greater willingness to share would help to answer a set of problems inherent within the pure model of the lone fieldworker. The challenge here is this. Even if one assumes that a single researcher really can cover the extent of empirical investigation that is claimed or implied within an all-encompassing ethnographic field trip, it is not clear that anthropologists can easily persuade the outside world of the validity of their evidence or of their conclusions. In the early period, this seemed less of an issue, partly because it was so obvious that the wealth of ethnographic material that could be provided by fieldwork was so exciting, and so novel. I was struck by this early triumph once again upon coming across the following letter in the archives of the Royal Anthropological Institute (RAI), commenting on the worth of the Malinowskian approach. Here, a tutor at Manchester University is replying to an initiative from Fleure (president of the RAI) and gently trying to sketch out that an alternative approach has come to the fore:

> April 8th 1946
>
> Dear Professor Fleure,
>
> I had a letter from Waller this morning asking me to write to you about syllabuses in Social Evolution. The letter says that you are interested in getting the RAI to issue "a pamphlet on schemes for Adult Education on 'Man and the Evolution of Society'".
>
> I should be very happy to do what I can, and in the mean while, here are my immediate responses to the stimulus:
>
> In spite of the Diffusionist bent in my training under Perry, Elliot Smith, Hocart etc., I have for the past 10 years or so, spent most of my lecturing time on functional studies of more or less contemporary societies, with the aim of interesting students in the comparative study of human societies and institutions.
>
> Hence you will see in my current syllabuses (some of which I enclose) that the problems of origin and development have been secondary. My view of each society was two dimensional and photographic rather than stereoscopic. I have found this to be a very useful introduction to most adult students.
>
> Functionalist fieldwork is of very good quality. . . .
>
> This lack of emphasis on origins fits in very nearly with the fact that most adult students approach a subject mainly for what light they consider important problems, esp. topical ones . . . in an outline syllabus . . . some concession would have to be made to this desire. . . .
>
> Yours sincerely
>
> G.A. Cheshire
>
> Manchester University Joint Committee for Tutorial Classes.
>
> (Ref. RAI A85)

Fast forward to today, and this confidence seems much less in evidence. In other words, something appears to have happened in the second half of the twentieth century that has made it difficult for social anthropology to be completely confident of its investigative validity, even as it has strived to become relevant or retain its relevance. One problem is that the proliferation of information about all societies in the world may make the anthropological approach appear redundant, however mistaken such a claim. Another impediment to research could be the profoundly anti-intellectual audit culture dominant within British universities, which means that there is no time, and increasingly little incentive, to produce in-depth anthropological investigation.

Yet another argument could be made that social anthropology could really function freely only in a very specific time period: after that point when colonial expansion had ceased (and therefore imperialism was no longer a dominant emotional impulse even within the empire) and before that point when modern media had made the gross inequalities that govern interaction in a global setting so blatantly obvious. In other words, just for a few decades anthropologists could work free of politics with good conscience: they did not feel part of the colonial governing apparatus and were not yet aware that inequalities were not going to be rapidly solved by global economic development. This appears to be the approach taken by Lienhardt (1964) in his tutor. (For an interesting overview of this period, see Riviere 2007.) Now, as Herzfeld notes afresh in this volume, it appears almost impossible to conduct fieldwork without being drawn into the wider conflicts that globalization is making obvious.

There is no easy way to capture such subtle shifts in the way that a discipline may change (though for a good recent account based on archival research, see Mills 2008). Nevertheless, it is of particular interest that social anthropology itself changed in its attitude toward science during this period. Individual practitioners do not necessarily reflect wider disciplinary perspectives, but it certainly appears to be the case that though the earlier modern social anthropologists embraced the Malinowskian movement and rejected the universalist evolutionary claims of the older generation, they retained a sense of the pursuit of a scientific endeavor. Today, there is an equally strong sense within social anthropology's self-image that the discipline should not be regarded a science in any precise sense. It has almost become routine to denounce science as "positivist" and view anthropology's place as simply to chart the way that science works in practice (see, for instance, Edwards, Harvey, and Wade 2007) rather than trying to work out what its findings may have to do with anthropological investigations today.

Sociologically speaking, it could be argued that such a change is a logical possibility within the model, so reliant on a single practitioner, which social anthropology adopted when it succeeded in institutionalizing itself in England. In other words, though Malinowski claimed to be practicing science, the fieldwork methodology he espoused could continue almost unchanged into a later era that preferred to see ethnographic investigation as more interpretive in nature. Evans-Pritchard is an illustration of this, in that he could produce *The Nuer*, and then *Nuer Religion*, out of the same series of field trips, even though the two works appear to lead in quite distinct intellectual directions. Evans-Pritchard himself led this change in emphasis, ironically in a Marett lecture (Evans-Pritchard 1950) that is still thought to be decisive in marking this shift for anthropology more generally. Looked at carefully, it is not at all clear that the way he opposes history and science is entirely valid. Nevertheless, it was extraordinarily effective, as was his influence on subsequent generations of anthropologists at Oxford.

Yet, in making his claim, Evans-Pritchard is assuming—something that gradually became generalized into social anthropology more generally—that science has to be purely concerned with generating natural laws and that it must be inductive in character. This is something that his predecessor Radcliffe-Brown certainly adhered to, and indeed a perspective that would have been entirely in sympathy with the approach of the universalist anthropologists at the RAI, such as Myres, who were the senior generation when Evans-Pritchard was making his way in the field as its secretary. It is comprehensible that Evans-Pritchard should have been frustrated with them and wished to disagree. Nevertheless, his subsequent dominance helped to polarize the debate within anthropology, so that there appeared for decades afterwards to be the two camps: the humanists, who did not believe in science, and the supposed positivists, who were scorned by them. Precisely at this time, though, the philosophy of science was becoming much more sophisticated through the exploration of deductive approaches. Its instigator, Popper, was at the forefront of attacking positivism and was equally notable for his use of "essentialism" as a criticism, for instance in *The Poverty of Historicism* (1957). In spite of Popper's obvious affinity with modern social anthropology in this respect, he has been largely overlooked by it (though see Rapport 2005), and the debate surrounding anthropology and science remains simplistically dismissive.

This is hardly the place to follow this up in more detail, but it does have an immediate relevance to our debate in comparing anthropology and archaeology. Archaeology finds itself in something of a similar dilemma, in that it has not yet worked out how to reconcile the exponential success of the archaeometry movement with an emphasis on the social creation of knowledge. Sadly, social anthropology does not have the luxury of a similar problem. Instead, rather than incorporating technological change within its practice, it appears to be ready to split into two: relegating to biological anthropology exploratory investigations based on recognized scientific practice, including explorations of evolution, and stripping social anthropology into a much narrower subject devoted almost entirely to engagement with social issues. This is accompanied with a frequently dense style of writing that is hardly attractive and often makes it difficult for academic social anthropology to be comprehensible to the outside world even as it claims to be its savior.

Yet social anthropology cannot be only political commitment. The reverse is possible in that a social anthropologist can be politically committed, and many have been. However, the two positions are distinct, simply because if the discipline of social anthropology is *only* commitment, then it loses the right to claim a privileged position because in doing so it leaves out the possibility of gaining the data to back up these assertions. Simply put, claims of political relevance can very easily become a substitute for results. Refusing to work in teams, with the implication that this has of the ineffability of anthropological data, hardly helps this claim to universal relevance, and it is surprising how little this contradiction is noted. It leaves us, indeed, with a paradox: just as social anthropology defines itself as being devoted to the public enlightenment of global inequalities, it has less material of its own that it can easily or convincingly share.

Conclusions

In conclusion, I am suggesting that the two streams of intellectual practice that we know as archaeology and social anthropology are separated by more than simply prejudice. This does not mean, however, that they are mutually incomprehensible. Far from it, there are areas of archaeology that have been demonstrably enriched by embracing social anthropology, resulting in a stream of initiatives and publications that shows no sign of ceasing. Social anthropology, equally, could potentially explore an endlessly creative vein by reembracing archaeology. In other words, it is time to repay the compliment and realize that just as archaeologists have learned a great deal from us, we have a great deal to learn from them.

However, in order to incorporate the broad stream of ideas often known as social archaeology, archaeology did have to adapt its traditional excavation techniques in quite significant ways and reconsider hierarchies within the excavation and the question of who generates archaeological knowledge for whom at any site. Social anthropology, in order to move closer to archaeology, equally would have to adapt its techniques in turn. One way of summing up these changes is that it would have to permit not just the single investigator but potentially multiple team members to participate in the way that the fieldwork is structured and would have to be far more open as to the origins and sources of knowledge as it emerges from any project.

A consequential benefit of this could be to reembrace a form of science—not the inductive Baconian positivism of Radcliffe-Brown but something much more fluid along the lines of Popper, which permits simultaneously academic rigor and the possibility of the social creation of knowledge. Far from meaning that anthropology becomes more detached from the inequalities that mar our contemporary existences, this would make it better equipped for advocacy because in doing so it would become more transparent and indeed, through a greater awareness, more modest in its claims. Precisely because of this, it could then become even more effective about what it can and cannot do in terms of the alleviation of problems, both intellectual and practical.

In the end, above all, social anthropology is an empirical subject or it is nothing. Our claim to be at the top table can only be because we are masters of a discipline that can help us to understand the contemporary social world better than other approaches. If we cannot demonstrate this, then we are reduced to hollow assertions that cannot be backed up when pressed. It is this dilemma, I believe, that is at least partly answered through a closer dialogue with archaeology.

References

Association of Social Anthropologists (ASA). 2003. *Directory of Members of the Association of Social Anthropologists of the Commonwealth 2003–4*. London: Association of Social Anthropologists.

Campbell, S. 2008. "Çatalhöyük: Multivocality in action?" *Antiquity* 82 (316): 497–500.

Duijzings, G. 1999. *Religion and the politics of identity in Kosovo*. London: C. Hurst.

Edgeworth, M., ed. 2006. *Ethnographies of archaeological practice, cultural encounters, material transformations*. Lanham, MD: AltaMira.

Edwards, J., P. Harvey, and P. Wade, eds. 2007. *Anthropology and science: Epistemologies in practice*. Association of Social Anthropologists Monographs 43. Oxford: Berg.

Elliot Smith, G., ed. 1928. *Culture: The diffusion controversy*. London: Psyche Miniatures.

Evans-Pritchard, E. 1950. "Social anthropology: Past and present, the Marett lecture, 1950." *Man* 50: 118–24.

Garrow, D., and T. Yarrow, eds. 2010. *Archaeology and anthropology: Understanding similarity, exploring difference*. Oxford: Oxbow Books.

Gellner, E. 1995. *Anthropology and politics: Revolution in the sacred grove*. Oxford: Blackwell.

Gokalp, A. 1980. *Têtes rouges et bouches noires: une confrérie tribale de l'Ouest anatolien*. Recherches sur la Haute Asie 6. Paris: Société d'Ethnographie.

Goody, J. 1995. *The expansive moment: The rise of social anthropology in Britain and Africa, 1918–1970*. Cambridge: Cambridge University Press.

Gosden, C. 1999. *Anthropology and archaeology: A changing perspective*. London: Routledge.

Hasluck, F. 1921. "Heterodox tribes of Asia Minor." *Journal of the Royal Anthropological Institute* 51: 310–42.

Hasluck, F. 1924. *Athos and its monasteries, by the late F.W. Hasluck*. London: K. Paul, Trench, Trubner.

Hasluck, F. 1929. *Christianity and Islam under the sultans*, ed. Mrs. F.W. Hasluck (née Hardie). 2 vols. Oxford: Clarendon.

Herle, A., and S. Rouse. 1998. *Cambridge and the Torres Strait: Centenary essays on the 1898 anthropological expedition*. Cambridge: Cambridge University Press.

Herzfeld, M. 1987. *Anthropology through the looking-glass: A critical ethnography in the margins of Europe*. Cambridge: Cambridge University Press.

Hodder, I. 1982. *The present past: An introduction to anthropology for archaeologists*. London: Batsford.

Hodder, I. 2005. "An archaeology of the four-field approach in anthropology in the United States." In *Unwrapping the sacred bundle: Reflections on the disciplin-*

ing of anthropology, ed. D. Segal and S. Yanagisako, 126–40. Durham, NC, and London: Duke University Press.

Ingold, T. 1992. "Editorial." *Man*, n.s., 27 (4): 693–96.

Kuklick, H. 1991. *The savage within: The social history of British anthropology, 1885–1945*. Cambridge: Cambridge University Press.

Leach, E. 1977. "The view from the bridge." In Spriggs 1977, 161–72.

Lewis, I. 1976. *Social anthropology in perspective*. London: Routledge.

Lienhardt, G. 1964. *Social anthropology*. London: Oxford University Press.

Marett, R. 1911. *Anthropology*. London: Williams and Norgate.

Meskell, L., and R. Preucel. 2006. *A companion to social archaeology*. Oxford: Wiley-Blackwell.

Mills, D. 2008. *Difficult folk? A political history of social anthropology.* Methodology and History in Anthropology 19. New York and Oxford: Berghahn Books.

Orme, B. 1992. *Anthropology for archaeologists*. London: Duckworth.

Popper, K. 1957. *The poverty of historicism*. London: Routledge and Kegan Paul.

Ramsay, W. 1890. *The historical geography of Asia Minor*. Supplementary Papers. London: Royal Geographical Society.

Ramsay, W. 1895. *Cities and bishoprics of Phrygia*. 2 vols. Oxford: Clarendon.

Ramsay, W. 1907. *The cities of St. Paul: Their influence on his life and thought*. London: Hodder & Stoughton.

Rapport, N., ed. 2005. "Democracy, science and the open society: A European legacy?" Special issue, *Anthropological Journal on European Cultures* 13.

Riviere, P., ed. 2007. *A history of Oxford anthropology*. Oxford: Berghahn Books.

Salmeri, G. 2004. "Frederick William Hasluck from Cambridge to Smyrna." In Shankland 2004a, 1:71–104.

Shankland, D. 1996. "The anthropology of an archaeological presence." In *On the surface*, ed. I. Hodder, 218–26. Cambridge: British Institute of Archaeology at Ankara, and Macdonald Institute.

Shankland, D. 2003. *The Alevis in modern Turkey: The emergence of a secular Islamic tradition*. London: Routledge.

Shankland, D., ed. 2004a. *Archaeology, anthropology and heritage in the Balkans and Anatolia: The life and works of FW Hasluck, 1878–1920*. 2 vols. Istanbul: Isis.

Shankland, D. 2004b. "Introduction: The life and times of F.W. Hasluck, 1878–1920." In Shankland 2004a, 15–67.

Shankland, D. 2009. "Scenes pleasant and unpleasant: The life of F.W. Hasluck (1878–1920) at the British School at Athens." In *Scholars, travels, archives: Greek history and culture through the British School at Athens*, ed. M. Llewellyn Smith, P.M. Kitromilides, and E. Calligas, 91–102. London: British School at Athens.

Spriggs, M., ed. 1977. *Archaeology and anthropology*. BAR supplementary series 19. Oxford: British Archaeological Reports.

Stocking, G. 1999. *After Tylor: British social anthropology 1888–1951*. London: Athlone.

Trigger, B. 2006. *A history of archaeological thought*. Cambridge: Cambridge University Press.

Ucko, P. 1987. *Academic freedom and apartheid: The story of the World Archaeological Congress*. London: Duckworth.

Wace, A., and M. Thompson. 1914. *The nomads of the Balkans: An account of life and customs among the Vlachs of Northern Pindus*. London: Methuen.

2

Big Revolutions, Two Small Disciplines, and Socialism

Chris Hann

Introduction

The concept of revolution is a loose one and a "bogey" in the opinion of philosopher of science Ian Hacking (1987, 45). According to Ian Jarvie (1964) the "revolution in anthropology" was preeminently the work of Bronislaw Malinowski. In succeeding decades critics have questioned Jarvie's analysis by pointing to continuities with the pre-Malinowskian era, including some in the work of the revolutionary himself. As a graduate student in Cambridge I discovered that organizational entropy also mitigated against revolution. Suggestions in the 1970s that social anthropology belonged with the new Social and Political Sciences (SPS) Faculty did not fall on fertile ground, and the department of Goody and Leach remained firmly in Archaeology and Anthropology. I was not the only student who attended more talks in SPS than in archaeology. It was perhaps obvious in my case, as I was preparing a fieldwork project in socialist Hungary, that the SPS library would have more to offer than the Haddon Library of Archaeology and Anthropology. The founding fathers of these disciplines—Durkheim, Marx, Tocqueville—had all addressed questions of revolution and transition, in their different ways. It did not occur to me to look for comparable inspiration in "arch and anth." The departments of this faculty were not researching closely together in any region or thematic field at this time, and I believe the same holds true today.

The reason for this lack of communication and the core of truth in Jarvie's argument both have a great deal to do with the "ethnographicization" (Stocking 1987; Urry 2006) of anthropology in the twentieth century. The prospect of doing fieldwork "behind the Iron Curtain" was certainly one of the main factors attracting me to the discipline after specializing in Eastern Europe as an undergraduate in politics and economics. I was suspicious of Cold War models of totalitarianism and the command economy: anthropology would allow me to understand how those societies really worked for their members. My impulse was almost as thoroughly presentist as Malinowski's project in the Trobriand Islands, no matter how greatly the Hungarian countryside differed from the "savage" or "tribal" society for which the ethnographic method was developed. There was not much room for any kind of history, let alone the longer perspectives of archaeology, in my research proposal.

Half a lifetime later I have published extensively on the contemporary history of one community in Hungary, but I have not found it easy to reach a satisfactory conceptualization of continuity and change. The villagers of Tázlár, with whom I lived for the best part of a year in the 1970s, could not help but have a strong sense of living in a one-party, socialist system since the 1940s. They had experienced an unwelcome intervention in the early 1960s, when they were put under great pressure to join new cooperative farms. Some of them also had a slightly earlier milestone in their heads: the failed uprising of 1956, classified by the ruling socialists as a counterrevolution, which even in this small rural community had brought a fatality. Other moments of rupture in the twentieth century included the "Republic of Councils" in 1918–19 and the Liberation and Land Reform of 1944–45. Nor did the events of 1989–90 lack their moments of drama on the national stage. And yet most villagers have consistently emphasized contexts of continuity to me, in political and economic domains as well as in religion and everyday life. Many processes of change continued incrementally under the new regimes of the 1990s, for example, in the sphere of consumption. Those who nowadays stress rupture in their discourses have not necessarily changed their habitus or "mental map." In some cases where the displacement of the ancien régime has brought sweeping changes, those affected seem perversely determined to assert the continued validity of the roles and norms they knew from the past.

A few years ago I carried out a modest restudy of this village, twenty-five years after the original fieldwork and more than a decade into postsocialism (Hann 2006). My friends were recognizably the same people, even if they no longer belonged to the same political party or worked for a nominally socialist cooperative farm. The immediate chaos of "transition" was long behind them, but I could not say that new norms and conventions had definitively replaced those of socialism. The anthropologist investigating postsocialism has, like those who studied socialism a generation before, to reconcile the evident facts of dramatic institutional change with multiple layers of resilience. In some contexts it is difficult to disentangle strands of continuity leading back into the socialist period from strands that lead back to presocialist years; that is, before the 1940s in the case of Eastern Europe, and before 1917 in the case of Russia. We evidently need to pay more attention to history as *process*, and to differential rates of change in the subsystems of a society.

All this may sound familiar, even to the point of banality. The best excuse that students of postsocialist societies can make for their excessive presentism until now is that the events unfolding before them in the field were often so startling that observing and reporting these used up all our energies. Twenty years later it is time to move beyond this presentism. Indeed this opening to history is already well under way.[1] In this paper I shall try to broaden the frame and ask how archaeologists have dealt with periodization and concepts such as revolution. By stretching our understandings of socialism in ways that would detach the fundamental impulse behind it from the details of modern European history, I shall argue that not only classical archaeological work on the emergence of social inequality but even work on the Paleolithic and the origins of our species can become relevant to the concerns of an ethnographer in rural Hungary. By the same token, the results of ethnography can help us to question the assumptions underlying influential stage models and to develop more complex accounts, particularly of forms of economic integration. Social science debates concerning the socialist revolutions of recent times may seem utterly incommensurate with the disputes of prehistorians, but I shall argue that these intellectual communities, which drifted apart for much of the twentieth century, largely as a consequence of the dominance of the ethnographic method, have much to gain in the twenty-first by resuming their dialogue. By doing so they can provide an essential corrective to a threatening "big revolution" driven by the so-called cognitive sciences.

Social Change, Revolution, and the Aftermath of Socialism

If the original Malinowskian ideal took exotic communities outside real history, the initiator of that alleged fieldwork revolution soon realized the futility of the salvage endeavor and instead did much to promote the investigation of social change in the last decades of the British Empire. Scholars such as Raymond Firth and Lucy Mair anticipated much of what came to be known as the modernization paradigm, which in turn helped to shape what became known as the anthropology of development. Like Malinowski himself in his time, his successors often subjected their predecessors to withering critique and insisted on the radical novelty of their own approach. With the benefit of hindsight it is easy to see deep continuities, just as we detect continuities in the rapidly changing societies that formed the objects of all this attention. But perhaps some progress was made, and we began to understand continuities in terms of dynamic processes in social organization, rather than rigid structure (Firth 1951).

When, if ever, might that bogey term *revolution* be warranted in anthropological analysis? How do we distinguish one age from another, an adaptation from a transformation, or a "structure" from the interminable sequence of historical "events" (Sahlins 1985)? Revisionist scholars have had no difficulty in describing powerful currents of continuity, as Eric Wolf did in his study (1969) of the protracted agonies of Mexico's revolutionary century. Ethnographers have sometimes been able to show that the success of a revolution movement may depend on the entrenched conservative beliefs of those mobilized to topple the previous power holders: David Lan (1985) demonstrated this memorably for Zimbabwe. In other cases the change may be real enough, but it is cyclical and disqualified on this ground from counting as revolution; Leach (1954) is the most famous anthropological demonstration of this kind of change. Max Gluckman (1965) was adamant that tribal societies could not experience revolution in its radical modern sense. But ethnographers working in other types of societies have frequently come to similar conclusions. The revolution that replaced the Ottoman Empire with a secular nation-state had not had much impact on Anatolian villagers when Paul Stirling went to study them a full generation after the rupture (Stirling 1965). Gradual processes of transition throughout the second half of the twentieth century did eventually bring far-reaching changes to Anatolian society, which Stirling documented in later work (1993). But the general lesson of the ethnographic studies seems to be that anthropologists are wary of concepts such as revolution, or even "punctuated equilibrium." Our reliance on ethnography, which initially restricted us to synchronic snapshots, as later refined in Manchester and elsewhere still seems to bias us toward theories of gradual change and to require skepticism toward the notions of caesura favored by other disciplines. The kinds of revolutions studied by political scientists (for example, Dunn 1972) generate much surface froth, but the anthropologist's deeper level of engagement with flesh-and-blood human beings leads ineluctably to an emphasis on continuities, even if the people we study themselves sometimes tell more complicated stories.

How does the collapse of Soviet socialism fit into these crude generalizations? Easier access from the 1990s allowed Anglophone anthropologists to engage with a part of the world and a type of society to which their discipline had not hitherto paid much attention. Following its demise they could begin to probe socialism itself more effectively, through archival sources as well as fresh memories. Most anthropologists were suspicious of other disciplines' focus on transition for the same basic reasons that they had critiqued modernization in earlier decades. They rejected a capitalist telos that flattened the world to fit a single template and emphasized transformation and multidirectionality in opposition to the standard assumptions of "transitology." There was a common understanding that all this flux formed part of a new neoliberal global order, yet even within subregions of Eastern Europe the varieties of capitalism have turned out to be very diverse. Few would now claim that that a new equilibrium, the sociological equivalent of Thomas Kuhn's (1962) "normal science," has been achieved, or can possibly be achieved. As the dust settles on socialism, as contemporary social dilemmas converge with those of neighboring regions and the former socialist countries are no longer so grossly underrepresented in our scholarly literature, it is time to ask what generalizations and theoretical implications can be drawn from the countless case studies. We can also assess the implications of "velvet," "orange," "rose," "tulip," and other fragrant convulsions in the aftermath of socialism for the concept of revolution.

In our work at the Max Planck Institute for Social Anthropology we have found that the search for patterns and more adequate theories leads ineluctably to a closer engagement with the past—and not just with the socialist past, which, beneath the ideological uniformities, was also substantially shaped by local and regional histories. In work on rural property we thus found it necessary to pay close attention not only to the particular form of collectivization but also to presocialist agrarian traditions, including the resilience of cooperatives or practices of land redistribution (Hann and the Property Relations Group 2003). Similarly, to understand the contemporary revival of the Russian Orthodox Church it is not enough to look carefully at what happened in the Soviet era. For some research questions it will also be important to take into account the role of Orthodox Christianity throughout the recorded history of East Slav populations and then to analyze the interaction of multiple "sediments" (Agadjanian and Rousselet 2010). Scientific atheism often meant the literal "domestication" of religion (Dragadze 1993), but this could have the effect that the active bearers of the religious "chain of memory" were *more* numerous than they might have been without the ideological pressures. Such issues can only now be addressed openly through empirical research. Throughout the former Soviet bloc, patterns have been more complex than a simple model of secularization theory would predict. In those locations, such as Eastern Germany, where the links between secularization and modernization seem to hold up rather well, the reasons again lie deep in presocialist history (see Hann 2010).

Many anthropological analysts of postsocialism have found elements of continuity with the socialist order to be of decisive importance in explaining outcomes. Some meanings may have changed, but seldom entirely; the processes are somehow cumulative. In the study of human societies the notion of a "zero hour" can never be taken literally (with the exception of cataclysms such as that of Easter Island). Even in the case of Germany's much-touted *Stunde Null* in 1945, it is easy enough with the wisdom of hindsight to point to countless continuities of which contemporaries were unaware or which they preferred to overlook through a kind of amnesia that has long been familiar to both anthropologists and historians. It is easier to change parliamentary laws than to change established institutions and practices, and it is very hard to alter certain engrained ideas inside people's heads. Formulations of this kind have become the new orthodoxy in the various disciplines of transitology, since it was the easiest way to explain the failures of shock therapy in the 1990s. If, in spite of all the benevolent advice received from the West, regions such as the Balkans, the Caucasus, and Central Asia failed to develop democratic civil societies, this could only be due to recalcitrant elements buried deep in their "cultures." Few anthropologists find this satisfactory. But our studies of postsocialism have yet to generate a general theory capable of explaining why it is that some things can change very quickly, while others seem hardly to shift at all (and when they do, the shift commonly turns out to be ephemeral, followed sooner rather than later by a relapse to the earlier state).[2]

This, then, is a major challenge: How can the work of sociocultural anthropologists in two decades of postsocialism contribute to a more satisfactory general theory of sociocultural change, and what place do concepts such as revolution and transformation have in this theory? In the remainder of the chapter I suggest that one way of going about the task is to stretch our definition of socialism in multiple ways and then to look to archaeologists as well as historians to help us avoid past pitfalls.

Stretching Socialism

In popular Euro-American understandings, socialism is defined fundamentally as collective ownership and is thought to originate in the writings of Karl Marx and Friedrich Engels in the middle decades of the nineteenth century. Some scholars will identify important precursors such as Robert Owen, Henri de Saint-Simon, and Charles Fourier, and it is sometimes alleged that the roots of twentieth-century totalitarianism can be found in the writings of Jean-Jacques Rousseau. There is a virtual consensus that socialism is somehow closely tied to the European Enlightenment as well as to that continent's industrial revolution (a phrase coined by Arnold Toynbee in 1884). Of course, humans have long embraced messianic religions, and heretical sects have experimented with many variants of utopia, in word and in deed. Socialism, however, is held to be modern and different from all of these, above all because of the manner of its imposition as a Hayekian "constructed rationality" and its basis in central planning. According to the conventional story, Marx and Engels simply got it wrong when they predicted that this big revolution would break out in the advanced industrial countries under the leadership of an impoverished proletariat. Instead, it took hold in backward Russia, thanks to a vanguard party that then went on to build up a brutal dictatorship and to export the ideology not to the capitalist West but to various regions of what is now known as the Global South (formerly the Third World). It seems that the revolutionary message was delivered to the wrong address (to adapt a phrase coined by Ernest Gellner in another context). All the horrors and misery associated with Communist Party rule in the twentieth century derive from this error. This explanation is attractive to committed Marxists because it allows them to maintain that *real* socialism has not yet been given a fair trial, since all efforts to date have been restricted to countries where the material and social conditions were not yet ripe.

Contrary to this narrative, evidence from other times and other places allows us to contextualize socialism differently, to detect forms of premodern socialism, while abandoning the teleologies of both bourgeois modernization theory and Marx's philosophy of history. For example, historians such as Esther Kingston-Mann (1999) have documented the strength of egalitarian, redistributive principles in prerevolutionary Russia. Stalinist collectivization and the aspiration to construct "factories in the countryside" may have constituted a rupture, but the most basic impulses behind socialism were familiar to Russian peasants.[3] This argument can be pushed much further in time and space. When political leaders such as Julius Nyerere of Tanzania attempted to build an African socialism on the basis of the alleged communal principles of traditional tribal societies, many Western observers scoffed; they saw instead a romantic exaggeration that led quickly to economic disasters for many postcolonial states. Indeed, Tanzania has paid a high price for the delusions of *Ujamaa*, and memories of the Nyerere era are distinctly ambiguous (Askew 2006). But what cannot be denied is the strong valuation placed on social equality in economic systems famously characterized by Hyden (1980) as "economies of affection." The defense of this value is often associated with accusations of witchcraft and sorcery. Indeed, such accusations can be viewed as the characteristic response to the forms of interpersonal inequality that were typical of sub-Saharan African societies. Sorcery functions here as the equivalent of modern socialism, which emerged in both its communist and its democratic electoral variants as the countercurrent to the enormous structural inequalities of the economically more complex societies of Eurasia (Goody 2003).

Stretching the definition of socialism away from a narrow focus on property rights toward questions of social equality immediately opens up possibilities for cooperation with archaeologists, for whom the evolution of complexity, hierarchy, and centralized power has always been central (Gledhill, Bender, and Larsen 1988). Above all, archaeologists can help to correct for the presentist bias that has accompanied the rise of the ethnographic method in the twentieth century. They have, for example, developed increasingly sophisticated approaches to understanding property relations and the inheritance of status, which help us to move beyond the simplistic contrasting of collective versus individual that has bedeviled theories of socialism. Many changes in human societies, such as the emergence of stratification and the early state, take place over a time span that cannot possibly be grasped by the fieldworking anthropologist, not even one who returns repeatedly to the location in a longitudinal study (regardless of whether or not the study embraces some moment of conspicuous rupture). From this perspective, continuous improvements in archaeological research technologies should prove conducive to the reaffirmation of old disciplinary complementarities (Marcus 2008).

Since the Malinowskian revolution, few anthropologists have acknowledged inspiration from an archaeologist, but Jack Goody (2006) has acknowledged his debt to the vision of Gordon Childe. According to a recent critic (Gamble 2007, chap. 2), Childe's (1942) concept of the Neolithic revolution was inspired by his brief visit to the USSR; it was regrettably infused with the typical Orientalist impulse to elaborate stereotypes of Asia in order to heighten the unique breakthrough of modern Europe. But whether or not Childe sought at some level to prise Europe and Asia apart, Goody insisted on welding them together in opposition to the societies he knew as an ethnographer in Africa (Goody 1976). He was particularly interested in Childe's focus on a second period of transition, the urban revolution of the later Bronze Age, which was certainly a phenomenon of the Middle East and Asia rather than Europe. In Goody's adaptation of the model, this was the breakthrough that eventually led societies right across the Eurasian landmass into more advanced agricultural systems (based on the plow) and at the same time toward more differentiated patterns of consumption and vertical systems for the *devolution* of property, notably dowry. Economic efficiency rose, together with increased individualization of landholding and status competition between households. Sub-Saharan African societies, though they participated in the earlier revolution that led to an intensification of food production, did not participate in this later revolution. Goody's adaptation of Childe proved fertile, and not merely for arcane theorizing about the distant past: the consequences of this divergence remain fundamental to understanding the contemporary condition of the African continent (see Hann 2008).

Societies of food collectors or hunter-gatherers offer particularly promising opportunities for cooperation between anthropologists and archaeologists. When Marx and Engels followed Lewis Henry Morgan and earlier European philosophers in proposing a classless, egalitarian condition for the original human society, they had virtually no empirical knowledge of modes of livelihood that were not based on some form of agriculture or pastoralism. We cannot do fieldwork in the Paleolithic, but much later in the twentieth century, thanks to pioneers such as Richard Lee (1979) and James Woodburn (1982), some features of the ideal type of "primitive communism" were confirmed in the ethnographic literature.[4] Of course, the romantic idealizations of nineteenth-century theorists were not borne out. Final agreement over the relevance of such ethnographic studies for evolutionary arguments may be difficult, even impossible, to achieve, given the paucity of material traces, but the archaeological contributions are nonetheless vital. It seems that at least some hunter-gatherer groups have developed effective mechanisms for preserving basic equality that have proved resilient down to the present day.

If the concept of a Neolithic revolution has become controversial and later archaeological accounts of the emergence of agriculture have been marked by "continuity thinking," some prehistorians are still willing to deploy the concept of revolution boldly. Thus, in a recent reassessment of arguments he developed over two decades earlier, Paul Mellars (2007) continues to speak of the "human revolution" in a robust singular. This did not take place in Europe, where older Neanderthal populations were replaced by newcomers. Defining revolution as an endogenously generated event, Mellars locates the emergence of modern humans in specific regions of southern Africa in a period of time that extended over tens if not hundreds of thousands of years. By comparison, Childe's Neolithic revolution is a mere camera click. However, other archaeological contributors to that volume, notably Sally McBrearty (2007), consider the very concept of a human revolution to be a "serious misnomer."

Prehistorian Clive Gamble (2007) is as unsympathetic to Mellars' notion of the human revolution as he is to Childe's notion of a Neolithic revolution. Questioning the very concept of the "anatomically modern human," Gamble argues that the experts have come up with very different answers to apparently straightforward questions. His own recommendation is to abandon the notions of revolution and origin altogether. The target is bound to remain elusive since all research in "Originsland" is saturated by the cultural and ideological conditions of contemporary archaeology and the wider academy. Gamble is thus dismissive of using diagnostic checklists in order to generate positivist knowledge of distinctive archaeological cultures. For him, cultures are ineluctably local; our universality is established not by the latest DNA analysis of the fossil record but by the abundant evidence we have for primal corporeal metaphors of nurture and the environment.

In emphasizing local social relations rather than a generalized individualist utilitarianism, Gamble takes theoretical inspiration from contemporary anthropologists, as well as the cultural theory of Raymond Williams.[5] These anthropologists in turn borrow from a wide range of academic specializations. Few are interested in the agenda they once shared with colleagues in archaeology and biology, including those questions of human origins and social equality. However, there are encouraging signs that this could be changing, for example, in interdisciplinary discussions of early human kinship (Allen et al. 2008). Kalahari specialist Alan Barnard (2009) distinguishes "at least three" revolutions, which he terms the signifying, the syntactic, and the symbolic, in the coevolution of language and kinship. While most scholars still prefer either to identify just one revolution, as does Mellars, or to reject the concept of revolution altogether, in the manner of Gamble and McBrearty, differentiation of the kind advocated by Barnard, deriving from classical anthropological theories, may offer a way forward.

Why Archaeologists, Historians, and Anthropologists Need to Work Together

How can the discussion of the preceding section be brought to bear on the challenges facing the postsocialist fieldworker? Before closing the argument I need to remind the reader of pertinent trends in other disciplines. The Victorian tandem of archaeology and anthropology cannot afford to ignore the sleek locomotive of the neo-Darwinian cognitive sciences, which is a very different vehicle from the cognitive anthropology of earlier decades. We may be facing a big revolution in our disciplinary fields, and if so we need to react appropriately.

If archaeologists and anthropologists follow Gamble's example and abandon Originsland, others are not afraid to rush in. Space does not allow even a cursory review here of the burgeoning field known as evolutionary psychology. We know from studies of our closest primate relatives that chimpanzees are capable of transmitting knowledge by cultural means, for example, concerning tool use. More or less sophisticated nongenetic learning is also characteristic of other, more remote species (e.g., parrots mimicking human sounds). But all this remains far removed from the ability of humans to use language and from the communicational capacities of human infants even before they have learned to speak. The work of Michael Tomasello (2008, 2009) has shown that both human and chimpanzee infants can work out ways to solve problems through cooperation. But only the humans have a notion that the reward of successful cooperation should be shared between the cooperating parties and not monopolized by whoever gets his hands on it first. A concern with the well-being of others and *fairness* seems fundamental to being human. This, rather than the formal legal character of property relations, is the source of what I have been calling the impulse behind socialism.

Research with food collectors has taken a new direction in recent years with the adaptation of experiments based on game theory in cross-cultural analysis (Henrich et al. 2004). In the course of this work it has been demonstrated that the !Kung Bushmen, studied by Lee (1979), are anything but generous in the offers that they make to each other when playing the Ultimatum game. Much variation has been uncovered, and it is clear that the explanatory models of orthodox, neoclassical economics are inadequate. Economists have been obliged to recognize what most ethnographers had known all along, namely that decision making often diverges from and may even contradict what the application of a strict utility-maximizing calculus predicts. Some economists have attempted to reconcile these findings with their axioms by concluding that human beings generally have a "taste for fairness" or an "aversion to inequality" (Fehr 1999).

This aversion to inequality can hardly be universal: humans do, after all, readily acquiesce in all manner of hierarchies. Marxist-Leninist regimes themselves were not particularly squeamish in enforcing new forms of hierarchy. But the normative impulse toward equality usually remained prominent under the modern socialist regimes, a commitment that went much further than the bourgeois principle of "equality of opportunity."

In any case it is clear that ideologies based on the ownership of the means of production must be superseded. Recent work at the interface of economics and the social sciences has shown that, where the rights and obligations are clearly specified, common property rights may well provide more efficient solutions than full privatization (Ostrom 1990). If Elinor Ostrom had ever declared herself to be a socialist, she probably would not have been awarded the Nobel Prize for economics in 2009. Her work is important because it demonstrates that systems based on community participation, often highly egalitarian in nature, can solve economic coordination problems in a wide variety of settings. Rather than confirm evolutionary trajectories between stages, whether culminating in the preponderance of private property, as in myths of liberal capitalism, or in state ownership, as in Stalin's version of socialism, such work shows the need to rethink property constellations as key components of a ubiquitous mixed economy.

Yet Another Transition?

Let me at this point return to the farmers of Tázlár on the Great Hungarian Plain to illustrate how the fieldworker can begin to engage with these larger issues. I selected this village for study because from the 1960s it had a form of collective known as the specialist cooperative. Although statistically unrepresentative, this institution came to exemplify the flexible economic policies pursued in Hungary after 1968. Without abandoning socialism, always defined primarily with reference to collective ownership of the means of production, power holders in Hungary introduced effective price incentives, above all for petty commodity producers in the countryside. When collectivized fields were returned to private ownership after 1990, the result was a severe contraction of production and gross inefficiency (Hann 2006). But in the last decades of socialism local interests were well served by a combination of a well-run socialist sector growing cereals, in large fields using the latest technologies, with the inputs of the rural household in labor-intensive vineyards and animal breeding. Labor incentives in both sectors were provided by the possibility of extending private ownership in the sphere of consumption, particularly of houses and motor vehicles. In short, this was a socialist mixed economy. Each of the "forms of integration" distinguished by Karl Polanyi (1944) was significant. *Redistribution* was managed through the state at various levels. Socialist planners still controlled some prices, but they granted increasing scope to the *market*. Meanwhile, the *household* was a key unit of production as well as consumption, at least in the rural sector, and complex ties of *reciprocity* linked these households to each other in both work and leisure activities. Hungary after 1968 represented a form of balanced "embedded socialism," following the dislocation ("disembedding") caused by land reform and collectivization in the preceding decades (cf. Hann 2009a).

This kind of market socialism obviously complicates any attempt to demarcate stages of history according to the mode of production in the usual Marxist sense (see the Appendix to this chapter). At the time of my fieldwork in the mid-1970s the means of production were still overwhelmingly in collective ownership (although a few individuals were just beginning to acquire larger items of equipment privately, including tractors). Contrary to the premise of most economists, and also to one of Goody's central assumptions in his work on the devolution of property in Eurasia, it was not necessary for the land on which food was grown to be privately owned in order to achieve efficient outcomes (Hann 2009b). Closer attention to the mix of forms of integration in Polanyi's sense is more fruitful than a simple classification on the basis of property ownership.[6] After 1990, the privatization of collective property in Tázlár was a protracted process that took more than a decade to complete. Given the relative poverty of local soils, a market in land has barely developed. There has been a significant shift toward the market, but the postsocialist state has retained most of its welfare responsibilities. Villagers see greater changes in the diminished importance of the household as a productive unit and in an associated decline in interhousehold reciprocity. But I think few of them have the sense that their recent *rendszerváltás* ("system change") amounts to a revolution.

How, then, are we to adjudicate between resilience and transformation and label eras? Are we to say that twentieth-century Hungary swung erratically between feudal, capitalist, and socialist modes of production? The rural populations of virtually all parts of Europe experienced massive changes in the course of the twentieth century, and the similarities (in terms of birthrates, out-migration, social security, etc.) seem from today's vantage point more striking than the differences introduced by socialist planning. If we as ethnographers trace the changes between the generations, should we embrace the continuity perspective of Gamble, perhaps together with the skeptical stance of sociologist W.G. Runciman (2009) toward all attempts to demarcate "ages and stages"? Runciman does not deny the utility of notions such as punctuated equilibrium, but he is surely right to draw attention to the hazards in their identification. The enormous influence of Marxist materialism on historiography and the historical social sciences poses special problems in the case of socialism, which is postulated as both the beginning and the end stage of this model. This tradition, including the Western Marxism of the 1960s and 1970s, remained fundamentally in thrall to Montesquieu and other pioneers of stage theories in the eighteenth century. Each new stage requires a new theory of transition to explain its emergence.[7]

The way forward cannot be to abandon periodization altogether but to develop better, less Eurocentric models for thinking about world history. I think Gamble is right to hold that the concept of revolution has been overworked and irredeemably devalued. Anthropologists, archaeologists, and historians cannot go on applying the same term to describe the emergence of the species, the urban revolution of the Bronze Age, the Industrial Revolution, the violent revolutions of 1789 and 1917, and the peaceful revolutions that ended Soviet socialism two decades ago and continue to generate colorful aftershocks. Instead, we need to join forces to understand complexity and overcome Eurocentricism. Socialism, in the sense of concern with fairness, equality, and solidarity, has been one component of humanity from the beginning; it was exactly that, one moral component, in the "actually existing socialisms" of Eastern Europe prior to 1989, and this did not disappear with the fall of the Berlin Wall.

Conclusion: Two Small Disciplines

Clearly we are still a very long way from understanding the exact workings of evolutionary, devolutionary, and revolutionary processes. I have argued that closer collaboration between anthropologists and archaeologists should help to counter the historian's proclivity for simplistic periodization, as well as the reductionism and ignorance of many in economics and the emerging cognitive sciences. Perhaps the most glaring example is that numerous scholars in evolutionary economics still proceed on the basis of nineteenth-century utilitarian theory; many still take it for granted that a society that procures its subsistence through gathering and hunting is enmeshed in a struggle for survival, despite a large literature in economic anthropology and archaeology that demonstrates the contrary. The experiments of Henrich and his colleagues, even when they involve native subjects in the field and not, as is usually the case in cognitive science, campus students, remain manipulative interventions. Despite all the charges that have been leveled against the ethnographic method in recent decades, it remains vital to observe the "natural" flow of social relations and to continue the cumulative comparative analysis of these findings. Archae-
and anthropologists can collaborate to historicize and humanize the models

of the emerging cognitive accounts; they can illuminate the precise mechanisms by which the postulated long-term changes have come about. The purpose is not to derail the sleek vehicle of cognitive science (actually more like a clumsy bulldozer) but to ensure that it does not obliterate the actual course of human history as it pursues its quest to understand our universals. To fulfill this mission the two small disciplines of archaeology and anthropology must develop their own theories and concepts. There is much on which we can build, including the legacy of Childe and Goody, but as we have seen they are by no means immune to criticism.

One source of confusion is the fact that the very same loose concepts, such as structure, transformation, and, in particular, revolution, which we use in our efforts to analyze human history, also figure prominently in our efforts to make sense of science and disciplinary history. For Hacking (1987) a "big revolution" in science is more than a change of structure or paradigm shift in the sense of Kuhn (1962, 1977). A big revolution is a rupture that affects whole swathes of scholarship and has a direct impact on the social world outside science; less momentously, it is accompanied by changes in the institutions of the sciences in question, such as the formation of professional associations and the patterns of their conferencing. In this sense, the revolution that Jarvie associates with Malinowski became "big" only with the founding of the Association of Social Anthropologists after Malinowski's death.[8]

It is sometimes argued that the contemporary digital revolution is already having consequences as far-reaching as the scientific revolution of the seventeenth century that ushered in the modern world. As far as the links between social anthropology and archaeology are concerned, however, the Darwinian revolution of the nineteenth century has the stronger claims. The fact that anthropology at the beginning of the twenty-first century is still often found in a single department or faculty with archaeology derives from academic divisions of labor first worked out in the lifetime of Charles Darwin. The two subjects went different ways quite early on. In the British case a good deal of the responsibility for the later divergence lies with Malinowski. But in places like Cambridge, faculty combinations, once established, are very hard to change. Here social anthropology remains wedded to archaeology (and also to biological anthropology; this component of the Trinity has not been explored here, though its enduring relevance is obvious). Contrary to my opinion at the time as a breathless young graduate student and junior lecturer, enthused by the study of the socialist present, I now think that the survival of this alliance is a very good thing. Hacking's big "probabilistic revolution" lasted some 130 years between 1800 and 1930. Perhaps the Malinowskian revolution, with its privileging of the ethnographic method, is better understood as an extended parenthesis in the big Darwinian revolution, which is only now, in a tight alliance with developments in cognitive science, reaching its climax in fields such as ours. If this diagnosis is correct, it is all the more important that social anthropologists work alongside archaeologists (and historians and historical sociologists) to ensure that seductive biological and cognitive models do not blind us to actual historical trajectories.

Notes

1. Some colleagues in this small community have already been taking advantage of improved access to accomplish innovative archival work; see Rogers 2009 and Kligman and Verdery 2011.
2. These issues are carefully discussed by West and Raman (2009), who distinguish in their subtitle between "revolution and transformation, restoration and continuation."
3. One of the most interesting conclusions of Kingston-Mann's (1999) research into late tsarist agrarian social structures is that adherence to the old moral principles was more conducive to economic innovation than the emerging capitalist alternatives.
4. This picture was confirmed in Soviet Marxist scholarship. For a detailed discussion of "the transition from the appropriative to the productive economy" see Kabo 1985. (My thanks to Peter Skalnik for this reference.)
5. It might be objected that his fundamental point owes more to another Cambridge scholar, historian E. H. Carr. Parts of Gamble's book read like a postmodern updating for archaeology of Carr's (1961) admonition to study the historian rather than the "facts." The past is necessarily a shifting target for each new generation of interpreters. This is surely unexceptionable, but it does not invalidate the enormous advances in knowledge that prehistorians have made in recent decades.

   Some of Gamble's more ambitious deconstructions are not entirely coherent for this reader. Apart from endemic confusions with the concept of culture, his use of "modernity" seems to introduce a "before and after" that contradicts his pro-continuity stance. Gamble implies a "big revolution" launched by the rationality of Descartes, most of whose work was deeply rooted in the scholastic traditions of medieval Christian philosophy. The postmodern prehistorian falls here into precisely those traps of Eurocentrism that Goody warns against.
6. When Karl Polanyi read Childe's *What Happened in History* he judged the basic assumptions (including the inherent conservatism of "tradition") to be narrowly rooted in nineteenth-century utilitarian psychology (Polanyi, "Notes—Economic Anthropology, 1947–1957," Container 22-3, Karl Polanyi Archive; I thank Gareth Dale for drawing my attention to this commentary). Perhaps the founders of the modern socialist movement are open to similar criticism. But what I observed in late socialist Hungary seemed very much in line with the maximizing assumptions of the economists: Accumulation did indeed proceed in a very economistic way but for reasons that had everything to do with the contingencies of Central European history in those decades. The same people have found themselves in a very different environment in the last twenty years, to which another Polanyian concept seems relevant, that of the "double movement." The abandoning of the socialist mixed economy in favor of a radical extension of the market principle has been accompanied by a shift to the political right and widespread xenophobia.

Even in Tázlár, where they are few in number, the Roma minority has experienced the brunt of this resentment.

7. One of my earliest book reviews for an anthropology journal tackled a collection edited by Marxist historian Rodney Hilton, called *The Transition from Feudalism to Capitalism* (1976). A century after Engels (1884) had codified the stages of historical materialism, serious historians were still scrutinizing transitions everywhere in the light of this model, including the "other transition," which had brought humanity across the threshold to feudalism (Wickham 1984). Neo-Marxists came up with their own variations on established European narratives of the Dark Ages and the Renaissance. Everyone acknowledged that modes of production did not change overnight, but Wickham thought he could pinpoint the collapse of the so-called ancient mode in Valentinian's imperial decree of 444. The pestilence of 1348 was sometimes cited as demarcating the end of the Middle Ages. By analogy, there is a prima facie case for viewing the revolutions of 1989 as the epicenter of yet another transition, one that impacted on a much larger area of the Eurasian landmass than that of 444. This is indeed the way in which the postsocialist transition has been conceptualized in many disciplines, but, as Runciman argues, the effects of such schemas are pernicious, especially when they imply a unilinear direction of change in all domains. In the case of the postsocialist countries, the very terms *transition* and *transformation* may have had powerful social effects, but they are a poor indication of deeper changes in "forms of integration" in Polanyi's sense. Hungarian peasant society experienced profound structural changes in the twentieth century, but the events of 1989–90 are little more than a blip in this story.

8. The succeeding sixty years of the Association of Social Anthropologists (ASA) seem to have been devoid of revolution and marked only by incremental changes in the scale of conference activities. The same is true of the American Anthropological Association (AAA). It would be difficult to claim that the launching of the European Association of Social Anthropologists at precisely the same time that socialist power collapsed confirms the diagnosis of a "big revolution"; on the contrary this seems to be a good example of *contingency* in history.

References

Agadjanian, A., and K. Rousselet. 2010. "Individual and collective identities in Russian orthodoxy." In *Eastern Christians in anthropological perspective*, ed. C. Hann and H. Goltz, 311–28. Berkeley: University of California Press.

Allen, N.J., H. Callan, R. Dunbar, and W. James, eds. 2008. *Early human kinship: From sex to social reproduction*. Malden, MA: Blackwell.

Askew, K. 2006. "Sung and unsung: Musical reflections on Tanzanian postsocialisms." *Africa* 76 (1): 15–43.

Barnard, A. 2009. "Social origins: Sharing, exchange, kinship." In *The cradle of language*, ed. R. Botha and C. Knight, 219–35. Oxford: Oxford University Press.

Carr, E. 1961. *What is history?* Harmondsworth, UK: Penguin.

Childe, G. 1942. *What happened in history.* Harmondsworth, UK: Penguin. (Orig. pub. 1936.)

Dragadze, T. 1993. "The domestication of religion." In *Socialism: Ideals, ideologies and local practice*, ed. C. Hann, 148–56. London: Routledge.

Dunn, J. 1972. *Modern revolutions.* Cambridge: Cambridge University Press.

Engels, F. 1884. *Der Ursprung der Familie, des Privateigenthums und des Staats: im Anschluss an L. H. Morgans Forschungen.* Hottingen-Zürich: Schweizerische Genossenschaftsbuchdr.

Fehr, E. 1999. "A theory of fairness, competition and cooperation." *Quarterly Journal of Economics* 114: 817–68.

Firth, R. 1951. *Elements of social organization.* London: Watts.

Gamble, C. 2007. *Origins and revolutions: Human identity in earliest prehistory.* Cambridge: Cambridge University Press.

Gledhill, J., B. Bender, and M. Larsen, eds. 1988. *The emergence and development of social hierarchy and political centralization.* London: Unwin Hyman.

Gluckman, M. 1965. *Custom and conflict in Africa.* Oxford: Blackwell.

Goody, J. 1976. *Production and reproduction: A comparative study of the domestic domain.* Cambridge: Cambridge University Press.

Goody, J. 2003. "Sorcery and socialism." In *Distinct inheritances: Property, family and community in a changing Europe*, ed. H. Grandits and P. Heady, 391–406. Münster, Germany: LIT.

Goody, J. 2006. "Gordon Childe, the urban revolution, and the haute cuisine: An anthropo-archaeological view of modern history." *Comparative Studies in Society and History* 48 (3): 503–19.

Hacking, Ian. 1987. "Was there a probabilistic revolution 1800–1930?" In *The probabilistic revolution*, ed. L. Krüger, L. Daston, and M. Heidelberger, 1:45–55. Cambridge, MA: MIT Press.

Hann, C. 2006. *Not the horse we wanted! Postsocialism, neoliberalism and Eurasia.* Münster, Germany: LIT.

Hann, C. 2008. "Reproduction and inheritance: Goody revisited." *Annual Review of Anthropology* 37: 145–58.

Hann, C. 2009a. "Embedded socialism: Land, labor and money in eastern Xinjiang." In *Market and society: The great transformation today*, ed. C. Hann and K. Hart, 256–71. Cambridge: Cambridge University Press.

Hann, C. 2009b. "The theft of anthropology." *Theory, Culture and Society* 26 (7–8): 126–47.

Hann, C., ed. 2010. *Religion, identities, postsocialism: The Halle Focus Group 2003–2010.* Halle, Germany: Max Planck Institute for Social Anthropology.

Hann, C., and the Property Relations Group. 2003. *The postsocialist agrarian question: Property relations and the rural condition.* Münster, Germany: LIT.

Henrich, J., R. Boyd, S. Bowles, C. Camerer, E. Fehr, and H. Gintis, eds. 2004. *Foundations of human sociality: Economic experiments and ethnographic evidence from fifteen small-scale societies*. Oxford: Oxford University Press.

Hilton, R., ed. 1976. *The transition from feudalism to capitalism*. London: New Left Books.

Hyden, G. 1980. *Beyond Ujamaa in Tanzania: Underdevelopment and an uncaptured peasantry*. Berkeley: University of California Press.

Jarvie, I. 1964. *The revolution in anthropology*. London: Routledge & Kegan Paul.

Kabo, V. 1985. "The origins of the food-producing economy." *Current Anthropology* 26 (5): 601–9.

Kingston-Mann, E. 1999. *In search of the true West: Economics and problems of Russian development*. Princeton, NJ: Princeton University Press.

Kligman, G., and K. Verdery. 2011. *Peasants under siege: The collectivization of Romanian agriculture, 1949–1962*. Princeton, NJ: Princeton University Press.

Kuhn, T. 1962. *The structure of scientific revolutions*. Chicago: University of Chicago Press.

Kuhn, T. 1977. *The essential tension*. Chicago: University of Chicago Press.

Lan, D. 1985. *Guns and rain: Guerillas and spirit mediums in Zimbabwe*. London: James Currey.

Leach, E. 1954. *Political systems of Highland Burma*. London: Bell.

Lee, R. 1979. *The !Kung San: Men, women and work in a foraging society*. Cambridge: Cambridge University Press.

McBrearty, S. 2007. "Down with the revolution." In *Rethinking the human revolution: New behavioural and biological perspectives on the origin and dispersal of modern humans*, ed. P. Mellars, K. Boyle, O. Bar-Yosef, and C. Stringer, 133–51. Cambridge, UK: McDonald Institute for Archaeological Research.

Marcus, J. 2008. "The archaeological evidence for social evolution." *Annual Review of Anthropology* 37: 251–66.

Mellars, P. 2007. "Rethinking the human revolution: Eurasian and African perspectives." In *Rethinking the human revolution: New behavioural and biological perspectives on the origin and dispersal of modern humans*, ed. P. Mellars, K. Boyle, O. Bar-Yosef, and C. Stringer, 1–11. Cambridge, UK: McDonald Institute for Archaeological Research.

Ostrom, E. 1990. *Governing the commons: The evolution of institutions for collective action*. Cambridge: Cambridge University Press.

Polanyi, K. 1944. *The great transformation: The political and economic origins of our time*. Boston: Beacon Press.

Rogers, D. 2009. *The old faith and the Russian land: A historical ethnography of ethics in the Urals*. Ithaca, NY: Cornell University Press.

Runciman, W.G. 2009. *The theory of cultural and social selection*. Cambridge: Cambridge University Press.

Sahlins, M. 1985. *Islands of history*. Chicago: University of Chicago Press.

Stirling, P. 1965. *Turkish village*. London: Weidenfeld and Nicolson.

Stirling, P. 1993. "Growth and changes: Speed, scale, complexity." In *Culture and economy: Changes in Turkish villages*, ed. P. Stirling, 1–16. Huntingdon, UK: Eothen Press.

Stocking, G. 1987. *Victorian anthropology.* New York: Free Press.

Tomasello, M. 2008. *Origins of human communication.* Cambridge, MA: MIT Press.

Tomasello, M. 2009. *Why we cooperate.* Cambridge, MA: MIT Press.

Urry, J. 2006. "The ethnographicisation of Anglo-American anthropology." *Sites*, n.s., 3 (2): 1–36.

West, H. G., and P. Raman, eds. 2009. *Enduring socialism: Explorations of revolution and transformation, restoration and continuation.* New York: Berghahn.

Wickham, C. 1984. "The other transition: From the ancient world to feudalism." *Past and Present* 103: 3–36.

Wolf, E. R. 1969. *Peasant wars of the twentieth century.* New York: Harper & Row.

Woodburn, J. 1982. "Egalitarian societies." *Man* 17 (3): 431–51.

Appendix

Human Sciences Bulletin: The Tázlár Socialist Culture

Scholars of the World Research Council at their Antipodean Center have completed their analysis of the remarkable find at Tázlár. The unique sand ecology of this location in western Eurasia, exactly halfway between the ancient Danube and Tisza Rivers, has preserved a rich collection of artifacts from the civilization that perished in the catastrophe of the year 0 (1986 in their own calendrical system). Our analysis sheds new light not only on the rudimentary living conditions of 1,200 years ago but also on the fragmented character of the human sciences of that era, before their consolidation in the course of the New Common Era (NCE). The 2,000 inhabitants of Tázlár lived in two nuclear centers and an additional 100 isolated farmsteads; evidence indicates that many more of the latter had been recently abandoned as their occupants moved to the two settlement clusters. Our excavations concentrated on the larger of these. Full documentation has been deposited in the global archive. The findings can be summarized as follows:

1. Two large constructions served cultic worship of the Christian God. The smaller of the two was more sparsely furnished and significantly older than the other, which could be dated precisely; this building, rich in colored glass and ritual objects, was erected in –30 NCE, shortly after the consolidation of the power

system known throughout this region as socialism. Moreover, records indicate that it was constructed by mutual aid, under the direction of a "socialist construction brigade." We do not know how this was possible in the light of all that is known about socialist repression of such cultic forms.

2. Another large building dating from the same decade can be attributed unambiguously to the socialists (on the basis of literature discovered in a small annex, which apparently served as the office of its director). It was known as the "Culture House." Artifacts found here indicate that these villagers were subject to ideological indoctrination from a very early age; however, other items were apparently used by very old people, known as pensioners. Evidently, by the time of the catastrophe, socialists had built up a comprehensive system of education and welfare that encompassed the entire life course.

3. It took researchers many months to identify the control center of this remarkable settlement. The breakthrough came when a host of red insignia and sacred socialist writings were uncovered in a small building that had apparently housed all their administrative offices. How such a small staff was able to exercise effective power over this dispersed settlement remains a puzzle.

4. Economic activities were coordinated in a separate building. Surviving artifacts include an abacus, presumably used by collective farm bookkeepers, and large stag antlers that may have decorated the office of the farm's leader ("chairman," to use the term we know from the comparative literature on the short-lived era of collective farming).

5. Apart from a few ancillary buildings with a public economic character, the main revelation of the traces found in Tázlár is the preponderance of private, residential buildings and the extraordinary disparities in wealth that they show. While about half of the reconstructed households had recently installed sanitary facilities of some luxury, the remainder lived in very primitive conditions. Similarly, about 45 percent had their own means of motorized transport, while most of the remainder relied on horse-drawn carts. The sources of private wealth are unclear, but the production and consumption of alcoholic beverages was certainly one major element in this local economy.

The interpretation of the Tázlár find has divided the experts of our Council as seldom hitherto. Surviving documents are scanty. Although almost all of them were written in the well-known "Latin" script, the "Hungarian" language was difficult to decipher for today's scholars (since none of its speakers survived the catastrophe). It was therefore a welcome surprise to discover in three private dwellings (but in no public locations) a copy of a work written in English and published only six years before the catastrophe, on the island of Britain. This book, apparently the work of a native of the island, C. M. Hann, who had lived for one year in Tázlár, provides considerable information about the living conditions of the villagers one decade before the catastrophe. The author makes it clear that they had considerable economic freedom and that many worked extraordinarily hard for the purposes of private accumulation; socialist political controls were strong, but they were weaker than they had been in the early decades of that era.

Our experts have been unable to reach a consensus on the nature of the enquiry conducted by Hann. Much of the detail seems superfluous to the concerns of any scholarly discipline; at any rate, no one in our team has been able to provide an adequate account. The author was apparently based at a "department of social anthropology" in the University of Cambridge, a significant center of learning at the time. It is known that this "anthropology" was linked to archaeology, a discipline which investigated societies of the distant past through their material traces. It seems (at any rate in the curious division of labor that prevailed in the last years before the catastrophe) that social anthropologists devoted themselves to the description of social relations as they observed them and paid rather little attention to history. Hann makes brief reference to earlier work by Hungarian archaeologists in Tázlár whose analysis of a burial ground confirmed that the settlement had been inhabited in the "Middle Ages," though it was later abandoned following conquest by another Turkic group (the name Tázlár is the principal evidence that the original settlers were Cumanian Turks rather than Hungarians). Hann's book is mainly about social relationships, with economic matters covered in greatest detail.

Our team has had much heated discussion about the classification of this site, bearing in mind both similarities and differences between this site and the more limited traces studied at sites at Khorezm and at Turpan from the same historical moment. The majority of us have opted to respect terms that were evidently of great importance at the time. "Socialist" meant that political power was in the hands of a single organ and that the means of production were in some form of collective ownership; the private accumulation of wealth in Tázlár, though based on a sophisticated market organization, seems to have been accomplished without the private ownership of land or of other productive equipment. The presence of large machines in a few private homes suggests this may have been in flux at the time of the catastrophe; significant changes may have taken place between Hann's observations and the moment of catastrophe just a decade later. Hann's work was published in a series entitled "Changing Cultures." The author does not explain the term culture (apart from describing the Culture House). It has continued to baffle our experts since the World Research Council was founded. However, it enjoyed an extraordinary popularity at the time throughout all the human sciences and among the general public. The Council has therefore decided to revive this term in its formal classification of the Tázlár find.

In dissenting opinions, several Council members placed on record their rejection of this revival of what they hold to be prescientific concepts. Some experts claimed that the concept of culture had led even the best human scientists to sterility and confusion before the catastrophe. Other colleagues questioned the use of the term of "socialist," since it was obvious that a good deal of Tázlár's economic organization fitted better with the rival concept of "capitalism." There was a consensus among Council members that the old theories of evolutionary stages had no place in our new science. Nevertheless, some found it helpful to state that the Tázlár economy as depicted in Hann's publication contained within it the seeds of a new "mode of production," which might well have become dominant within a few years but for the catastrophe. The majority felt that the evidence compiled by Hann and corroborated by the findings from the site confirmed the axioms of our new human science, revealing the dual human impulses in exceptionally vivid forms. We marvel at the effort invested by our precursors in distorting these universal impulses to fit theories of stages, as if basic propensities to sympathize and cooperate could be transformed by changes in institutions. A proposal to call this culture "transitional" was speedily rejected. Nonetheless, several members continued to hold that a "caesura" in the form of radical political and economic change was only a few years away at the time of the catastrophe.

Thus, "the Tázlár socialist culture" was the formulation on which most council members could finally agree. Professor Müller was unable to accept this compromise and has resigned from the World Research Council in protest. It was agreed to place on record his opinion that "by adopting this nomenclature the scholarship of the New Common Era is returning to all the muddles of the pre-catastrophe era."

3

Whose Rights to Which Past? Archaeologists, Anthropologists, and the Ethics and Aesthetics of Heritage in the Global Hierarchy of Value

Michael Herzfeld

Social anthropology and archaeology are today discovering common ground of a relatively novel kind. For the latter, this was perhaps less of a revelation than it was for social anthropologists, who do not have to confront the problem I have called that of "evidential scarcity" to the same degree (Herzfeld 1992, 66). Archaeologists rather obviously cannot go back and talk to the people who created the objects found in excavations. That gap is widening; with the growth of both literacy and technology, many of the people who have served as social anthropologists' informants continue to stay in touch by e-mail and telephone. And so archaeologists must think ever harder about how to establish the meaning of their data—which does not mean that social anthropologists, with all the assurance of plenty at their disposal, have been better at getting it right.

It is thus salutary to think what social anthropology would be like were it constrained by these limitations that archaeologists must always confront. What can we learn from the evidential scarcity that characterizes much work on the past, and does it suggest priorities that we might usefully consider as our present-day research sometimes appears to founder under the sheer weight of undigested and multimedia data? And is the corollary of evidential scarcity an obsession with the material preservation of what does survive? In other words, if circumstances breed mutually complementary forms of disciplinary excess, can these two interrelated disciplines perhaps serve as instructive mirrors to each other, generating a discourse that today, more than ever before, would seem to be truly urgent: how to avoid a glut—of monumental testimonies on the one side and of precious chatter on the other? In other words, can our data actually reach a point of excess that might fatally harm our analytic, aesthetic, and ethical judgment?

The answers to these questions lie, I suggest, in an orientation that for social anthropology, at least, has long been an article of epistemological faith: that significance lies in how objects and concepts are *used*. The centrality of use theories of language to the emergence of a semantically responsive anthropology cannot be underestimated. We cannot therefore judge what is excessive until we know what we hope to achieve by using it. If, for example, we argue (improbably as it might be) that the public interest is best served by the monumentalization of swathes of hitherto residential city spaces, presumably there is no such thing as a glut of monuments. But if it is simply scientific avarice that will not allow any supposed archaeological remnant to be absorbed into the urban fabric or reused in completely new ways, it is time to rethink the role of scholarly approaches to conservation. Conversely, if the exponential growth of web-based archives of purely oral material serves the political interests of exclusionary ideologies and practices in the name of safeguarding "local tradition," such data may actually become a pernicious presence. I suggest that one socially useful role for both social anthropology and archaeology is the critical management of a public debate about the *uses* of "finds" and "data" in the larger political arena—a debate that has real consequences for people who live in spaces designated as historic.

It was perhaps inevitable that the morality of an archaeology stoutly defending the importance of preserving the remains of the past could hardly avoid clashing with an equally intransigent social anthropological ethics of respect for living populations. And it has become increasingly clear that the material remains of the past, no less than the so-called intangible heritage with which—especially—nineteenth-century nationalist folklorists were concerned, would furnish tools of both domination and resistance. As a result, neither discipline can ever honestly claim political neutrality. Yet archaeologists, perhaps more than social anthropologists, have on the whole, for reasons linked to the more obvious materiality of their data, more tenaciously resisted the idea that their discipline was *necessarily* political than have social anthropologists.

They have certainly commented, often disapprovingly, on the exploitation of archaeology to justify pernicious ideologies; important recent work on nationalism in archaeology (especially Kohl and Fawcett 1995) has its roots in Grahame Clark's (1939) principled and early critique of the Nazis' uses of archaeology. Modern commentators from the anthropological side have remarked, often controversially, on the archaeological creation of politically expedient factuality (e.g., Abu El-Haj 2001). But the idea that archaeology *must* be at least potentially political at all times seems to be more difficult to cultivate within the discipline itself; the very circumstances that have lent archaeological findings so eclectically to various forms of nationalism, for example, did not favor an open admission that this resolutely concrete, materially based discipline could not be ideologically neutral. The materiality of language, by contrast, was rarely taken seriously by a discipline that has often seemed determined to embrace a version of the fallacy of misplaced concreteness. Yet even some of the earliest archaeologists sensed that this concreteness was misleading; Mortimer Wheeler's (1954, 15) early recognition that excavation always entailed some measure of destruction (see also Lucas 2001) parallels precisely Claude Lévi-Strauss's (1997) rueful recognition that he could not take a photograph without including material evidence of what first contact brought in its train.

Institutionally, archaeology has been greatly strengthened by its utility for the goals of nation-states; this accounts for both its greater public popularity (in relation to social anthropology) and its often massive financial backing by various state organizations. In countries like Greece and Israel, where archaeology plays a vital role in shaping the argument that continuous inhabitation constitutes evidence of a collective right to the land, national archaeological services have become "states within the state" and have wielded extraordinary moral authority as well as political clout. Such institutional motives also reinforce the idea that archaeology must be "scientific" in the sense that it deals with supposedly incontrovertible facts—"facts on the ground," for example. Weaker groups have little choice but to respond in kind to the positivistic and materialist models favored by powerful nation-states. North American and other "first nations," the Palestinians, and many other groups have slowly discovered that collective identities depend on being able to take on the accoutrements of the nation-state. Anti-immigrant, fascist groups similarly play up the role of "heritage" and demand that it satisfy criteria of radical factuality.

Such factuality, moreover, easily translates into the language of territorial conquest and control. The model of the nation-state is derived, as Richard Handler has pointed out in his work on Quebec nationalism (1985, 1988), from the early-modern European model of the possessive individualist—of a person, in other words, defined as such by the single fact of owning property. And if one is going to "have a culture," to invoke Handler's wry allusion to this connection, the key, clearly, is to reify it—or, better, to reveal its timeless materiality in the form of archaeological remains. Obviously, this does not in itself make archaeology morally objectionable.

But it does sometimes expropriate certain amenable types of archaeology for exclusionary ends, in ways that for a modern social anthropology—or, indeed, for the new social archaeology—would almost certainly never be acceptable. On the other hand, simply pointing out such processes conceals its own moral dangers. When we deconstruct them, we are also engaging in a political choice. That might seem relatively innocuous, or even salutary, if the state in question is a powerful player such as the United Kingdom, the United States, or China. But very different issues are at stake if the group that is struggling for recognition is a small indigenous tribe that is trying very hard to resist genocide or forced assimilation at the hands of a repressive government (Jackson 1995), or a regional government resisting the assimilationist goals of an encompassing state. And the dilemmas do not stop there; while we may find a nation-state's policies toward minorities to be objectionable or insensitive, these policies may well have their origins in a still larger frame of political domination; we may be blaming a perpetrating agent for a situation born, at least in part, of the latter's victimization by larger and external forces. The slave traders of Africa responded to the increasingly exigent colonial demand for free labor; today's antiquities trade is sustained economically by the wealthiest members of the very societies that institutionally condemn tomb robbers and antiquities dealers to opprobrium and punishment for desecrating the sacred heritage.

To understand is not necessarily to condone. Many a local population, resentfully facing the precariousness of the present-day employment and housing situations and the retreat of the traditional political left (see, e.g., Herzfeld 2009; Molé 2010; Muehlebach 2009), finds itself attracted to a racist ideology that claims to justify violent responses against supposedly invasive immigrants and asylum seekers. This is particularly likely to happen when middle-class evictees discover the difficulty of garnering sympathy for their plight; their condition proves to be insufficiently picturesque in contrast to that of the "huddled masses," and their failure to mobilize public support all too easily turns into an especially bitter form of racism. Something similar happens in the United States, a country that ideologically takes great pride in its immigrant origins but also in its middle-class identity, when its disgruntled mainstream flirts with draconian forms of exclusion and segregation with regard to newcomers. We can understand these unattractive stances as the product of economic, political, or even religious fear, without subscribing to them or refraining from expressing our concern.

For "structural violence" (see, e.g., Farmer 2003) reproduces itself at multiple levels. In one such process, the proliferation of monuments becomes a means of essentializing and perpetuating categorical exclusions while subjecting the larger polity to a still broader form of geopolitical domination—to, for example, demarcations between the West and the Rest. Take, as one example that has implicated both archaeological and social-anthropological practices, the case of modern Greece. The label *modern* is itself diagnostic; what are the implications of the fact that without such a prefix any reference to things Greek risks being viewed automatically as being about the ancient past, especially given the pervasive Greek concern with high antiquity? This focus on antiquity is historically a foreign importation. All the more dangerous, then, for any Westerner to risk questioning the thesis of unbroken continuity with the ancient past in the manner of the Tyrolean pan-Germanist and pro-Ottoman pamphleteer Jakob Philipp Fallmerayer (1830, 1836), or to doubt the Greekness of that past in the idiom of Martin Bernal (1987). When Bernal's *Black Athena* was published, it was actually the more conservative end of the Greek intellectual spectrum that was most indignant. Right-wing nationalists now found themselves confronting a Westerner castigating them for their failure to conform to a model ultimately invented in, and imposed from, the imperial countries of Western Europe (notably Britain and France). In the grand scheme of things, this certainly must have seemed very unfair.

It also shows clearly that in such contexts any stance of academic neutrality can only be hypocritical. The slightest engagement with the archaeology of Greece is fraught with political sensitivities, as many archaeologists—several of them Greek—have come to realize (e.g., Hamilakis 2007; Hamilakis and Yalouri 1996; Yalouri 2001; see also Stroulia and Sutton 2010). An ethics of practice demands recognition of the fact that the remains of the past lie among living people for whom their significance may be far removed from that of academic research, but who deal with the implications of official historiography in their everyday lives—and often mine it for politically useful materials (see Herzfeld 1991). There is simply no way to avoid taking sides, because the fact of doing archaeological research is always already a political act. The same is true for ethnographic research, and this is compounded when the latter is focused on the impact of historic conservation and archaeologically directed zoning laws on the lives of local residents.

Thus, when I started working within Rome in a district—Monti—inhabited by people who were not particularly poor but who were being rooted out of this wonderful area in the center of Rome by a combination of forces that included rich proprietors, churches, the underworld, and politicians and banks, I was faced with a clash between my rather simplistic sense of outrage at the rash of evictions then taking place and my distaste for some of the political alignments that seemed to share my indignation. The people with whom I was particularly associated were getting a rather bad odor with the left, to whom I was myself far more sympathetic, simply because they had allowed the far-right National Alliance (Alleanza nazionale) Party to offer them assistance.

So I made an attempt to get some of the leftist politicians in the area on board as well. While the residents were eventually unable to avoid being evicted, the political and ideological broadening of their support base may have helped to increase awareness of the real injustice taking place. After two centuries of basically living at very low rents, a whole population was without warning faced with the total disruption of their lives. And while those who might have been expected to be more sympathetic, the leftists, often sneered at these evictees' relative prosperity, it did not escape notice that some of the people who came to replace them at vastly inflated rents were in fact leftist intellectuals and politicians. It is also important—and timely—to recall that Italian fascism has almost always had a social-activist dimension. That aspect of the involvement of the more extremist right-wing elements allowed the latter to make significant electoral inroads into the leftist domination of Roman politics.

The choices I made at the time were certainly motivated by my own political preferences. But even had I chosen to take a backseat and confine myself to observation, I would in effect have joined forces with the surprisingly laissez-faire elements on the far left of the political spectrum who paradoxically dismissed any attempt to resist eviction as a failure to realize the inevitability of market processes! Just as their hands-off attitude had political implications, any refusal on my part to get involved would have signaled a similar vicarious fatalism—an exhortation to accept the necessity and logic of the capitalist market. Gramsci would surely have appreciated the irony!

One of the classic arguments for not getting involved, aside from the usual attempts to shore up an increasingly unpersuasive academic purism, is that of the right of foreigners to interfere in political processes. To be sure, one must always consider the possibility that the most well-meaning intervention can be construed as an act of imperial meddling. But I would argue that—unless one has a strictly state-oriented understanding of the nature of culture—there is also an obligation to weigh the consequences of both action and inaction for those on whom we depend for our knowledge and therefore for our careers.

This issue confronted me in Thailand, when I began research there, almost from the start (see Herzfeld 2003). In Italy I could at least lay some claim to participatory rights as a citizen of the European Union (I hold a British passport). In Thailand, I had no such formal basis for claiming the right to participate in political action. Here, however, I found some inspiration in a distinction that has always been very much in the forefront of discussions in which I took part in Italy—that between the generically political (*politico*) and the institutionally party-political (*partitico*). I would certainly be reluctant to participate in an interparty feud, although my attempt to bring in the center-left in Rome was certainly oriented toward party politics (and revealed the surprising extent to which politicians of opposite factions would utilize such a moment to carry on the informal conversations on which in practice the governance of their unruly country actually depends; see Herzfeld 2009, 270–71).

But in a broader sense it was actually useful to distinguish myself from the party hacks. In fact, when I first went to visit the Pom Mahakan community where I came to do most of my Bangkok fieldwork to date, I was asked whether I would help the community fight for its right not to be evicted. Initially floored by the question, I then responded that I could promise nothing without further investigation—because I was not a politician! After two or three weeks, I was convinced that the community both satisfied the criteria I had set for a site at which I would conduct research and had a legitimate grievance that I was interested in helping them pursue. They were being expelled from their long-standing residential site in the name of a history in which they wanted to be considered full participants.

This is not the place to rehearse their various claims of relationship to the site itself or the counterclaims made by the bureaucrats to deny them recognition as a community. The issues are complex, involving questions of law as well as cultural identity, and have engaged the attention of a wide range of scholars as well as politicians and the United Nations Habitat agency—this last body being also, and simultaneously, concerned with the situation in Rome (see Advisory Group on Forced Evictions [AGFE] 2005). For a community of some 300 souls, Pom Mahakan has achieved an emblematic status that may eventually determine the fate of a far larger number of people as the logic of whatever happens to this community is likely to be extended nationally and even beyond the Thai borders.

What concerns me here instead is the impossibility of treating their predicament in any meaningfully apolitical sense. The history in which they wish to participate is itself heavily laden with political significance; in an age in which criticisms of the institution and persons of the monarchy are met with a draconian law against lèse-majesté, their attempts to remain on a site of great significance to the dynasty's own history compel them to work within the terms of a strictly dynastic and official understanding of the Thai past. Moreover, they must celebrate their collective presence in terms of "Thai-ness" (*khwaam pen thai*), overlooking the irony that such Thai-ness is based on a historically Western-derived, bourgeois model of national identity (Peleggi 2002a). It would be disingenuous—indeed, experientially untrue—to say that it had very little to do with the everyday lives of ordinary Thais. But its significance for them was partly determined by political decisions they made to exploit the model for their own ends while recognizing the risks that this entailed. The more they embraced it, and especially when they agreed to take part as extras in the shooting of a historical film on the site, the more clearly they acknowledged a Baudrillardian vision of a world framed by simulacra (see Baudrillard 1994)—but that did not make any of it less real. It was, however, real because they made it so, not because it was the inevitable state of the world into which they were born. They *chose* to take part in a historical drama that emphasized the archaeological and architectural framework of their site and thus also reframed, or rather intensified the already dominant mode of framing, their everyday lives as part of a historical documentary. That process was still further enhanced by their growing association, as representatives of a quintessentially and historically Thai lifestyle, with a neighboring royal institution (the King Prajadhipok Museum); their involvement with the museum's activities in documenting traditional communities eventually led to their actually meeting a core member of the royal family in a ceremony conducted at the museum itself. I was directly involved in forging some of the connections that made this happen, yet I was also uneasily aware that it was a process that risked co-opting the residents in a vision of past, present, and future that repressed much of what made them a distinctive community. Their leaders, I discovered, were experiencing similar qualms. But the alternative would have been collective annihilation. So the political gains of such an engagement are, it appears, almost always necessarily partial and provisional, and the greatest risk lies in letting the provisionality of everyday life disappear into the bureaucratic stillness of official history.

Provisionality offers its own special challenge to anthropological ethics; it contests the premise of final resolution that positivistic planners always hope to be able to perfect. The commitments one makes in situations like that of Pom Mahakan never go away. One of the leaders, early in our acquaintance, asked me whether I would continue to be interested in the community if the residents were eventually evicted and dispersed. His question gave me a moment of shocked recognition of how easy—and how irresponsible—it would be to abandon them to the oblivion meted out to them by the bureaucratic state. It was also a moment in which I realized that I could not, in good conscience, go on studying the impact of the past on the present, or the everyday management of historical and archaeological sites, if I acted in such a self-serving and indifferent fashion. I did respond that even a cynical view of the matter would have me coming back to the residents for follow-up since I would want to know what had happened to their views of history after—and, implicitly, as a result of—the eviction. But that, like my refusal to make "political" promises, actually seemed to reassure him about the integrity of my intentions, and I confess that the realization afforded me no small amount of comfort.

The issue seemed to me, in any case, to be a rather simple one. I had no real compunction about getting involved, in the main because I felt that it was a very weak community faced with massive action by a city government that simply wanted to press forward with its plans to construct an uninhabited park on the site. Perhaps, too, the authorities felt that the idea of dedicating the park to Queen Sirikit would silence any opposition. But there are many ways of articulating political critique that do not stray into the dangerous territory of lèse-majesté. The sheer banality of a park, the main feature of which was an enormous, empty lawn—one, moreover, that soon filled up with puddles of mud in the one segment that was constructed—did not seem to offer a compelling moral alternative to a scheme that would allow the residents to remain as guardians of the historic site and the living representatives of what in fact was very much the official vision of the true Thai cultural essence.

There is another compelling argument against the idea that foreigners should avoid engagement with local political issues. That is the fact that even the most nationalistic of states today embraces some form of global engagement. As a representative of something vaguely called "the West," I felt that the constant invocation of values—aesthetic, political, and moral—attributed to that entity implicated me, and by extension every other Western scholar, in a process of cultural engineering that misrepresented allegedly Western values and practices while also forcing ordinary people into economic and physical misery. The authorities' declared goal of turning Rajadamnoen Avenue, the street connecting Pom Mahakan to the sacred space of the old royal palace grounds (Sanam Luang), into "the Champs-Elysées of Asia" exemplifies this dynamic. It is hard to imagine that tourists would visit this upstart version of Baron Haussmann's ceremonial avenue except, perhaps, to buy expensive souvenirs from the government-sponsored shops planned to replace the jumble of offices, restaurants, and private homes that currently lines the street and its side alleys. But the authorities determinedly ignored any suggestion that these same tourists would have taken great delight in visiting "traditional" communities so conveniently located in the very heart of the old city.

The key term invoked by the authorities to justify their decisions was "beauty" (*khwaam suay ngaam*). Not only were the criteria of this aesthetic manifestly of Western origin, which certainly fits with the larger pattern of Thai public life (Harrison and Jackson 2009; Peleggi 2002b); they also reflected a desire to conceal aspects of Thai life felt to be incompatible with true "civilization" (*khwaam siwilai*, on which see Thongchai 2002). Because Thai officialdom finds any departure from this model to be embarrassing and potentially damaging to the kingdom's self-presentation, the techniques as well as the structural forms of surface design are almost always of Western origin even when certain decorative features (spirit hooks, house frames, and the like) are stereotypically Thai. These also accompany urban policies that uncannily resemble Haussmann's plans for Paris; by effectively placing the symbolic center under military surveillance and guaranteeing fast access to tanks and armored cars, and by banishing both potentially unruly student populations (as in the move of Thammasat University to Rangsit) and the poor residents of the various communities lining Rajadamnoen Avenue for most of its length, these policies reinforce a "civilizing process" (Elias 1978) of which any colonial power would have been proud—and this in a country that has long boasted of having never labored under the colonial yoke.

The conjuncture of concealment and a Western facade is not coincidental. Because the claim to civilized status is politically important, it is often—although here Greece furnishes a more dramatic case study than Thailand—enacted by means of aggressively Western-derived and modernist cultural features that concomitantly serve as instruments of concealment. This is why the metaphor of a facade is so appropriate.

If concealment represents a reaction to an increasingly globalized set of values (what I have elsewhere dubbed the "global hierarchy of value"; Herzfeld 2004) and the desire to measure up to these as the price of acceptance, it is often concealment of the most intimate dimensions of everyday sociability and cultural form—aspects of a long social history that today clash inconveniently with this world aesthetic. Globalization, moreover, compounds the phenomenon. UNESCO, for example, while representing a global hierarchy of aesthetic value, is an institution made up of nation-states and cannot realistically be anything more than the sum total of those nation-states. Nation-states are heavily invested in both concealing and protecting those aspects of everyday life that belong to the zone of cultural intimacy and that are often considered embarrassing in a moral universe still massively defined by what was once a colonial sensibility (Herzfeld 2005). Institutional globalization therefore locks into place, on a worldwide scale, the suppression of cultural features that do not please the (often self-appointed) defenders of national purity and dignity.

This tendency feeds on a rich tradition of self-censorship—especially in nineteenth-century Europe, where newly emergent nations vied with each other to attain to standards of Victorian respectability established as the yardstick of civilization by the colonial powers. The same process was repeated in the twentieth century as new nations emerged from the colonial system, demonstrating that the demise of colonial occupation did not bring with it the disappearance of the colonial aesthetic. Indeed, that aesthetic—which became the basis for ranking populations on a sliding scale of nearness to civilization or otherwise (Raheja 1996)—gained a new lease on life as the largely Eurocentric standards of UNESCO were rendered visible and monumental through the creation of the UNESCO World Heritage list (Askew 2010).

Eastern Europe was an early experimental laboratory for such cultural purism. The nineteenth-century Greek folklorists, for example, cleaned out all the obscenities and dirty jokes, treated all expressions of local history as corrupt derivatives of a national master narrative, and firmly rejected anything that could be attributed to Arabic, Turkish, Albanian, or Slavic influence. One notorious essay traced all Balkan domestic architecture to the alleged form of the ancient Greek *megaron* (Kyriakides 1955). Folk songs were traced to epic poems and ancient dramas, and

more improvisatory forms such as the Cretan assonant couplets (*mandinadhes*) almost disappeared from the "national" collections of folklore, although they resurfaced in local compilations that expressed a somewhat dissident identity that both
reinforced and contested the hegemony of national models; moreover, folklorists
developed something of an allergy to improvisational forms in general, since they
resisted the kind of museological reductionism that served the goals of national
consolidation (see now Sykäri 2011). I recall that during the repressive days of
the military regimes of 1967–74, the Folklore Archive of the Academy of Athens
did maintain boxes of unsorted *mandinadha* texts; other song texts were placed in
carefully labeled files, but the archive's functionaries viewed the *mandinadhes* with
helpless perplexity since they could not discipline these riotously varied texts into
a manageable taxonomy.

Predictably, UNESCO became the means of both driving "unofficial" forms of
folklore even further underground and at the same time reifying the rest as "folklore," "local knowledge" (see Gupta 1998), and "national treasures." The model
remained one of resolutely simplistic materialism. Early folklorists had spoken of
"monuments of the word," thus peremptorily dismissing from the canon anything
that could not be fenced around like the monuments enclosed by the framing devices of modern urban planners. UNESCO perpetuated this model; the category of
intangible culture rendered some things vastly more tangible than before, leaving the
messy, living aspects of everyday culture in the limbo of unclassifiability (Herzfeld
forthcoming). In short, the taxonomic imperatives of bureaucracy took over from
social life and rendered it invisible, while charges of disrespect for a national past
were sometimes treated as tantamount to treason.

This dangerous turn notably characterized Greece under the military regimes of
1967–74, despite the colonels' notorious ineptitude in neoclassical Greek and their
highly selective and frequently absurd representation of the national past. Yet the
image of the ancient past for which they demanded such unctuous respect was one
they had carefully censored and retooled themselves. So sensitive were they to the
perceived need to calibrate national culture to the Western ethos, in fact, that they
even censored ancient Attic comedies by Aristophanes on the grounds of suppressing
obscenity. Classes in high schools and universities were conducted in a purist concoc-
tion (*katharevousa*) that few citizens—and certainly not the colonels themselves—
really ever mastered. Concealing the evidence of alternative forms of Greekness
became a national virtue, and, like the purist language itself, this self-censorship
has left identifiable marks on the understanding of national culture even in today's
more enlightened and less straitjacketed times. As a result, in an age when a bust of
Dionysus can still appear as a meaningful ornament on the neoclassical exterior of
a bar in South Korea, there remains a general—if today more inchoate—sense that
the Greek nation's strongest claim on global respect is its ability to resuscitate the alleged ethical and aesthetic values of high antiquity. Hybridity is not a welcome guest
at this global cultural feast.

And yet hybridity is nothing new in Greece, or anywhere else for that matter. In religious affairs it is known as syncretism—a term that fell into some disrepute, but that has recently (Shaw and Stewart 1994) been somewhat restored to favor because it suggests useful analogies with processes in other domains of social life (in politics, for example; Stewart 1994). Such syncretism also has ancient antecedents; the myth of pure national culture is, after all, rather recent, and the denial of minority identities is a historically recent product of political expediency.

Thus, for example, a Greek archaeologist, Amy Papalexandrou (2003, 2010), has done insightful studies of the *spolia*, the remnants of the classical past, that are built into Byzantine churches. The general view until she did her work seems to have been that the Byzantines had no respect for the pagan past—that in fact they were out to destroy it—and that this was simply evidence of their indifference to it. She shows that these *spolia* are inserted into the walls in extremely systematic ways; even their apparent disorder suggests that *spolia* concentrated within themselves a generalized sense of varied, ancient cultural sources deserving of respect and suffused with the divine, and that their eclectic variety reproduces the literary pattern of "encyclopedism" that characterized much of the writing of that time (2010, 63–64). Papalexandrou thereby shows that this systematicity is clear evidence of a deep respect, not for the religion of the ancient Greeks, but for their artistic capacities and for some sense of continuity between that culture and the modern, probably a much more convincing continuity than the much more obviously constructed one favored by nineteenth-century Greece.

Current concern with concepts of agency poses its own risks in interpreting such phenomena; as Brown and Hamilakis (2003, 14) rightly remark, it "tends to prioritize the role of calculating and manipulative agency over the inertia or momentum of assembled precedent." But Papalexandrou's work nicely sails between Scylla and Charybdis; she does not attempt the impossible (guessing what the Byzantines really understood the *spolia* to represent) but shows that some patterns of use do suggest at least an attitude of acceptance and perhaps admiration. It may well be that the relative vagueness of her conclusion more accurately reflects the actual state of affairs when the *spolia* were affixed to churches than any attempted generalization about their precise meaning could achieve.

If monuments can resist the allure of bureaucratic or positivistic obsessions with definition, moreover, the same ought to be true, a fortiori, of those cultural phenomena that have been classified as intangible heritage. What to a philologist is a vernacular text that bears witness to ancient memories might be nothing more, or less, than a familiar song or tale or a commemoration of local events for the ordinary citizen. In fact, this is also true of domestic architecture despite attempts to monumentalize it as heritage; individual memories reconstruct social relations and reframe them in largely presentist and often significantly contested terms (Bahloul 1996; Slyomovics 1998). And domestic architecture strengthens my argument in another sense; although it is not intangible in the sense that UNESCO attributes to folklore, it complicates the sense of semantic permanence that most people associate with the big monuments, since everyone knows that private homes often get drastically restructured. (That said, we should not forget that the same thing does also happen to some of the world's most imposing architectural structures, as in the conversion of mosques into Christian churches and Hindu temples and vice versa.)

Even the imposing structures or historically significant sites that we most easily classify as monuments do not always mean the same thing to everyone, even at a single given moment within a small and tightly knit community. To archaeologists, the altar of Caesar in the Roman Forum is a historically significant monument; to those neofascists who continue to evoke Mussolini's exaggerated classicism and the ideals of *romanità*, it is a place to leave flowers in an act of homage that apparently speaks more to current political dynamics than to the historical personage of Julius Caesar himself or to the religious system that deified him. To many Romans, again, the arch of Titus is an imposing monument built by one of the more practical and successful ancient emperors, but its scenes of the pillage of Jerusalem in 70 B.C.E. make it anathema to observant Jews, themselves a symbolically crucial population that allegedly preserved much of the ancient culture of the Eternal City; they will not accept the subjection symbolized by passing under the arch.

Sometimes politicians are more determined to reify certain monuments, and to isolate them from the common people whose heritage they supposedly represent, than are even the scholar-practitioners charged with their preservation. In the case of Pom Mahakan in Bangkok, the central dispute revolves around whether the roughly 300 residents of the site—an important segment of the eighteenth-century city fortifications—should be evicted to make way for a carefully manicured park or remain as both guardians of the site and representatives of older Thai lifestyles. The bureaucrats have been adamant that the residents must go. Less clear was the position of the Fine Arts Department, one of whose representatives, an archaeologist who visited the site to make an assessment, expressed the view that it would arguably be preferable for the site to be inhabited by caring and traditionally minded people. In addition, one of the community's most fervent advocates, and more generally an advocate of poor people's rights, is a now-retired professor of archaeology from Thammasat University, Pthomrerk Ketudhat.

At one point, a few houses were indeed torn down, and the area closest to the citadel (*pom*) that gives the community its name, an area the residents had used for communal meetings and as an exhibition area to publicize their cause, was covered with the expanse of lawn that I have already mentioned as poorly maintained. Meanwhile, despite difficult physical conditions and extremely limited financial resources, the residents maintained a spotlessly clean environment in the still-inhabited section. They thus made their case by demonstrating their capacity to deliver on their promises of responsible site management. In short, they have made an inspiring argument for their right to survival as a community quite literally in situ. Those archaeologists and social anthropologists who have expressed support for that case have taken a stand on both pragmatic and ethical grounds, whereas the bureaucrats' response is almost entirely grounded in legalistic arguments.

A purist might nevertheless argue that people should not be allowed to take pieces of monuments and incorporate them in a settlement or in buildings that reflect a present-day identity. Papalexandrou's treatment of the Byzantine use of *spolia*, however, reminds us that reuse is itself a cultural practice of great antiquity—in, we might add, many parts of the world. To oppose a project that is *both* an attempt at conservation *and* an insertion of that attempt in a project of communal development is to take a very narrow view indeed of the public good—the ethical argument usually raised in defense of the purists' view. And in some cases—consider, for example, the Navajo artists who made sand paintings and whose successors now argue that these paintings should be allowed to fall apart because this is part of the prescribed ritual sequence (see Parezo 1983)—the purists' goals conflict directly not only with present-day desires but with the intentions of the original creators of the works in question. Bureaucratic understandings of conservation may result in the survival of monuments that would otherwise have disappeared, but the failure to heed present-day social contexts is surely an abuse of archaeology as a human science.

When that context is a nationalist project, whether it affects physical monuments or popular lore, it is relatively difficult for a small local community to stand up for an alternative vision. Archaeology in the service of the national state can be extremely destructive to the interests of marginal or minority groups. In such works as the important volumes edited by Bond and Gilliam (1994; especially Hall 1994) and by Kohl and Fawcett (1995), we can easily track the impact of ideology on typology, and of typology on sometimes highly selective techniques of excavation and analysis. In particular, nationalist ideologies that elide the presence of minority interests find archaeology a useful tool (see Abu El-Haj 2001). That being the case, and even allowing for a degree of spirited internal debate, should we not be suspicious of global institutions that do little more than intensify the impact of such selectivity? That is the most serious objection to UNESCO's attempts to codify and legalize its classifications of archaeological monuments (see De Cesari 2010a, 2010b). If a single nationalist edifice is hard to resist, or conversely creates fertile grounds for the resentment that so easily produces exclusionary ideologies of more or less fascist stamp, what can we expect of an international organization that by its very constitution cannot transcend the shared ideals of all nationalist projects?

The necessarily partial and perhaps unsatisfactory—and certainly provisional—answer lies in what we might call "empirical reflexivity." That UNESCO and other bodies save monuments is not to be denied. Less clear, however, is for whom and to what ends they save them. The Western colonial powers—drawing on the emergent and successful project of scientific urbanism—could congratulate themselves on a liberal vision that incorporated and even monumentalized the architectural remnants of a defeated otherness (see Herzfeld 1991, 197; Rabinow 1989, 299–301). This is not to say that the underlying motives are always simply the projection of a discomfited liberal conscience, but there often seems to be an element of self-justification involved, especially as such acts of preservation also entail *spatial taxonomy*—fencing, territorial mapping (Thongchai 1994; Wilkinson 1951), charging admission fees, and so on.

How, then, are we to resist the kind of closure that comes with these taxonomic interventions? The latter cluster largely around four key terms: heritage, monumentality, history, and preservation. All of them invoke the idea of permanence, though they may also be contrasted in terms of the specific modalities they suggest—as, for example, Daniel (1996, 25–27) has done in comparatively treating heritage and history as the diagnostic strategies of Tamils and Sinhalese, respectively, in Sri Lanka. The difficulty with this kind of binarism is that it easily becomes circular and, in the process, reinforces the authority of the dominant member of the pair. While such solipsism is far from what Daniel intended, it is hard to imagine that slippage could be avoided for long. My own distinction between social and monumental time (Herzfeld 1991) runs the same risk; the nation-state's monumental time is itself a form of social time, albeit of a kind that often creates the illusion of permanence.

A key problem is that we tend to assume, as do many nationalist folklorists contemplating the relation between written and oral texts, that the literary, official way of talking about the past furnishes the models for the vernacular equivalents. That is not necessarily true. As I have frequently noted, the Greek usage of the word *istories* means "histories," but it also means "differences" and "quarrels." Who is to say that the orientation toward local gossip implied by such a usage follows rather than precedes the creation of official historiography? If monumental time is social, so, too, is the idea of a fixed and unchanging national identity. Moreover, the mask of unity often conceals a complex set of mutually contrasted and contesting ideologies, performatively realized as *istories*, disputes. History is pluralized by differences of opinion, and it is this plurality, as much as particular versions of local or dissident history, that nation-states typically prefer to suppress or to disguise with bromides about "unity in diversity" and the like.

But vernacular usages like this suggest that there may be more historiographies than are dreamed of in official thinking. How, for example, would the four terms I have just listed appear from a Thai point of view? For heritage, what about "uncanny recognitions"; for monumentality, "merit-making"; for history, "dynastic stability"; and for preservation, "reincarnation"? I have deliberately constructed this list of alternatives to evoke the concerns of modern Thai Buddhism, and I suggest that these offer an infinitely more interesting way of decoding the supermodern city of Bangkok—a city that, while it has lost much of its original grounding in the logic of the mandala (Tambiah 1976, 102–31), is still shaped on the ground to a significant degree by Buddhist values (see Taylor 2008, 18–23). These values arguably contradict or subvert the urban planners' Western orientation as this emerges in, for example, the widely derided intention, already mentioned, of transforming Rajadamnoen Avenue into the Champs-Elysées of Asia.

But a more playful application of these four re-readings is to reimport them into the analysis of European cultures. If "uncanny recognition," for example, works in Thailand because of the ubiquitous fascination with ghosts (e.g., Klima 2002), what are we to make of Roman claims that the ghost of Messalina (the emperor Claudius's ill-fated wife) still walks through the streets of the historic core (Herzfeld 2009, 68)? Should we take such claims less seriously only because of the self-ascribed rationalism of Europeans? It is true that Romans do not describe these supernatural encounters as "heritage" (*patrimonio*), a term that for them derives from official usage, but it would appear that they afford a means of symbolizing a sense of belonging to a past that is Roman rather than Italian and that is embedded in the very stones and pavements of their ancient quarter. The fact that sightings of Messalina were mentioned in a setting that includes the Colosseum and the Forum, on a street that has been continuously inhabited in some form for at least two millennia, implicitly ties what the state regards as the national *patrimonio* to extremes of localism (*campanilismo*) and invests the grandiose history of the ancient empire with the resonance of cultural belonging.

"Merit-making" poses an interesting point of comparison. Thais—especially Thai monks—refurbish temples in much the same way that Greeks refurbish icons. That is, they will make them as brightly colored as possible because brightness is associated with divinity in both traditions. Thais show little concern with using the original materials in beautifying temples and other religious buildings; Greeks encrust icons with silver and gold. In both cases the goal is to glorify the divine; whether one professes belief in reincarnation or in final rewards in the hereafter, that goal is motivated by an underlying concern with personal salvation (or the salvation of loved ones). The refurbishment of a venerated material object in the present serves as both the vehicle and the metaphor of that salvation.

We can go further. In Thailand the doctrine of reincarnation not only requires the dynamic of refurbishment rather than of conservation but also means that the materiality of a given monument is less important than its identity; the retention of original materials—for example, in plans to rebuild some of the houses at Pom Mahakan— has an economic rather than a symbolic value. When we turn this perspective on the use of icons and other religious images in Greece, we find that a small trace of the original material is all that is required to establish a continuity of identity since it is the repository of a transcendent grace that can infuse an infinity of images (e.g., Danforth 1989, 169–74). In short, a comparison of the two cases demonstrates that the pursuit of personal or collective salvation in the here and now animates decisions about the treatment of the sacred far more than static models of pure reproduction. In semiotic terms, the links are as much indexical as they are iconic; they are embedded in social dynamics rather than in the kind of collective image of culture that nationalism seeks. This, too, is why nation-state bureaucracies generally try to extract monuments and other venerated objects from their social contexts and specify, through fencing or placement in museums, that their new role is to emblematize the permanence of the collectivity.

In some cases this entails forgetting the origins of the state itself. Modern Thailand and Greece both emerged from polities very different from the Westernized models that animate their bureaucratic structures today. Dynastic stability in Thailand and claims to cultural continuity with the ancient past in Greece both lay claim to a permanence that is best represented in the material conservation of monuments. In both countries, for example, the old association of temples with markets and with everyday political and social interchange is increasingly erased by monumental enclosures and other acts of what we might call "classification on the ground." In Athens, the present-day framing of the Acropolis exemplifies this process; the adjacent neighborhood of Anafiotika, long threatened with extinction because it posed a conceptual threat to the lofty classicism of the Acropolis, was saved from destruction only because an emergent new aesthetic led to its reconfiguration as an example of the vernacular national heritage—at which point gentrification also began to drive out many of the original residents' families (Caftanzoglou 2000, 2001, 2010). What had changed was the permitted *content* of "Greek heritage," not the pervasive attempt to represent the past by suppressing plural histories and the inconvenience that their living bearers pose for official strategies of representation.

Again, however, it is important to remember that the monumental is also social; its claims to permanence are, paradoxically, the product of a process. Özyürek (2004) has nicely documented this in the context of museum representations of an idealized national image of the Turkish family. What Palumbo (2003, 305) calls "philological correctness"—the scholarly literalism that officialdom so often uses to legitimize its choices and occlude their contingent character—is similarly subject to changing criteria of evaluation; scholarly legitimation is itself a social process, just as the practice of bureaucracy is one of rendering contingent choices as incontrovertible outcomes. The stance of scholarly disinterestedness is another example of such a process masquerading as factual fixity. Both as analysis and as ethics, it serves us poorly: as analysis, because it is precisely the phenomenon that we should be studying and thus cannot serve as an instrument of that analysis; and as ethics, because it plays into the hands of those who wield official power.

One move that can usefully discommode this complicity is the strategy I have advocated here: that of viewing more familiar cultural settings from the perspectives we gain elsewhere, not so much in an ethno-archaeological sense, but, more provocatively, by using comparison to suggest interpretations that do not emerge from the assumptions embedded in our disciplines' own cultural origins. Such an approach, however, will take us only so far. We cannot do "archaeology from the native's point of view," to paraphrase Clifford Geertz (1983, 55–70); still less can we be sure how the natives of one part of the world would interpret the experiences we observe in another. The problem of evidential scarcity is especially acute here. The erstwhile denizens of an archaeological site cannot comment on what we say about them, while there is also the risk that today's residents might see our well-meaning attempts to connect with them as little more than a disguise for academic self-interest. Nevertheless, that is a risk we have to take; and it is one increasingly taken.

What I am suggesting is that some of the archaeological work done in collaboration with local populations (e.g., Stroulia and Sutton 2010) can complement the cross-cultural analyses of historicity to produce an enhanced understanding of the multiplex past, an understanding that also responds to an ethic of political engagement with those on whose local generosity and knowledge we depend. Despite the risk of unintended condescension, which is in any case something we can turn into a genuinely reflexive ethic as long as we can sustain our awareness of it at all times, our willingness to involve local residents in our projects opens up new questions that are at once epistemological and ethical. Engaging local residents in the production of a video of local life, for example, addresses both dimensions (e.g., Nixon 2010). That, I suggest, is the crux of the matter; for a project that is conceived in purely epistemological terms, without regard to its ethical implications (or with a self-satisfied completion of some bureaucratic ethics requirement), ultimately surrenders to the discursive closure that is the hallmark of the official world and renders the scholar complicit in official control of the local. To those who would argue against any sort of political engagement on the grounds that this is not the work of the true scholar, and especially of the scholar working in a foreign country, I would therefore respond that a stance of disinterestedness is itself both political and resistant to critique (see also Herzfeld 2010).

Local people's relationship with a landscape may be obvious when one is working in a city, as I was in Rome or Bangkok. But for many scholars working in the countryside, that relationship has proved strangely harder to discern. While social anthropologists have generally noted peasants' attitudes to the land, for example, it was not until they learned to appreciate what local people actually said about the land as a form of *knowledge* that these attitudes became less of an exotic curiosity and more of an intellectual resource. A decisive contribution to this shift, a volume co-edited by Feld and Basso (1996), has had more of an impact on social anthropology than on archaeology, as is also true of Gupta's (1998, 156–290) effective debunking of the radical conceptual separation between so-called indigenous and scientific forms of knowledge. In archaeology, some of the essays collected in the recent volume edited by Stroulia and Sutton (2010) document an encouraging shift. More particularly, the work of the Kalaureia Research Programme addresses this problematic in a notably useful way, in one case by examining the local use of photographic images in a frame extended to include those employed by archaeologists (see Hamilakis and Anagnostopoulos 2009; Hamilakis, Anagnostopoulos, and Ifantidis 2009).

This is not an argument against professional expertise; a preference for something called local knowledge over professional expertise merely reproduces the pernicious old binary opposition in a mirror image. Gupta's (1998) fine analysis shows precisely why we should be careful not to reify indigenous knowledge as necessarily superior to the scientific brand; his point is precisely that both are hybrids, both are grounded in experience, and both are context dependent. Working in the context of current debates about the historiography of Thailand, Thongchai (2001) has made a comparable point about the risks of elevating local above national history, thereby replacing the tyranny of one reification with the equally repressive dominance of another model. And in the present context, Hamilakis and Anagnostopoulos (2009, 81) have pointed out the political consequences of such moves with great acuity: "For example, in Europe today the concept of the indigenous (along with claims of ancestry and continuity) is invoked to support racist attitudes towards recent economic and political immigrants." Far-right movements are quick to take advantage of discontent with national governments by cultivating especially hateful forms of racism on the grounds of preserving authenticity, indigeneity, and local heritage (Herzfeld 2009, 231).

None of these reservations, however, should be taken to mean that local people should not be invited into the discussion of the archaeological and ethnographic study of the places they inhabit. Quite to the contrary, serious discussion on equal terms entails a principled and well-argued rejection of the more unpleasant manifestations of local pride. For the same reason, archaeologists should not be expected to abandon their authority or claims to technical expertise simply on the grounds of a false rendition of political correctness. Rather, all parties to such engagements should, without exception, be held accountable for their views and for the social consequences of those views. There may well be situations in which philological correctness and local understandings actually converge; there may be others in which the residual colonialism of much scholarship is matched by thoroughly internalized attitudes of contempt, often disguised by a rhetoric of civility, for minorities and other disadvantaged groups.

In all these situations, scholars should never forget that what distinguishes the best work, especially in social anthropology, is the capacity to listen and observe rather than to ask only leading questions or try to direct the local production of culture. As a leader of the community with which I am currently working in Bangkok observed to me recently (2010), it is sometimes better to sit at the back and listen than to dominate the discussion—this, from a man whose leadership style has repeatedly saved his small urban enclave from destruction by hostile authorities and who has never hesitated to adopt a strong style of leadership when emergencies such as mass eviction threatened. As I try to learn from him and relish the insights he garnered from his stance, I also hear clearly his adoption of a perspective indexed by his use of anthropological terms (for example, he repeatedly uses the word *boribot*, "context," a true learnedism, in his current conversations) and realize with pleasure that our pedagogy is genuinely mutual and, as a result, mutually beneficial.

In the management of community affairs, scholars who study both the material context and the social environment are themselves stakeholders. But they do not have to live with the consequences of their interventions to the extent that local people must; such is the nature of the differential in access to political and economic resources. We must assess our attitudes both to the desirability of historic conservation and to the benefits of critical dissection in light of this difference (on the latter, see also Jackson 1995). In the community of Pom Mahakan in Bangkok, where I have been conducting field research over the past several years, there is now a small building that functions as a community museum. Its purpose is announced by an elegant, traditionally lettered red and gold board announcing that it houses the "Local Knowledge of the Pom Mahakan Community." This, clearly, is reification in the idiom of intangible heritage. The residents felt constrained to project their presence in this way because the idea of "local knowledge" has gained considerable traction in the context of nation-state positivism within which they must establish their legitimacy. But what does this building actually contain? It houses a huge portrait of the king but also a treasure trove of documentation of their resistance to the authorities' attempt to evict them. They have thereby rendered their struggle both visible and forceful. It would do no good, and might actually do a great deal of harm, to criticize their construction of this museum as simply yielding to the false consciousness of an identity modeled on that of the state and its institutions. Their own awareness of these conceptual traps is a far better protection of their intellectual and political integrity than any outsider intervention could possibly afford.

Conversely, when we look at museums created for and by elite institutions in the West, deconstruction of their ideological underpinnings serves a similar purpose of raising and sustaining awareness, and of encouraging reflection on the colonial origins of so much of what we automatically take today as beneficial intervention. The ethnological museums of Oxford, Cambridge, and Harvard Universities have all served as excellent illustrations and bearers of staunchly evolutionist frameworks. Today, however, they also incorporate material on why they have changed. They are, in other words, intentionally reflexive, and, as reflexive museums, they encourage a sustained critical perspective on the motivations that animate so much current engagement by anthropologists in the practical problems of far-flung places. Moreover, with digital media we can also unite art history and ethnological museums so that art historians begin to see paintings and statuary from European "high culture" as ethnographically revealing, while anthropologists might start to pay greater attention to the historical development of form and aesthetics (see Herzfeld 2007). By thus challenging some of the binary assumptions that underlie our organization of knowledge—what we might ironically call our own local knowledge—we can make our received categories productively uncomfortable and, in consequence, generative of new insights and reorderings.

If celebration allows marginalized groups to find a space within the parameters permitted by national authorities, critique is more productive within the power structure itself. A few years ago, the city administration of Rome, in a fascinating display at the Ara Pacis in Rome, displayed images showing how Mussolini had brutally destroyed significant parts of the medieval city in order to construct the spaces that allowed him to play the role of the new Caesar. Such reminders of the fallibility of power also work against the archaeological and conservationist version of the fallacy of misplaced concreteness: reconstructions and other evocations of authenticity are themselves parts of ongoing cultural processes, always liable to reversal or revision and always subject to the necessary corrosion—or cleansing—of doubt.

It is much easier to sell certainty to any public, and especially to a consumerist public. Reification and essentialism are seductive precisely because they represent efforts already made and concluded, demanding nothing further from us save acquiescence. How much easier it is to accept a seemingly perfect fake—the Parthenon in Nashville, Tennessee, for example—than to enjoy the in-your-face provisionality of conscientious archaeological restoration and the commemoration of inconvenient events, or to face difficult choices balancing—for example—heritage and housing against each other. It is the Sisyphean task of social anthropology and archaeology together to resist the siren lures of false perfection and to reinstate the desirability of inconvenience. Responsible restoration is self-critical; restoration should show how artifacts and monuments—super-*spolia*, as it were—are being reused in their modern contexts. Responsible ethnography similarly focuses, as I suggested at the beginning of this essay, on the use of categories rather than on the categories themselves. Both also attend to their own practices, not as a vehicle of self-congratulation, but as a salutary reminder that we, too, are engaged in the processes that we document; and the renewal of dialogue between the two fields can only strengthen this commitment to critique.

The evidential scarcity faced by archaeologists and the informational excess faced by social anthropologists are both cross-cut by chances and choices—by the chances of preservation in the archaeological record and of informant attitudes in the ethnographic experience, and by the choices dictated by the professional and ideological predilections we bring to our analyses. It is in this area that the interests of social anthropologists and archaeologists must engage both each other and the social realities within which they operate. They must serve as checks on each other's modalities of scarcity and excess. While their moral compass should prevent an explosive development of the heritage industry from becoming an obstacle to the provision of housing and of the other necessities that make life bearable, it should also oppose the populism that seeks to eradicate the plural heritages of those who lack the power to defend their own interests.

That complex goal is achievable only when scholars also resist the essentialisms—puristic readings of the past—through which authorities around the world justify their most repressive invocations of eminent domain. Such interventions may range from the theological—what Stewart (2010) wittily calls "immanent domain"—to the legalistic, but they are all exercises of power that purport to serve a collective and morally justifiable goal. While some interventions may indeed serve a sense of the common good on which citizens can largely agree, and may genially remind these citizens of the impermanence of both monuments and governments, others, more wedded to the interests of power, threaten instead to stifle argument, often invoking the supposedly international values of the global hierarchy in order to reinforce their authority. In that scenario, the reductionist and atemporal hand of bureaucracy builds, in the name of conservation, perfectly restored walls around cities no less perfectly dead.

References

Abu El-Haj, Nadia. 2001. *Facts on the ground: Archaeological practice and territorial self-fashioning in Israeli society.* Chicago: University of Chicago Press.

Advisory Group on Forced Evictions (AGFE). 2005. *Forced evictions: Towards solutions? First report of the Advisory Group on Forced Evictions to the executive director of UN-Habitat.* Nairobi, Kenya: Advisory Group on Forced Evictions.

Askew, Marc. 2010. "The magic list of global status: UNESCO, world heritage and the agendas of states." In *Heritage and globalization*, ed. Sophia Labadi and Colin Lang, 19–44. Abingdon and New York: Routledge.

Bahloul, Joëlle. 1996. *The architecture of memory: A Jewish-Muslim household in colonial Algeria, 1937–1962.* Cambridge: Cambridge University Press.

Baudrillard, Jean. 1994. *Simulacra and simulation*, trans. Sheila Faria Glaser. Ann Arbor: University of Michigan Press.

Bernal, Martin. 1987. *Black Athena: The Afroasiatic roots of classical civilization.* Vol. 1. New Brunswick, NJ: Rutgers University Press.

Bond, George Clement, and Angela Gilliam, eds. 1994. *Social construction of the past: Representation as power.* London: Routledge.

Brown, K. S., and Yannis Hamilakis. 2003. "The cupboard of the yesterdays? Critical perspectives on the usable past." In *The usable past: Greek metahistories*, ed. K. S. Brown and Yannis Hamilakis, 1–19. Lanham, MD: Lexington Books/ Rowman and Littlefield.

Caftanzoglou, Roxane. 2000. "The sacred rock and the profane settlement: Place, memory and identity under the Acropolis." *Journal of Oral History* 28: 43–51.

Caftanzoglou, Roxane. 2001. "Shadow of the sacred rock: Contrasting discourses of place under the Acropolis." In *Contested landscapes: Movement, exile and place*, ed. Barbara Bender and Margot Winer, 21–35. Oxford: Berg.

Caftanzoglou, Roxane. 2010. "Producing and consuming pictures: Representations of a landscape." In Stroulia and Sutton 2010, 159–78.

Clark, Grahame. 1939. *Archaeology and society.* London: Methuen.

Danforth, Loring M. 1989. *Firewalking and religious healing: The Anastenaria of Greece and the American firewalking movement.* Princeton, NJ: Princeton University Press.

Daniel, E. Valentine. 1996. *Charred lullabies: Chapters in an anthropography of violence*. Princeton, NJ: Princeton University Press.

De Cesari, Chiara. 2010a. "Creative heritage: Palestinian heritage NGOs and defiant arts of government." *American Anthropologist* 112: 625–37.

De Cesari, Chiara. 2010b. "World heritage and mosaic universalism: A view from Palestine." *Journal of Social Archaeology* 10: 299–324.

Elias, Norbert. 1978. *The civilizing process*, trans. Edmund Jephcott. Vol. 1. New York: Unizen Books.

Fallmerayer, Jakob Philipp. 1830, 1836. *Geschichte der Halbinsel Morea während des Mittelalters*. Stuttgart and Tübingen, Germany: J. G. Cotta.

Farmer, Paul. 2003. *Pathologies of power: Health, human rights, and the new war on the poor*. Berkeley: University of California Press.

Feld, Steven, and Keith H. Basso, eds. 1996. *Senses of place*. Santa Fe, NM: School of American Research Press.

Geertz, Clifford. 1983. *Local knowledge: Further essays in interpretive anthropology*. New York: Basic Books.

Gupta, Akhil. 1998. *Postcolonial developments: Agriculture in the making of modern India*. Durham, NC: Duke University Press.

Hall, Martin. 1994. "Lifting the veil of popular history: Archaeology and politics in urban Cape Town." In Bond and Gilliam 1994, 167–84.

Hamilakis, Yannis. 2007. *The nation and its ruins: Antiquity, archaeology, and national imagination in Greece*. Oxford: Oxford University Press.

Hamilakis, Yannis, and Aris Anagnostopoulos. 2009. "What is archaeological ethnography?" *Public Archaeology* 8: 65–87.

Hamilakis, Yannis, Aris Anagnostopoulos, and Fotis Ifantidis. 2009. "Postcards from the edge of time: Archaeology, photography, archaeological ethnography (a photo-essay)." *Public Archaeology* 8: 283–309.

Hamilakis, Yannis, and Eleana Yalouri. 1996. "Antiquities as symbolic capital in modern Greek society." *Antiquity* 70: 117–29.

Handler, Richard. 1985. "On having a culture: Nationalism and the preservation of Quebec's *Patrimoine*." In *Objects and Others*, vol. 3 of *History of Anthropology*, ed. George Stocking, 192–217. Madison: University of Wisconsin Press.

Handler, Richard. 1988. *Nationalism and the politics of culture in Quebec*. Madison: University of Wisconsin Press.

Harrison, Rachel, and Peter Jackson, eds. 2009. *The ambiguous allure of the West: Traces of the colonial in Thailand*. Hong Kong: Hong Kong University Press; Honolulu: University of Hawaii Press.

Herzfeld, Michael. 1991. *A place in history: Social and monumental time in a Cretan town*. Princeton, NJ: Princeton University Press.

Herzfeld, Michael. 1992. "Metapatterns: Archaeology and the uses of evidential scarcity." In *Representation in archaeology*, ed. Jean-Claude Gardin and Christopher S. Peebles, 66–86. Bloomington: Indiana University Press.

Herzfeld, Michael. 2003. "Pom Mahakan: Humanity and order in the historic center of Bangkok." *Thailand Human Rights Journal* 1: 101–19.

Herzfeld, Michael. 2004. *The body impolitic: Artisans and artifice in the global hierarchy of value*. Chicago: University of Chicago Press.

Herzfeld, Michael. 2005. *Cultural intimacy: Social poetics in the nation-state*. 2nd ed. New York: Routledge.

Herzfeld, Michael. 2007. "Fusion museums: On the importance of preserving an embarrassing genealogy." *Res* 52: 37–43.

Herzfeld, Michael. 2009. *Evicted from eternity: The restructuring of modern Rome*. Chicago: University of Chicago Press.

Herzfeld, Michael. 2010. "Engagement, gentrification, and the neoliberal hijacking of history." *Current Anthropology* 51 (suppl. 2): S259–67.

Herzfeld, Michael. Forthcoming. "Intangible delicacies: Production and embarrassment in international settings." *Ethnologies*.

Jackson, Jean E. 1995. "Culture, genuine and spurious: The politics of Indianness in the Vaupés, Colombia." *American Ethnologist* 22: 3–27.

Klima, Alan. 2002. *The funeral casino: Meditation, massacre, and exchange with the dead in Thailand*. Princeton, NJ: Princeton University Press.

Kohl, Philip L., and Clare Fawcett, eds. 1995. *Nationalism, politics, and the practice of archaeology*. Cambridge: Cambridge University Press.

Kyriakides, Stilpon P. 1955. *The northern ethnological boundaries of Hellenism*. Thessaloniki, Greece: Institute for Balkan Studies.

Lévi-Strauss, Claude. 1997. *Tristes Tropiques*, trans. John and Doreen Weightman. New York: Modern Library.

Lucas, Gavin. 2001. "Destruction and the rhetoric of excavation." *Norwegian Archaeological Review* 34: 35–46.

Molé, Noëlle J. 2010. "Precarious subjects: Anticipating neoliberalism in northern Italy's workplace." *American Anthropologist* 112: 38–53.

Muehlebach, Andrea. 2009. "*Complexio oppositorum*: Notes on the left in neoliberal Italy." *Public Culture* 21: 495–515.

Nixon, Lucia. 2010. "Seeing voices and changing relationships: Film, archaeological reporting, and the landscape of people in Sphakia." In Stroulia and Sutton 2010, 331–72.

Özyürek, Esra. 2004. "Wedded to the republic: Public intellectuals and intimacy oriented publics in Turkey." In *Off stage/on display: Intimacy and ethnography in the age of public culture*, ed. Andrew Shryock, 101–30. Stanford, CA: Stanford University Press.

Palumbo, Berardino. 2003. *L'UNESCO e il campanile: Antropologia, politica e beni culturali in Sicilia orientale*. Rome, Italy: Meltemi.

Papalexandrou, Amy. 2003. "Memory tattered and torn: Spolia in the heartland of Byzantine Hellenism." In *Archaeologies of memory*, ed. Ruth M. Van Dyke and Susan E. Alcock, 56–80. Oxford: Blackwell.

Papalexandrou, Amy. 2010. "On the shoulders of Hera: Alternative readings of antiquity in the Greek memoryscape." In Stroulia and Sutton 2010, 53–74.

Parezo, Nancy J. 1983. *Navajo sandpainting: From religious to commercial art*. Tucson: University of Arizona Press.

Peleggi, Maurizio. 2002a. *Lords of things: The fashioning of the Siamese monarchy's modern image*. Honolulu: University of Hawaii Press.

Peleggi, Maurizio. 2002b. *The politics of ruins and the business of nostalgia*. Bangkok: White Lotus.

Rabinow, Paul. 1989. *French modern: Norms and forms of the social environment*. Cambridge, MA: MIT Press.

Raheja, Gloria Goodwin. 1996. "Caste, colonialism, and the speech of the colonized: Entextualization and disciplinary control in India." *American Ethnologist* 23: 494–513.

Slyomovics, Susan. 1998. *The object of memory: Arab and Jew narrate the Palestinian village*. Philadelphia: University of Pennsylvania Press.

Stewart, Charles. 1994. "Syncretism as a dimension of nationalist discourse in modern Greece." In Stewart and Shaw 1994, 127–44.

Stewart, Charles. 2010. "Immanent or eminent domain? The contest over Thessaloniki's Rotonda." In Stroulia and Sutton 2010, 179–200.

Stewart, Charles, and Rosalind Shaw, eds. 1994. *Syncretism/anti-syncretism: The politics of religious synthesis*. London: Routledge.

Stroulia, Anna, and Susan Buck Sutton, eds. 2010. *Archaeology in situ: Sites, archaeology, and communities in Greece*. Lanham, MD: Lexington Books/Rowman & Littlefield.

Sykäri, Venla. 2011. *Words as events: Cretan mandinádes in performance and composition*. Studia Fennica Folkloristica 18. Helsinki: Finnish Literature Society.

Tambiah, Stanley J. 1976. *World conqueror and world renouncer: A study of Buddhism and polity in Thailand against a historical background*. Cambridge: Cambridge University Press.

Taylor, James. 2008. *Buddhism and postmodern imaginings in Thailand: The religiosity of urban space*. Farnham, UK: Ashgate.

Thongchai Winichakul. 1994. *Siam mapped: A history of the geo-body of a nation*. Honolulu: University of Hawaii Press.

Thongchai Winichakul. 2001. "Prawatisat thai baep rachaachaatniyom: Chak yuk anaanikhom amphrang su rachaachaatniyom mai roe latthii sadet phaw khon kradumphi thai nai pachuban." *Silapawathanatham* 23 (1): 56–64.

Thongchai Winichakul. 2002. "The quest for *siwilai*: A geographical discourse of civilizational thinking in the late nineteenth and early twentieth-century Siam." *Journal of Asian Studies* 59: 528–49.

Wheeler, R.E.M. 1954. *Archaeology from the earth*. Oxford: Clarendon.

Wilkinson, H.R. 1951. *Maps and politics: A review of the ethnographic cartography of Macedonia*. Manchester, UK: Manchester University Press.

Yalouri, Eleana. 2001. *The Acropolis: Global fame, local claim*. Oxford: Berg.

–4–

Archaeology and Anthropology: The State of the Relationship

Ian Hodder

I cannot pretend to be able to pronounce on the nature of truth, the theme of the E. H. Young Memorial Lectures, but I do wish to make some comments, which I hope will be more true than false, about the current state of the relationship between archaeology and anthropology. I intend to do this through the lens of Çatalhöyük in central Turkey, where I have been working since 1993. I intend to broach three themes from this vantage point: matter and materiality, scales of temporality, and archaeology and ethnography.

Matter and Materiality

Çatalhöyük is a mound, or tell, in central Turkey dated to 7400–6000 B.C.E. About twelve hectares in size, it consists of over eighteen levels of occupation. In each level up to 3,500 to 8,000 people lived in houses so densely packed together that there were no streets and the inhabitants moved around the "town" on the roofs, entering the houses down ladders. The houses were made of upright timbers and sun-dried mud brick, internally plastered and sometimes painted with narrative scenes involving the teasing and baiting of wild animals. The heads and horns of cattle and other wild animals were often set as installations in the houses. Beneath the floors the dead were buried, with sometimes as many as sixty-two burials in one house (Hodder 2006).

When we excavate the buildings we often find the walls of the houses leaning at perverse angles. Most of this leaning happened during the Neolithic, and we see many attempts were made to hold them up, by using upright posts, by placing walls inside or outside existing walls to provide support, or by adding buttresses. Indeed, the clustering of houses close together, wall set against wall, at Çatalhöyük may have been designed to help hold up the walls of individual houses. Each house rested against its neighbor and gained support from it. Nevertheless, there is much evidence of bending and buckling of bricks in the walls, and there was much instability in the architecture.

To some degree this instability resulted from the use of unfired clay as a building material, but the architectural problems at Çatalhöyük partly resulted from the use of a particular type of smectitic clay. Smectite-rich soils are found in many semiarid environments that have a local volcanic geology. Çatalhöyük is in a semiarid zone, and the site is surrounded by alluvial soils. These derive from volcanic regions to the southwest. We know these alluvial soils were used for building houses since we have found the extraction pits right by the site. Smectites are prone to very quick expansion with water, and very high shrinkage when dry, and this property continues when they are used as construction materials. It is this material that caused the stresses and strains in the architecture of Çatalhöyük in an environment with seasonal rain and very high annual and diurnal temperature variation.

We have put several of the Neolithic Çatalhöyük houses on display in situ. To the visitor they seem stable and permanent, but this apparent stability is produced by the extensive use of conservation chemicals, consolidants, and grouts. In the Neolithic, different solutions were found to create an apparent permanence and stability for the house. As already noted, the walls were supported with large wooden posts. The inhabitants also recruited the ancestors to help hold up the house—in one case placing a human skull at the base of an upright post. Other solutions included frequent replastering of the walls to protect them. In the upper levels of the site there may have been a dearth of large trees and timbers, and so the walls were widened with bigger bricks and internal buttresses. During the sequence there was also a shift to sandier mixtures of clay for bricks, the sand minimizing the effects of the smectite clays.

Obtaining sandier clays for larger bricks probably involved traveling farther from the site. As a result it became less possible to make bricks at the house construction site, and so bricks were made closer to the clay sources and the dried bricks were carried to the site. All this required more labor and more organization of labor. So people increasingly got entangled or trapped at Çatalhöyük. Dealing with smectitic clays led to various implications and entanglements with things that increasingly trapped people in further relationships with things. The relationships between molecules in the clay produced relationships between people in society.

Similar unfired mud-brick building is a key component of the early Neolithic farmers in Middle East from the Pre-Pottery Neolithic A (PPNA) onward. It is only one example of the increased investment in made things—artifacts—during this period. The Neolithic witnesses an explosion of the amount of made material culture—ceramics, polished axes, grinding stones, bone tools (Renfrew 2001). These made artifacts entrapped people in long-term relationships of material investment, care, and maintenance—people became entangled with and domesticated by things.

The best example of this process is the increased dependence of humans on cereals during the Epipalaeolithic and into the Neolithic. Once the tough rachis had been selected for, the wheats and barleys depended on humans for their regeneration. Cereals and people had become co-entangled—the cereals had entangled people and domesticated them (Fuller, Allaby, and Stevens 2010). People domesticated animals, but the costs of herding and dealing with the diseases that were transferred to humans meant that people, too, were domesticated by animals—as much as they were by houses, bricks and mortar, and artifacts.

Expanding out from my Neolithic example, it has often been argued that the difference between anthropology and archaeology is a difference between a focus on people and a focus on material things. The back-and-forth relationship between archaeology and anthropology has often involved nestling archaeology within the broader remit of the anthropological focus on people. After all, who wants to just study things? So, especially in the United States, archaeology has been closely tied to anthropology. Anthropology saved archaeology from cultural historical minutiae, from fossils and from being fossilized. In Britain from the 1960s onward, archaeologists aped those anthropologists who offered general schemes that could be applied widely, especially if they emanated from Paris or, second best, from University College London.

In recent decades, the archaeological desire to put the faces of people on pots and potsherds led to the embrace of phenomenology in Britain, and more widely there has been a widening influence of the University College London focus on material culture. We have seen many broader discussions of the theme of materiality (e.g., Meskell 2005; Miller 2005). One might have thought that this recent emphasis on material culture and materiality would have brought anthropology and archaeology closer together, and in various ways it has. But I have also been struck by the way in which the "archaeological" is absent in many of these discussions of material culture and materiality. The ways in which archaeologists pay attention to the detailed recording of things rarely find their way into the ethnographic studies in the *Journal of Material Culture*, and the chemical and physical composition of things—what we might call their archaeometry—rarely is part of discussions of materiality. Most discussions of materiality in both archaeology and anthropology, and I realize that I overgeneralize, focus on how people construe things, how they construe matter, how things or thing networks have a human-like agency. Many discussions try to explore how matter enters into social worlds of being. But beyond the theoretical stance, the physicality of things remains unstudied, or is left to the archaeometrist and archaeological scientist to study as a separate and seemingly unrelated area of analysis.

In archaeology this inability to link material science to material culture and materiality is perhaps linked to the ways in which Heidegger has been read. In considering the hammer as an example of something that is "ready-to-hand," Heidegger explored the silent ways in which we are embedded in tools and things, and, in a similar way perhaps to the recent work of Latour, Heidegger (1971) looked at networks of things related in an equipmental totality (Olsen 2010). The way Heidegger has been taken up in archaeology has been to remain focused on the human side of this human–thing set of interactions—on the human "being." But we can also look at the craftsperson from the point of view of the hammer—at how the hammer creates a particular type of person. While archaeologists have tried to move in this direction, especially influenced, for example, by Ingold's (2000) account of how the weaver responds to fibrous material in the weaving of a basket, there has been a reluctance to go very far down this road. To understand how humans and things co-inhabit a lived world we need to enlist the scientists who study the engineering potentials and performance characteristics of smectitic brick, and the botanists who study the processing of domesticated wheats, and the material scientists who know how dried reeds bend and behave in basket-making. We need to turn to behavioral archaeology and to human behavioral ecology, where the material worlds in which humans get entangled are explored in all their detailed intricacy and physicality, where issues such as the energetic costs and expenses of obtaining sandy clay are quantified in relation to the costs and on-costs of going farther to get trees for house posts.

Of course, most of us on the interpretive side tend to balk at this. But if there is to be real rapprochement between archaeology and anthropology, then we have to accept that contemporary archaeology is firmly grounded in the natural sciences. Over recent years it has become increasingly sophisticated in its use of natural science techniques, from forensics to stable isotopes, aDNA and food residues in pots. Real progress in linking archaeology and anthropology needs to grapple with the dregs of the old culture wars and to confront our apparent inability to move beyond the objectivist/subjectivist split. I know many will feel that this is an old call, and that many or most of us have made that move. But in my view the absence of archaeological science from theoretical debate about material culture is one example that suggests this is not so. In my view we still need to develop a theory that explores the entanglements between people and things in a more symmetrical way. Andy Jones (2004), in leading a debate in the journal *Archaeometry*, has made a similar point (and see also Ingold 2007). We need to locate matter in materiality. Perhaps the end result will look very much like Latour and actor network theory, but I agree with the critique made by Lemonnier that even here there is a lack of archaeological sensitivity (Lemonnier and Latour 1996). What is missing is a full account not only of the ways in which people depend on and construe things they have made but also of the ways in which things depend on and produce humans. We need to be able to explore the full entanglements and entrapments into which humans are drawn as things run out and fall apart—these entanglements are irreducibly both physical and material as well as social and cultural.

So my first charge for a truly integrated archaeology and anthropology is to break the prejudices that still separate the scientific study of matter from the interpretation of materiality. There is potential for a renewed focus on the links between humans and the science of matter—whether it be of smectitic clay or mitochondrial DNA—without falling back, as we all fear, into materialism and objectivism.

Scales of Temporality

In the deep stratigraphies at Çatalhöyük we can observe how houses were built on top of each other over the 1,400 years of occupation at the site. There was remarkable repetition in the internal layout of houses (Hodder 2006). The arrangement of activities inside the houses "remembered" earlier layouts over spans of at least 400–500 years, and similar results have been found at the earlier site of Aşıklı Höyük (Esin and Harmankaya 1999).

At Çatalhöyük these repeated houses were used to construct histories, partly by the reliving of earlier arrangements of activities and more consciously by passing down objects. The objects that were passed down included human skulls and other body parts removed from bodies buried beneath house floors. In one case a severed skull was plastered to remodel facial features. In addition, plastered bull and other wild animal heads were installed in houses in memory of feasts and social ceremonies. In these ways some houses amassed a history, and we have come to call such houses "history houses" (Hodder and Pels 2010). These history houses have more burials in them, and they are architecturally more elaborate than other houses, but they do not seem to have controlled production or had more storage than other houses. Their primary role was to look after the ancestors and the history of an extended social "house" (extending beyond the bounds of an individual material house).

And yet all this was achieved at some cost. We have already seen that the walls of the houses kept buckling and leaning over so that investment in them as long-term markers of a social group struggled with the unwillingness of the smectitic clays to stand up for long. Other problems emerged from the "history house" system. As people killed and collected wild bulls to make feasts, wild cattle may have become less common on the Konya plain around the site, and we observe a shift to greater reliance on domestic sheep, and increasingly on the secondary products of sheep (wool and milk). It also seems likely that domesticated cattle were introduced in the upper levels of the site. This all meant more herding and tending and milking; and also more processing of animal products. We know from the residues found in the pots that cooking pots were used for the processing of meat, bone marrow, grease, and fat, probably largely from domestic sheep and goats.

Cooking pottery was introduced halfway up the sequence at Çatalhöyük. Cooking pots may have been introduced because they allowed more efficient use of time in the domestic unit. As the economy intensified, time-saving devices for cooking sheep and goat bones and obtaining grease were developed. So a new technology was introduced—thin-walled cooking pottery (Atalay 2005). This allowed pots to be delegates for humans—the pot sitting on the hearth cooked the food while humans were involved in other tasks. But this change created further change as new sources of clay and temper were sought and as energy was invested in making and firing pots.

As things went awry people fixed them, but this just extended the networks of entanglement and intensified the linkages. As humans and things got more widely and more intensely connected, when something went wrong or ran out or needed management, then yet more things had to change just so that people could stay in the same place. The rate of change increased because of the complex interconnectivity of things and humans, things and things, and humans and humans.

In the upper levels of Çatalhöyük the rate of change does indeed increase. Houses are rebuilt more quickly, the history house system begins to transform (dominant houses become less concerned with amassing history and more concerned with amassing stored goods and controlling production). There are new technologies (e.g. in lithics and stamp seals), new pottery types, new cooking technologies, new economic ventures.

Stepping back and taking a very broad perspective, we can say that there was a massive buildup of made material culture in the Neolithic and a concomitant massive increase in the rate of change. Childe (1951) long ago identified a package of ten material attributes that were introduced in and defined the Neolithic in the Middle East (ground stone, polished stone, pottery, domesticated plants, settled villages, and so on). Humans came to depend increasingly on things they had made or interfered with. As they did so, the things they depended on started to go wrong or run out (walls falling down, wild cattle running out, existing methods of cooking being too time-consuming). As people tried to fix these problems, they became yet more invested in material things and new technologies that themselves had their problems, all leading to change at an ever faster rate. From Aşıklı Höyük to the end of Çatalhöyük, that is, from 8500 to 6000 B.C.E. in central Turkey, there is a marked increase in the rate of change. This increase in the rate of change occurs throughout the Neolithic of the Middle East and Europe.

This increased rate of change can be compared with the very slow pace of change in the Upper Paleolithic. For example, the Franco-Cantabrian styles of cave art continue with remarkable continuity for more than 15,000 years (Valladas et al. 2001). By the time of Aşıklı Höyük in the Neolithic there are strong continuities over just 1,000 years, and by the upper sequence in Çatalhöyük changes in styles are occurring in less than 100 years. As people became more and more entangled in made things, the rate of change increased.

Expanding out again from my Neolithic example, it is noteworthy that anthropologists, philosophers, and social theorists often argue that material culture stabilizes—that it creates permanence and helps to produce duration within social structure. For example, Michel Serres (1995, 87) states that "our relationships, social bonds would be airy as clouds were there only contracts between subjects. In fact, the object . . . stabilizes our relationships. . . . For an unstable band of baboons, social changes are flaring up every minute. . . . The object, for us, makes our history slow." The political philosopher Hannah Arendt (1958, 137) suggested that "the things of the world have the function of stabilizing human life."

Perhaps it is the case that in the short term, material things do help to create Maurice Bloch's (2008) transcendental social. The social becomes objectified in things (Miller 2005). But over the longer term, the archaeological evidence suggests that material things accelerate change. This seems true of the Neolithic, but it also seems evident that rates of cultural change have increased over the span of our species. Whether there has been a gradual increase, or a highly punctuated process in which the Neolithic and industrial revolutions played a major part, remains to be documented. The amount of material that we have as a species transformed in some way or another—the amount of artifacts and our appetite for resources to make arti-facts—has increased in a similar exponential way over the same span. As the amount of made material culture has increased, rates of cultural change have also increased, and the snapshot we see at Çatalhöyük is just part of a wider trend. If material culture stabilizes, one might have expected the opposite to happen—that as we became more and more dependent on things, the speed of change would have slowed down.

Rates of cultural change and the degree of dependence on made material culture may not be causally related, but I would like to suggest that they could be. We may over the short term try and construct social stability in material things we have made (such as the "houses" of people in the material "history houses" at Çatalhöyük). But these things we have made tend to fall apart. And they tend to run out. And these things are connected to other things in an increasingly vast network. Somewhere in this network things are always going wrong. Things need maintenance, repair, investment. Things go wrong in the complex scheduling of things in relation to each other. As things fall apart we have to run faster to fix things, innovate, introduce new solutions. The rate of change increases the more we become entangled with things. In the short term, social theorists, philosophers, and anthropologists may be right that material culture stabilizes, but over the long term it appears to destabilize. This is just one of many examples where the longer-term perspective provided by archaeology provides a different and complementary view.

Archaeology and Ethnography

Sadrettin Dural was a guard from the local village who worked at Çatalhöyük in the 1990s. He took advantage of the site and the project by building a café outside the entrance gates. As well as being a guard he showed people around the site and began asking the archaeologists questions about it and about the Neolithic and the origins of agriculture. He said he wanted to write a book giving his view of the site and the project, and this has now been published in English (Dural 2007).

For me it seemed important to hear Sadrettin's voice in this way as I had been so used to seeing the rows of hundreds of local workers standing in the photographs from the great excavations of the Middle East conducted by Mallowan, Woolley, and oth-ers. Such workers on archaeological sites, often highly skilled, had remained silent for too long. It seemed important that Sadrettin felt empowered to write back and to express his own perspective on the work of a foreign-run project close to his village.

Sadrettin would not have written his book if there had not been anthropologists and ethnographers on the project with whom he could talk. They helped Sadrettin and the archaeologists understand each other; they facilitated the process. In many ways the Çatalhöyük project has intruded into the lives of the local communities near

Çumra in central Turkey but also into the regional, national, and global communities who feel they have a stake in the site (Hodder 2006). At the local level, one social anthropologist who worked with us, David Shankland, helped us understand how local people saw the mound before the archaeologists came. He also helped us understand the role of the state in relation to its museums, sites, and monuments. Another ethnographer, Ayfer Bartu, helped us with seminars in which the local community was involved, in dialogues about how the site should be excavated and developed, in education programs, and in community development projects. She also helped us understand how and why the global goddess community was so fascinated by and at times appalled by the archaeological work at the site. Ayfer Bartu also helped when conflicts between the various stakeholders emerged, particularly between the goddess community and the local community and the national Turkish government. She also helped Sadrettin learn about the site and write his book.

Understanding all these stakeholder currents would not have been possible without the support of people trained in dealing with the in-depthness of social life—without people being willing to live in the village and attempt to understand the impact of the project. Without these ethnographers I think the long-term existence of the project would have been threatened as the tensions grew between, for example, traditional Islamic communities and goddess worshippers. The in-depth engagement with the local community in particular has recently been extended by community-based participatory research coordinated by Sonya Atalay (Atalay et al. 2010).

Expanding out from the example of the Neolithic Çatalhöyük for the third time in this paper, we can note that archaeology and anthropology are similar in that both to some degree produce and transform the object they study. But archaeology does this in a very particular, material, and intrusive way. Archaeologists sprout material things from the ground that grow and multiply and decay so that they require regulation, management, and negotiation. Archaeology is a place-making discipline. It makes concrete places and things—and it also energizes these places and things with histories.

Archaeology produces places and histories that intrude into people's lives. This production creates responsibilities that need to be dealt with in multidisciplinary teams. There is much discussion of memory and monuments nowadays across the disciplines, as well as debates regarding the role of heritage in postconflict healing and in shared pasts. The key issues include whether the past has to be owned—or whether it can be shared, whether there are universal values and universal rights to heritage, or whether heritage should always be locally, or nationally, managed (Meskell 2009; Schmidt 1996).

In my view, the key is not to trust in universal principles wielded by international agencies, but to trust in the process of heritage making itself—that is, to have trust in the possibilities of negotiation around the stakeholder table. These negotiations are best conducted in a cosmopolitan framework—by cosmopolitan here I mean a complex blending of the global and the particular in ways that do not replicate

Western perspectives (Meskell 2009). The cosmopolitan interactions that now surround discussions of heritage rights make use of local, national, regional, and global networks to enhance heritage claims. In all this complexity, archaeologists are most effective when working alongside multisited ethnographers as part of multidisciplinary teams—archaeologists trained as ethnographers or archaeologists and ethnographers working side by side using a closely linked discourse about rights, memory, the cosmopolitan, healing, and reparation.

Conclusion

In attending talks by cultural anthropologists at Stanford I note that they often do not show images or slides—in fact, they sometimes seem to think a PowerPoint is where you plug the computer in. Theirs is a narrative art, often absorbed by the intricacies of subjectivities, words, and thoughts. Archaeologists, on the other hand, hang their accounts on images. Indeed, one sees the total panic in their eyes if for some reason the PowerPoint slide presentation does not work. How can they talk without the pictures?

These two modes of presenting lectures iconically represent the narrative-based accounts of anthropology and the material object-based studies of archaeology. But cross-cutting this divide, I have tried to point to three areas in which archaeology and anthropology can work together and contribute in a symmetrical relationship: matter and materiality, scales of temporality, archaeology and ethnography. But I do not want to underestimate the gap that has opened up between archaeology and anthropology. A large component of archaeology is based in the natural sciences. Many social and cultural anthropologists may feel that they have broken through the subject/object barrier. But, in my view, most of the supposed solutions avoid a thoroughly symmetrical position. Material culture studies, materiality, and material agency all seem to me to avoid the material grain and the archaeological sensibility. They often strive to avoid or dismiss evolutionary studies and adequate consideration of the long term.

As a result, it has become difficult for archaeologists and anthropologists to work together both in their home institutions and in the field although of course there are many distinguished exceptions. As an example of the potentials and the difficulties, in recent years we have tried at Çatalhöyük to bring archaeologists and anthropologists together. The archaeologists at the site have invited a group of anthropologists to work with them at the trowel's edge. Each year for the last three years anthropologists such as Webb Keane, Peter Pels, Maurice Bloch, and Harvey Whitehouse have spent a week at the site getting to know the data firsthand and contributing to our interpretations as we dig. This has been a wonderful experience, and we have together come up with new ideas for the site, such as the idea of "history houses," as well as new ideas about wider accounts of the early farmers in the Middle East (Hodder

2010). The experience has been so successful that it has now been expanded, with continued Templeton funding, for a further three years with a new group of anthropologists.

It is because of the success of this experiment that I remain a strong and hopeful devotee of the possibilities of close interaction between archaeology and anthropology. But, also in my view, what has been hard in this experiment has been the initial gap that existed. There was an initial lack of comprehension on the part of the anthropologists, not about ideas at all, but about how each of us works. Our methods have long diverged. We struggle to see how we each come to conclusions. The image-less and image-full lectures encapsulate these differences. And underlying them there are distant traces of the culture wars that I think we all assumed we had surpassed. The anthropologists involved in the Çatalhöyük collaboration initially seemed taken aback at all the advances that have taken place in archaeometry, forensics, and archaeological science. They initially struggled to see how scientific data on lipid residues and fecal matter could be linked to theories about materiality and memory. As LeRon Shults put it, what was he to make of "the tiniest piece of preserved poop" (Hodder 2010, 351)? In my view, collaborative progress depends on finding more satisfactory ways of exploring how matter contributes to materiality, on elaborating on how the long and short terms interact, on working together in joint programs in the field. By doing this we may in the future be better able to teach students how two separate and independent disciplines work, deal with data, and truly contribute to each other.

References

Arendt, H. 1958. *The human condition.* Chicago: University of Chicago Press.

Atalay, S. 2005. "Domesticating clay: The role of clay balls, mini balls and geometric objects in daily life at Çatalhöyük." In *Changing materialities at Çatalhöyük: Reports from the 1995–99 seasons*, ed. I. Hodder, 139–68. British Institute of Archaeology at Ankara Monograph 39. Cambridge, UK: McDonald Institute for Archaeological Research.

Atalay, S., D. Çamurcuoğlu, I. Hodder, S. Moser, A. Orbaşlı, and E. Pye. 2010. "Protecting and exhibiting Çatalhöyük." *TUBA KED* (Cultural Inventory Journal of the Turkish Academy of Sciences) 8: 7–18.

Bloch, M. 2008. "Why religion is nothing special but is central." *Philosophical Transactions of the Royal Society* 363 (June): 2055–62.

Childe, V. G. 1951. *Man makes himself.* London: Watts. (Orig. pub. 1936.)

Dural, S. 2007. *Protecting Çatalhöyük: Memoir of an archaeological site guard.* Walnut Creek, CA: Left Coast Press.

Esin, U., and S. Harmankaya. 1999. "Aşıklı in the frame of Central Anatolian Neolithic." In *Neolithic in Turkey: The cradle of civilization. New discoveries*, ed. M. Özdoğan and N. Başgelen, 115–32. Istanbul: Arkeoloji ve Sanat Yayınları.

Fuller, D. Q., R. G. Allaby, and C. Stevens. 2010. "Domestication as innovation: The entanglement of techniques, technology and chance in the domestication of cereal crops." *World Archaeology* 42 (1): 13–28.

Heidegger, M. 1971. *Poetry, language, thought*, trans. A. Hofstadter. London: Harper.

Hodder, I. 2006. *The leopard's tale: Revealing the mysteries of Çatalhöyük.* London: Thames and Hudson.

Hodder, I., ed. 2010. *Religion in the emergence of civilization: Çatalhöyük as a case study.* Cambridge: Cambridge University Press.

Hodder, I., and P. Pels. 2010. "History houses: A new interpretation of architectural elaboration at Çatalhöyük." In Hodder 2010, 163–86.

Ingold, T. 2000. *The perception of the environment: Essays on livelihood, dwelling and skill.* London: Routledge.

Ingold, T. 2007. "Materials against materiality." *Archaeological Dialogues* 14 (1): 1–16.

Jones, A. 2004. "Archaeology and materiality: Materials-based analysis in theory and practice." *Archaeometry* 46 (3): 327–38.

Lemonnier, P., and B. Latour. 1996. "Lettre à mon ami Pierre sur l'anthropologie symétrique." *Ethnologie Française* 26 (1): 17–31, 32–37.

Meskell, L., ed. 2005. *Archaeologies of materiality.* Oxford: Wiley-Blackwell.

Meskell, L., ed. 2009. *Cosmopolitan archaeologies.* Durham, NC, and London: Duke University Press.

Miller, D., ed. 2005. *Materiality.* London: Duke University Press.

Olsen, B. 2010. *In defense of things.* Walnut Creek, CA: AltaMira.

Renfrew, C. 2001. "Symbol before concept: Material engagement and the early development of society." In *Archaeological theory today*, ed. I. Hodder, 122–40. Cambridge, UK: Polity.

Schmidt, P. 1996. "The human right to a cultural heritage. African applications." In *Plundering Africa's past*, ed. P. Schmidt and R. J. McIntosh, 18–28. Bloomington: Indiana University Press.

Serres, M. 1995. *The natural contract.* Ann Arbor: University of Michigan Press.

Valladas, H., J. Clottes, J.-M. Geneste, M. A. Garcia, M. Arnold, H. Cachier, and N. Tisnérat-Laborde. 2001. "Palaeolithic paintings: Evolution of prehistoric cave art." *Nature* 413: 479.

No More Ancient; No More Human: The Future Past of Archaeology and Anthropology[1]

Tim Ingold

The year is 2053, and the Association of Social Anthropologists is celebrating its centennial with a big conference. As scholars are wont to do on such occasions, a number of contributors to the conference have been dwelling on the past century of the discipline with a mixture of wistfulness, curiosity, and hubris, wondering why their predecessors hung on with such tenacity to forms of argumentation that now seem rather quaint. Everyone recognizes that the title of the association is a relic of past times. Social anthropology is not what it was, for it is distinguished neither by a preoccupation with social phenomena nor by the axiom that such phenomena are the exclusive preserve of a categorical humanity. The discipline has become, rather, a principled inquiry into the conditions and potentials of life in a world peopled by beings whose identities are established not by species membership but by relational accomplishment.

By this year of 2053, the term *archaeology*, too, has become an anachronism, for the subject that still goes by that name has long since lost its association with antiquity. It is not that archaeologists have ceased to dig down for evidence of past lives, any more than ethnographers have ceased to participate in the lives that are going on around them, in what we call the present. But they have dropped the pretence that what is past is any older, or more ancient, than the present, recognizing that the occurrences of the past are not deposited at successive moments while time moves on but are themselves constitutive of that very movement. Between archaeology and social anthropology, then, there is no longer any difference of principle. They have, in effect, converged in a science of life whose overriding concern is to *follow what is going on*, within dynamic fields of relationships wherein the forms of beings and things are generated and held in place.

No More Ancient

In short, both the *archaeo-* of archaeology and the *anthropo-* of anthropology have lost their former appeal. To show why this has come about, I shall examine these disciplinary prefixes in more depth. Starting with *archaeo-*, we could pose the following question: What does it mean to ask how old something is? Or, to put it another way, what kinds of assumptions do we make about a thing for such a question even to make sense? How old is a mountain, a river, a stone? How old is the wind, a cloud, a raindrop, or an ocean wave? How old is a tree, a person, a building, a pot, a piece of furniture? "Ah, that writing desk," you exclaim with some relief, "I can tell you *exactly* how old it is." For you are a specialist in antiques, and an expert in such matters. A little bit of detective work allows you to deduce when it was made. Let us say that it dates from 1653. Remembering that we are now in the year 2053, you conclude that the desk is exactly 400 years old.

But if we judge the age of a thing by the elapsed time from the moment it was made to the present, does this mean that for us to ask how old it is, the thing must at some time have been *manufactured*? Is "How old is that?" a question that can be asked only of artifacts? Even if we answer, perhaps with some unease, in the affirmative, this only begs a host of further questions. The desk is made of oak, which was once hewn from a living tree and seasoned well before being cut into planks. Why should we not say that the desk is as old as the oak? After all, in substance if not in form, there is no more, and no less, to the desk than the wood of which it is made. Then how old is the oak? The tree was not manufactured; it grew. Is it as old, then, as the acorn from which it sprang? Is the oak, in other words, older than the wood from which the desk was made? Then again, the desk has not remained unaltered by use. Generations of writers have worn and scratched its surface. Here and there, the wood has cracked and split, due to fluctuations of temperature and humidity, or has been restored with filler and glue. How can we distinguish those alterations that result from use and repair from those that are intrinsic to the process of manufacture?

The answer, of course, is that something is deemed to have been made at the point when its form matches a conception that is supposed to have preexisted in the mind of a maker. The notion that making entails the bringing together of a conceptual form (*morphe*) and material substance (*hyle*) has, ever since Aristotle, been one of the mainstays of the Western intellectual tradition. What goes for the writing desk also goes for the pot: When we ask how old it is, we count its age from the moment when form and substance were united in the allegedly finished thing. The clay, we suppose, is shaped in the potter's hands to a final form that, once hardened and fired, it retains in perpetuity. Even if the pot is now smashed, we identify its "finishing" with the instant of original formation, not that of fragmentation and discard.

So it is with the building, though at this point we might feel rather less sure of ourselves. What a difference, in English, the article makes! Building is an activity; it is what builders do. But as soon as we add the article and speak of *a* building, or even of *the* building, the activity is abruptly brought to a close. Movement is stilled, and where people had once labored with tools and materials, there now stands a monument to human endeavor, solid and complete. Yet as all inhabitants know, buildings are never really finished. "A 'building,'" observes the inventor and designer Stewart

Brand, "is always building and rebuilding" (1994, 2). The work of building goes on, in the day-to-day activities of repair and maintenance and in the face of the inundations of animals, plants, and fungi and the corrosive effects of wind, rain, and sunshine.

If, for this reason, it is difficult to state with conviction how old a building is, how much more difficult it must be once we turn from buildings to people! Of course, if you ask me how old I am, I can tell you right away. I was born in 1948, which means that since the year is 2053, I am presently 105 years old. But wait. In all probability, I died a few years ago, though I cannot tell you exactly when. Why, then, did you not start counting from the day I died? Why do we always count how old people are from their date of birth rather than death? Surely, at least for as long as people are still alive, they are not yet finished. Just as buildings are always building and rebuilding, and trees always budding and shooting, are not people always peopling, throughout their lives and even thereafter?

I think there is a reason why we count the years from a person's birth rather than from his or her death. It is the same reason why we count the age of the writing desk from when it was made, and the age of the oak from the germination of the acorn. There is a sense in which we believe that the person is finished even before his or her life in the world has begun. Though we conventionally date this finishing moment to birth, it would be more accurate to date it to that of conception. Indeed, it is no accident that the inauguration of a new life should be known as the moment when the child is *conceived*, since it conforms to a logic identical to that of the Aristotelian model of making. According to this logic, a person is created in advance—or, as we say, *procreated*—through the unification of a set of ideal attributes with bodily substance. And if we ask where these attributes come from, the answer that social anthropologists would have provided, up to and even following the first decades of the twenty-first century, would have been: *by descent*. That is, each generation receives the rudiments of person-composition from their ancestors and passes them on, with greater or lesser fidelity, to their descendants. But the life of every person is expended *within* each generation, in being the person he or she is. For as we have seen, all the creative work has been done in advance, through the mutation and re-combination of transmitted attributes.

What I have described is the essence of the *genealogical model*, namely, that persons and things are virtually constituted, independently and in advance of their material instantiation in the life world, by way of the transmission of ready-made but mutable attributes in an ancestor-descendant sequence (Ingold 2000, 136). I hope to have shown how closely this model is linked both to the idea that constitution involves the unification of form and substance and to the possibility of asking—of both persons and things—how old they are. If we return to my original list, which ran from mountains, rivers, and stones through winds, clouds, raindrops, and waves to trees, people, buildings, pots, and furniture, the tendency in thinking about antiquity has always been to start at the end and to push back as far as one can go. It is to think of things early in the list, like raindrops and clouds, as though they were part of the furniture.[2] Yet already with people and buildings, we run into the problem that this way of thinking cannot countenance how people build buildings, and buildings people, throughout their lives. Once we move on to things placed earlier in the list, such problems become insurmountable.

We are talking here of things that grow and wither, swell and abate, flow and ebb, whose forms emerge from the movements and circulations of earth, air, and water. Yet these things are as much a part of the inhabited world as are people and artifacts. One of the oddities of archaeology, as late as the first decade of the twenty-first century, was that it imagined the entire material world, barring the people themselves, as furnished accommodation. It was as though people, buildings, and the artifacts to be found in them comprised *all there is*. In such a world, however, there would be no air to breathe, no sunlight to fuel organic growth, no moisture or soil to support it. Without these things, life would be impossible. And it was at the very moment when it began to dawn on archaeologists that the world they had imagined was crippled by inertia, but when they were still prisoners of the idea that things are constituted through the unification of form and substance (as in the classic concept of "material culture"), that they came up with the notion of *agency*. The word was introduced to fix an insoluble conundrum: How could anything happen in a world of solid and immutable forms? The answer was to endow them with an intrinsic, but ultimately mysterious, capacity to act. Huge efforts and millions of words were expended in the futile search for this capacity. Fortunately, we can now put all that behind us.

For what has taken place, during the first half of the twenty-first century, has been a genuine sea change in our thinking. One way of putting it would be to say that where, before, the tendency was to start from the end of our list and work backward, we would now—in 2053—be more inclined to start from the beginning and work forward. This is to think of a world not of finished entities, each of which can be attributed to a novel conception, but of processes that are *continually carrying on*, and of forms as the more or less durable envelopes or crystallizations of these processes. The shape of the mountain and the banks of the stream attest to processes of erosion that are still going on now, as they have in the past. The rounded forms of pebbles on a shingle beach arise from their abrasion under the constant pounding of the waves, which are still breaking on the shore, even as sea levels have risen and fallen. Ocean waves have the same basic forms now that they did hundreds, thousands, or even millions of years ago, as do storm clouds and raindrops. We may say of these forms that they *persist*. Of a pot, however, or even of a body buried in a peat bog, we would say that it is *preserved*. It is the focus on persistence rather than preservation that distinguishes current archaeology from that of earlier times.

It would be fair to say that traditional archaeology was more interested in pots and bog bodies than in mountains or clouds. For only such things as were deemed to have been preserved qualified for entry in what was called the "archaeological record." It is a record comprised of fragments that, having once broken off from the flow of time, recede ever further from the horizon of the present. They become older and older, held fast to the moment, while the rest of the world moves on. But by the same token, the things of the archaeological record do not persist. For whatever persists carries on, advancing on the cusp of time. Waves continue to break, and raindrops continue to form and to fall on the mountainside, filling streams that continue to flow. In focusing on such things—persistent but not preserved, experientially ever-present yet ever absent from the record—current archaeology is interested not in their antiquity, not in how old they are, but in what we could call their "pastness,"[3] recognizing them as carryings on along temporal trajectories that continue in the present. From the fixed standpoint of antiquity, what carries on also passes, and is thus ephemeral. If our interest is with pastness, however, it is the things that carry on that last, whereas the enduring constituents of the archaeological record, comprising the castoffs of time and history, are ephemeral.

Persistent things have no point of origin. Rather, they seem to be originating all the time. For contemporary archaeologists, this is fundamentally the way things are. The world we inhabit, they say, *is* originating all the time, or undergoing what we might call "continuous birth" (Ingold 2006, 3–4). And if that is true of mountains, rivers, and clouds, then why should it not also be true of persons? Instead of comparing persons to buildings, pots, and writing desks, and concluding that all are endowed with agency, we could compare them to mountains, rivers, and clouds, recognizing that all are immersed in the continuous birth of the world. This is to think of the life of the person, too, as a process without beginning or end, punctuated but not originated or terminated by key events such as birth and death, and all the other things that happen in between. And it is to find the locus of creativity not in the novelty of conception, to be unified with substance, but in the form-generating potentials of the life process or, in a word, in *growth*. And pushing this way of thinking as far as we can, we could wonder whether it might not give us a better understanding of things like buildings, pots, and furniture. Insofar as their forms, too, emerge within processes of material flow and transformation, cannot they also be said to grow? Even our writing desk could be considered as a phase in the pastness of oak!

No More Human

This is the point at which to return from the *archaeo-* of archaeology to the *anthropo-* of anthropology. Where the former prompted us to ask what it means to say of a thing that it is ancient, the latter raises a different but related question: What does it mean to say of a being that it is human? I have already connected the time-honored archaeological concern with antiquity, with how old things are, to the genealogical model of classical social anthropology. Of course, the genealogical model was never *confined* to social anthropology but was rather characteristic of thought across a range of disciplines. One of these was biology, reconfigured in the wake of the Darwinian revolution as the study of genealogically related life-forms, and concerned above all with tracing the phylogenetic pathways along which species adapt, through variation under natural selection, to their respective conditions of life. Understood in these terms, the human is just another species, conventionally known as *Homo sapiens*. "What is a human being," you ask? The answer is "an individual of the species," to which we might add that on an evolutionary timescale the species has not been around for very long. For this reason extant human beings are remarkably similar genetically, despite manifest differences in outward appearance. This similarity does not, however, amount to identity, as the following example shows.

Every human being has a protuberance in the center of the face with two holes that allow the inhalation and exhalation of air. We call it the nose. Yet look around, and you would be hard-pressed to find two noses of the same size and shape. Not only does the form of the nose differ from one individual to another; there also seem to be significant differences between populations. Should we suppose, then, that the basic architecture of the nose—a kind of generic ground plan—is identically keyed into all humans, as part of their genetic makeup, to which interpopulational differences, along with individual idiosyncrasies, are added by virtue of environmental experience? Anyone conversant with modern biology would have to say "no." Did not Darwin refute, once and for all, the essentialist doctrine that for every species there exists a preestablished template or design? All of us have noses, and the more closely related we are genealogically, the more they share a family resemblance. But there is no such thing as the universal nose. As Darwin showed, it is not formal identity but genealogical proximity that unites the individuals of a species. Were it not for the intrinsic differences among individuals of common descent, natural selection could not occur. And if natural selection had not occurred, then neither *Homo sapiens* nor any other species could have evolved.

But at the very moment when biologists turned their attention from morphology to behavior—from what human beings look like to how they act, think, and feel—something strange occurred. In 1978 the founder of sociobiology, E. O. Wilson, published an influential book entitled *On Human Nature*, in which he claimed that the entire course of history could be understood as a preordained outgrowth of behavioral predispositions common to all humans and coded in the "genetic capital" of the species (Wilson 1978, 88–89). Psychologists were quick to pick up the same tune. In their manifesto for the brave new science of evolutionary psychology, John Tooby and Leda Cosmides were moved to assert that, until differentiated by experience and upbringing, "infants are everywhere the same" (Tooby and Cosmides 1992, 33). All human newborns, they insisted, come into the world endowed with exactly the same, genetically prescribed capacities, regardless of how they might be expressed—if at all—in their subsequent development. Although not yet walking, they all have the capacity for bipedal locomotion; although not yet talking, they all have the capacity for language. In the name of Darwinism, it seems, sociobiologists and evolutionary psychologists were vigorously promulgating an essentialist conception of human nature completely at odds with the scientific paradigm in which they claimed to work!

What are we to make, then, of an individual of human parentage who is congenitally crippled or born deaf and dumb? Remember that for modern biology, reconstructed along Darwinian lines, the criterion for species membership is genealogical. Basically, this means that you are a human being if your parents are. On this criterion, both the cripple and the deaf-mute, though they lack what are supposed to be essential attributes of human nature, are just as qualified to be counted as human beings as anyone else. Indeed, it seems that any attempt to define the human being in terms of the possession of one or another essential capacity is destined to fail, since whatever capacity you choose, there is bound to be some creature born of man and woman in which it is lacking. And, conversely, there is bound to be some creature not so born in which it is present—if not now, then at some time in the future. Why, then, have biologists and psychologists persisted in their appeal to such alleged universals as bipedalism and language while attributing their evolution to a theory—of variation under natural selection—that works only because the individuals of a species are endlessly variable? To find the answer we have to return to the question posed at the beginning of this section: What does it mean to say of a being that it is human?

There are really two questions lurking here, of which we have so far touched only on the first, namely, "What is a *human* being?" But this question cannot sensibly be asked, let alone answered, unless we have already both asked and answered the second question: "What is it to *be* human?" Where the first question is empirical, the second is ontological. It is a question of being. And if we are to proceed to ask the empirical question, then the ontological one has to have been answered in a particular way. The required answer is that "human" denotes not a species of nature but a condition of being that *transcends* the natural. To return to the nose: As the organ of what has long been regarded in the Western tradition as the inferior sense of smell—a sense shared by most quadrupedal mammals and often more developed in the latter—the nose is not implicated in the establishment of the human condition. Comparing the noses of different creatures entails crossing no ontological threshold. With bipedalism and language, however, it is quite different.

From classical antiquity through to the naturalists of the eighteenth and nineteenth centuries, and the evolutionists of the twentieth, Western thinkers have repeatedly insisted that there is more to bipedalism than a certain way of getting around, and more to language than a compendium of communicative signals. They have speculated on how the ability to stand and walk on two feet must have freed the hands from the function of supporting the body, allowing for their co-option as the instruments of an intellect increasingly liberated from its moorings in the material world (Ingold 2004b; Stoczkowski 2002, 86–89). Unlike the quadruped, with four feet firmly planted in the ground of nature, the biped is held down by only two, while the hands become answerable to the call of reason. "Man could not have attained his present dominant position without the use of his hands," wrote Darwin in his book *The Descent of Man and Selection in Relation to Sex*, "which are so admirably adapted to act in accordance with his will" (Darwin 1874, 76–77). And if the hands were seen as the instruments of reason, then language was its armature. For it was precisely in their reference to concepts rather than objects, to the domain of ideal representations rather than material manifestations, or, in short, to mind and not nature, that words were said to exceed the nonverbal gestures of nonhuman animals.

Thus when the sociobiologists and evolutionary psychologists of the late twentieth century reclaimed the human universality of bipedalism and language, they were not announcing a new, evidence-based scientific discovery but rather retelling a very old story for which there was no evidence at all. This story served, in effect, as a quasi-mythical charter for the practice of their own science, establishing as it did a baseline for what it means to be human of which the very idea of human nature was of course a corollary. Carolus Linnaeus must surely have been aware of this when, almost three centuries ago, he struggled to find a set of anatomical descriptors that would, reliably and unequivocally, distinguish individuals of the genus he had christened *Homo* from the apes. Eventually he settled for a word of advice, *nosce te ipsum*, "know for yourself." Do you want to know what makes us human? The answer, for Linnaeus and his fellow philosophers of the Enlightenment, lies in the very fact that you ask the question. It is not one that nonhumans ask of themselves. To be truly human, then, is to look into the mirror of nature and know ourselves for what we really are.

Nor was the mirror cracked by the controversies that followed, a century and a half later, in the wake of Darwin's theory of evolution by natural selection. Rather, in the principle of natural selection, science saw the perfect reflection of its own reason. Darwin himself never wavered from the mainstream view that it was humans' possession of the faculty of reason that allowed them to rise above, and to exercise dominion over, the world of nature. Where Darwin did differ from most (but by no means all) of his predecessors was in claiming that the possession of reason—or the lack of it—was not an all-or-nothing affair, distinguishing all humans from all nonhumans. In evolutionary terms, he thought, reason advanced by a gradual, if accelerating, ascent, and not by a quantum leap. But this implied, too, that reason was not equally advanced in all human populations and indeed that, in some, it had scarcely advanced beyond the level manifested in the most intelligent of apes.

After a shaky start, Darwin's stock grew throughout the twentieth century to the point at which he had become a virtual saint among scientists. The celebration, in 2009, of the bicentenary of his birth spawned a glut of hagiography. We could not, it seemed, have enough of it. Yet the history of anthropology's flirtation with Darwinism had been far from glorious. Up until the outbreak of World War II, prominent physical anthropologists, drawing chapter and verse from *The Descent of Man*, were continuing to maintain that what were known as civilized and savage races of man differed in their hereditary powers of reason in just the same way that the latter differed from apes, and that interracial conflict would inevitably drive up intelligence by weeding out the less well-endowed groups. In 1931 Sir Arthur Keith, distinguished physical anthropologist and erstwhile president of the Royal Anthropological Institute, delivered a Rectorial address at my own institution, the University of Aberdeen, in which he maintained that interracial xenophobia was to be encouraged as a way of selecting out the weaker varieties. The war of races, Keith declared, is nature's pruning hook (Keith 1931).[4]

But the second war in a century to break out among the supposedly civilized races of Europe, itself fueled by xenophobic hatred, put paid to such ideas. In the wake of the Holocaust, what was self-evident to Darwin and most of his contemporaries—namely, that human populations differed in their intellectual capacities on a scale from the primitive to the civilized—was no longer acceptable. Darwin's view that the difference between the savage and the civilized man was one of brainpower gave way in mainstream science to a strong moral and ethical commitment to the idea that *all* humans—past, present, and future—are equally endowed, at least so far as their moral and intellectual capacities are concerned. "All human beings," as Article 1 of the Universal Declaration of Human Rights states, "are endowed with reason and conscience." To emphasize this unity, scientists reclassified extant human beings as members not just of the same species but of the same subspecies, designated *Homo sapiens sapiens*.

Yet if these beings are alike in their possession of reason and conscience—if, in other words, they are the kinds of beings who, according to orthodox juridical precepts, can exercise rights and responsibilities—then they must differ in kind from all other beings that cannot. *Homo sapiens sapiens*, then, was no ordinary subspecies. Doubly sapient, the first attribution of wisdom, the outcome of a process of encephalization, marked it out within the world of living things. But the second, far from marking a further subdivision, registered a decisive break from that world. In what many late twentieth-century commentators took to calling the "human revolution" (Mellars and Stringer 1989), the earliest representatives of the new subspecies were alleged to have achieved a breakthrough without parallel in the history of life, setting them on the path of ever-increasing discovery and self-knowledge otherwise known as culture or civilization. Human beings by nature, it was in the historical endeavor of reaching beyond that very nature that they progressively realized the essence of their humanity. Half in nature, half out, pulled in sometimes contrary directions by the imperatives of genetic inheritance and cultural tradition, their double-barreled subspecific appellation perfectly epitomized the hybrid constitution of these creatures.

It was with this cast of unlikely characters, known to science as "modern humans" (as opposed to the "archaic" variety, so-called Neanderthals, who had not made it through to the second grade of sapientization), that the evolutionary anthropology of the late twentieth century populated the planet. The first such humans were portrayed as archetypal hunter-gatherers, people whom history had left behind. *Biologically* modern, they were supposed to have remained *culturally* at the starting block, fated to enact a script perfected through millennia of adaptation under natural selection. It was a script, however, that only science could read. Between the hunter-gatherer and the scientist, respectively pre- and post-historic, was supposed to lie all the differ-ence between being and knowing, between the adaptive surrender to nature and its subjugation in the light of reason. In this scenario, it was the achievement of *cultural* modernity that provided science with the platform of supremacy from which, with no little hubris and profound contradiction, it asserted that human beings were part and parcel of the natural world.

Dismantling the Machine

Indeed, by the late twentieth century it had become apparent that in this contradiction lay the very meaning of "the human." Referring neither to a species of nature nor to a condition of being that transcends nature, but rather to both simultaneously, it is a word that points to the existential dilemma of a creature that can know itself and the world of which it is a part only through the renunciation of its being in that world. Writing at the turn of our present century, the philosopher Giorgio Agamben argued that the recognition of the human is the product of an "anthropological machine" that relentlessly drives us apart, in our capacity for self-knowledge, from the continuum of organic life within which our very existence is encompassed (Agamben 2004, 27). To resolve the contradiction—that is, to comprehend knowing as being, and being as knowing—calls for nothing less than a dismantling of the machine. Far from tacking on a second *sapiens* to mark the onset of fully fledged humanity, it was necessary to move in a direction opposite to that of twentieth-century science, and to attend to the generic *Homo* itself. And that was the direction anthropology took. By the first decades of the twenty-first century, it had become obvious that the concept of the human would have to go.

Why was anthropology brought to such a pass that it had to relinquish the very *anthropos* from which the discipline had taken its name? The answer is that it came from thinking with, and about, children. In fact, children had always posed a problem for anthropology. Apparently delivered into the world as natural beings, devoid of culture and civilization, they had somehow to be provided with the rudiments of identity that would make them into proper social persons. Childhood, wrote Walter Goldschmidt sixty years ago, is characterized by "the process of transformation of the infant from a purely biological being into a culture-bearing one" (1993, 351). As the offspring of human parents, the newborn baby was acknowledged as a human being from the start but as one that had still to reach the condition of being human. On their way from infancy to adulthood, children appeared to be biologically com-plete but culturally half-baked. Indeed, their status came to closely resemble that of prehistoric hunter-gatherers, likewise suspended in a liminal phase in the transition from a natural to a fully cultural life.

The resemblance is no accident. For in both instances the anthropological ma-chine was at work, producing the human by regarding as not yet fully human an already human being (Agamben 2004, 37). Some humans, it transpired, were more human than others: grown-ups more than children, scientists more than hunter-gatherers. Moreover, this same machine, dividing body and soul, generated a point of origin as the moment when these components were conjoined in the definition of a historical project, whether for the individual human being or for humankind as a whole. We used to speak, without batting an eyelid, of "early man" and of the child's "early years." It was as though the antiquity of prehistoric hunter-gatherers could be judged, like the ages of preschool children, by their proximity to their respective origins. Just as the child was deemed to be closer to its origin than the adult, so likewise, early humans were thought to be closer than later ones to that mighty moment when humanity began. Yet despite their best efforts, prehistorians failed to find this moment. And this was for the simple reason that it never existed. Nor indeed is there any such moment in the life of the child.

In reality, as we all know, children are not half-baked hybrids of biology and culture but beings who make their way in the world with as much facility and hindrance, as much fluency and awkwardness, as grown-ups. They are in the process not of becoming human but of becoming the people they are. In a word, they are *growing*, in stature, knowledge, and wisdom. But the child's life does not start from a point of origin, nor is his or her "early" life closer to such a point than later life. Rather than being literally descended from ancestors, as posited by the genealogical model, children follow in the ways of their predecessors. They carry on. Of course there are key moments in life, but these are more akin to handovers in a relay than points of origin. And so it is with the history of the world. It, too, carries on, or persists, without beginning or end. Its inhabitants may follow where others have passed before, but none is more ancient than any other, nor others more modern. Or, to put it another way, the world we inhabit is originating all the time. Yet the anthropological machine, as it drives the recognition of the human, also splits conception from materialization, form from substance, and in so doing establishes the idea of their hylomorphic reunification in an original moment of procreation. Whenever we ask how old things are, the machine is operating in the background. To take it apart is thus to do away not only with the concept of the human but also with the question of antiquity. Abandon the concept, and the question disappears with it. No more human; no more ancient.

Afterword

In 2009, the system of international finance that had fueled the unprecedented prosperity of the preceding decades abruptly collapsed. It had always rested on shaky foundations, dealing as it did in a world of virtual assets, visible only on computer screens, which were ever more tenuously related to the material transformations wrought by real working lives. Once the pretence on which it rested was finally exposed, the whole apparatus fell like a house of cards. The fall was followed, in the immediately ensuing years, by the equally precipitous collapse of big science. For this, too, was found to rest on the pedestal of illusion and conceit. The particle physicists who believed that with one final throw of their collider, in the biggest and most expensive machine ever built, they would finally explain the structure of the universe, were pilloried as reckless and arrogant fools, like the bankers before them. And the bioscientists, who had abandoned the real world of living organisms for the computer-based modeling of large genetic data sets, went the same way. It was a messy, bitter, and contested implosion that cost many once-distinguished careers. The funders of research were left in disarray.

Amid the wreckage, however, a handful of small and adaptable disciplines that had never lost their footing began to thrive. Like tiny mammals in the dying days of the dinosaurs, they were ready to seize the opportunities opened up by the extinction of the megafauna that had once ruled the scientific world. They had a different strategy of reproduction. It was not to lay as many eggs as possible in the hopes that a tiny minority might survive in a fiercely competitive environment, but to treat the germs of knowledge with the same reverence as life itself, to be grown, nurtured, and cared for. These mammalian disciplines recognized, as their reptilian predecessors had not, that knowing is itself a practice of habitation, of dwelling in a world undergoing continual birth. For them, knowledge grows from the ground of our engagement with the world. They saw that to be is to know, and that to know is to be. And among these disciplines, I am pleased to say, were anthropology and archaeology. That is why, in this year of 2053, we are still here to celebrate their success.

Notes

1. This chapter started life as a plenary address presented to the 2009 Conference of the Association of Social Anthropologists of the United Kingdom and the Commonwealth, on Anthropological and Archaeological Imaginations: Past, Present and Future, held at the University of Bristol, April 6–9. Following some revision, it was first published in *Archaeology and Anthropology: Understanding Similarity, Exploring Difference*, edited by Duncan Garrow and Thomas Yarrow (Oxford: Oxbow Books, 2010, pp. 160–70). It has been further revised for the present volume.

2. In a famous painting, entitled *Poison* (1939), René Magritte highlighted the surreal consequences of this way of thinking about things by depicting a cloud making its entrance through the door of a room.

3. For this term, I am indebted to Cornelius Holtorf. In his presentation to the ASA Conference, Holtorf argued that the "pastness" of things depends not on the determination of a date of origin but on our being able to tell trustworthy stories linking them to the present. Of things preserved in the archaeological record, these would be stories of preservation, or perhaps of recovery.

4. Elsewhere (Ingold 2004a) I have told the story of this lamentable episode in the history of anthropology at Aberdeen.

References

Agamben, G. 2004. *The open: Man and animal*, trans. K. Attell. Stanford, CA: Stanford University Press.

Brand, S. 1994. *How buildings learn: What happens to them after they're built*. Harmondsworth, UK: Penguin.

Darwin, Charles. 1874. *The descent of man and selection in relation to sex*. 2nd ed. London: John Murray.

Goldschmidt, W. 1993. "On the relationship between biology and anthropology." *Man*, n.s., 28: 341–59.

Ingold, T. 2000. *The perception of the environment: Essays on livelihood, dwelling and skill*. London: Routledge.

Ingold, T. 2004a. "Anthropology at Aberdeen." *Aberdeen University Review* 60 (3): 181–97.

Ingold, T. 2004b. "Culture on the ground: The world perceived through the feet." *Journal of Material Culture* 9 (3): 31.

Ingold, T. 2006. "Rethinking the animate, re-animating thought." *Ethnos* 71 (1): 1–12.

Keith, A. 1931. *The place of prejudice in modern civilization*. London: Williams and Norgate.

Mellars, P., and C. Stringer, eds. 1989. *The human revolution: Behavioural and biological perspectives on the origins of modern humans*. Edinburgh: Edinburgh University Press.

Stoczkowski, W. 2002. *Explaining human origins: Myth, imagination and conjecture*, trans. M. Turton. Cambridge: Cambridge University Press.

Tooby, J., and L. Cosmides. 1992. "The psychological foundations of culture." In *The adapted mind: Evolutionary psychology and the generation of culture*, ed. J.H. Barkow, L. Cosmides, and J. Tooby, 19–136. New York: Oxford University Press.

Wilson, E.O. 1978. *On human nature*. Cambridge, MA: Harvard University Press.

–6–

Sacred Architecture: Archaeological and Anthropological Perspectives

Richard D. G. Irvine, Nick Hanks,
and Candace Weddle

Many of our field sites are marked and shaped by buildings constructed in order to express and mediate the religious practice of social groups and individuals. Churches, monasteries, shrines, and other buildings of these types transform the landscapes in which many of us work, and the social effects of these sites can continue long after they cease to be used for their original purpose. How should we approach these structures? Can religious buildings, the ways they are built, and the architectural form they take help us to understand the religious practice and beliefs of individuals and groups? In order to approach these questions, we will examine ways in which anthropologists and archaeologists might be able to inform one another's practice when seeking to understand sacred architecture. Drawing on a number of case studies from the Hellenistic world to the contemporary moment, we will explore ways in which human use (rather than aesthetic features) might be mapped out. Methodologically, we ask whether methods from archaeology might aid the anthropological analysis of sacred space, while also asking to what extent ethnographic methods could aid interpretation of archaeological remains of religious buildings. Theoretically, through our concern with use patterns, we seek to analyze the way in which an understanding of architectural form might help us to map out life cycles, changing styles and forms of ritual, the interaction between the sacred and the profane, and the maintenance of proximity and distance.

Mapping Sacred Space: Case Studies from Bristol

In order to consider how the forms of sacred spaces both dictate and are affected by their ritual use, it is vital to develop methods that allow us to analyze and express in a concrete form the organization of the spaces and the implications of their design. During 2004 Nick Hanks conducted a study of eight religious buildings of different faiths in Bristol, England: Baha'i, Buddhist, Christian, Druid, Hindu, Jewish, Muslim, and Sikh. For the purposes of this chapter, we shall refer primarily to the Baha'i Centre, the Hindu Mandir Bristol, and the Sikh Gurdwara Singh Sabha,[1] each of which was converted from a previous secular use. The Baha'i Centre was a converted two-story late nineteenth-century shop, with the ritual space located on the second floor.[2] The Hindu Mandir was a converted former Methodist Chapel built in 1864, with the ritual space located around the balcony, with views down into the ground floor, which was used as a community hall. The Sikh Gurdwara was a converted former canteen for Bristol Omnibus built in the early twentieth century and later used as a Lloyd's Bank. It was extensively altered to insert a new floor that became the ritual space, with a kitchen and function room below. It is important to note that the nature of the physical environment being used can itself lead communities to adapt their practice in ways that are specific to that location; as Markus (1993, 9) has noted, practices are often more easily molded to the space than the buildings to the practices. For example, at the Hindu Mandir the main shrine cannot be placed in the center, due to the lack of any floor to support it there, so it is placed at one end, and the practice of circular processional movement is toward and away from the main shrine at this balcony level instead of around it. In each case, study of the physical conversion and ritual use of the spaces yielded information on social relationships both within the framework of the religion and between the members of the faith groups and society in general.

The approach taken by Hanks was a combination of interviews and observation of activity within the building. The activities were then mapped onto the spaces using the method of "permeability mapping," as set out by Hillier and Hanson (1984) in *The Social Logic of Space* as a way of analyzing the social use of space from a ground plan. It records the potential movement that people have between rooms within a building. Hanks extended this method to spaces defined by furniture and bodies within the largest spaces that were used for ritual. Such a method can be rapidly applied if need be, with Gould (1999) putting it forward as a valuable method for capturing data about a building before it is lost to development. As can be seen from the very simple examples (Figure 6.1), alterations in the positions of doorways can radically change the experience of visiting a building. Building E has rings of freedom of movement, whereas D has separate branches, one with a controlled door. Both buildings have three layers of depth. Permeability mapping shows how the access is controlled, and how much depth the building has. This method was used extensively by Markus (1993) in his book *Buildings and Power*, although the fact that this comprehensive work did not engage with religious buildings was the catalyst for Hanks to carry out his work. Markus (1993, 13) writes that buildings are designed for two groups: the "inhabitants" and the "visitors," and that "the raison d'être of the building is to interface the two groups and exclude strangers." With religious buildings the regular users of the building are the "visitors," and the "strangers" are those who do not use the building. When the buildings house permanent residents, as in the case of Buddhist monks, these have different routes and levels of access than other users of the space. This is a similar situation to that found within other building types that have two classes of inhabitant, for example, English country houses (West 1999)

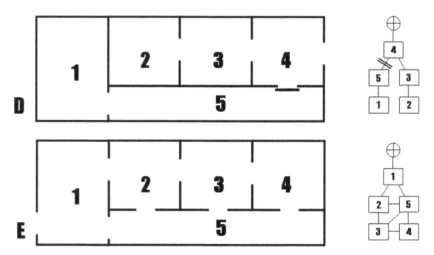

Figure 6.1 Simple plans with permeability maps based on Hiller and Hanson's work (1984).

with the separation of the family and their servants; we will return to such separations later when we turn our attention to Catholic monastic architecture.

Of course, our understanding of access and movement in a sacred setting must consider more than the physical. Hillier and Hanson (1984, 146) state that "an inhabitant is, if not a permanent occupant of the cell [building/room], at least an individual whose social existence is mapped into the category of space within that cell: more an inhabitant of the social knowledge defined by the cell than of the cell itself." In the work of mapping buildings used for religious purposes, it becomes apparent that the divine or other sacred presence within the space also needs to be considered an inhabitant.

When this method of permeability mapping, adapted to the purposes of sacred space, was applied to the eight buildings, it immediately became apparent that each had spaces that corresponded to the three phases of ritual activity as refined by Victor Turner (1969) from Van Gennep's famous work on rites of passage: *separation* (lobby/reception room), *transition/liminal* (main ritual room), and *incorporation/ reaggregation* (community/socializing room). Though for some buildings the community spaces are not present in that actual building, they are instead represented in other buildings used after the main ritual activity. These features and other common elements noticed by Hanks are drawn here as a simplified permeability map (Figure 6.2).

The reception spaces help to facilitate *separation* of sacred and profane in two ways. Here visitors prepare themselves before entering the main ritual space: removing shoes, changing clothing, washing, and putting aside objects/materials that are not permitted. Thus they distance themselves from the world and thoughts of it by changing from their everyday appearance and leaving worldly things here. The

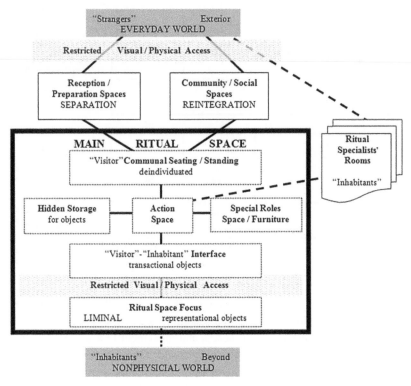

Figure 6.2 Nick Hanks's liturgical ritual space permeability model, incorporating ideas from Markus (1993), Marshall (2002), Nash (1997), Turner (1969), and others.

reception space also acts as a means of *separation* from the outside world by creating physical distance and restricting both visual and physical access. We will explore this need to exclude strangers later in this paper.

The other connection to the exterior world is provided by the community spaces. These aid the visitor in the incorporation of the ritual experience into their lives, prior to returning into the exterior world. These spaces often provide literature and objects for visitors to take home to carry the beliefs and practices beyond the sacred space and into other spaces. Here the sense of group belonging is increased by sharing food and socializing, returning to more physical and worldly activities. They are also the spaces used outside of times of rituals for social and educational events that complement or support the visitors' *belief* and *belonging*, which Marshall (2002), building on Durkheim's work in *Elementary Forms of the Religious Life* (1915), has described as the primary aims of ritual. These social and educational spaces that are more connected with the world are places where strangers are most likely to appear, and they often require separate entrances to avoid passing through the main ritual space. In the Sikh, Hindu, and Baha'i examples, the reception and community spaces were located on the first (ground) floor, with the main ritual space removed to the second floor.

The main ritual spaces studied have the majority of their area devoted to visitor seating or standing. This creates an emphasis on communality. Participants gather together in large groups facing the same direction, toward the focus of the ritual space; indeed, in some cases (as in the Sikh Gurdwara), there is even a prohibition on turning your back on this space. Being together en masse in communal seating allows for synchronizing of movement and voice (Hillier and Hanson 1984, 191); as Marshall (2002) would put it, *de-individuating* and *co-presencing* the visitors to increase the sense of *belonging*.

Between the visitors' communal seating and the focus of the ritual space is a space where actions can be directed toward that focus. Significance is given to the actions by their close proximity to the ritual focus, and their high visibility in the area toward which all are looking. It is the point of closest approach for visitors to the ritual space focus. The ritual space focus is that point to which the visitors look, move, voice, and make actions. Also, as this space for actions is only occasionally used, it adds a sense of distance between the ritual space focus and the visitors, as well as heightening the significance of actions carried out there. Some people, of course, may have a temporary or permanent role separate from the group. This role may be indicated by a piece of furniture, such as a lectern or platform.

The physical objects at the ritual focus have two roles: "transactional" and "representational." Representational objects, according to Scarry (1985, 314), are intended to have a psychological effect, be it to act as a reminder or to inspire with awe and mystery. They are not considered to "be" what they represent. They point to something beyond or are accessed by something beyond. Then there are the offerings, of artwork, food, or money (but also nonmaterial offerings such as praise), which Grimes (1982, 94) observes are primarily transactional and made toward the ritual space focus from which the visitors seek to gain benefits. There may be adjacent or combined locations for the transactional and representational objects, for example, a table before an image. Though transactional objects were present in all eight cases, the representational objects were not. The ritual space focus is a material aid to the attentional focusing behavior that, according to Marshall (2002, 363), is an essential part of ritual's objective of removing attention from the self and creating immersion in the group. However, the need to focus attention is more important than the subject of that attention (Marshall 2002, 361); hence, the ritual space focus can be physically empty in some cases, particularly when the visitors are in a circle facing the center, which is strongly defined by the obvious geometry. The Baha'is, for example, had only a small table at the focus of their circular space.

It has been noted by Renfrew and Bahn (2000, 406), among others, that ritual has both a "conspicuous public display" element, with the highest concentration of ornamentation being at the ritual space focus, and a "hidden mystery element," or, as Nash (1997) described it, "restricted visual access." Both of these seemingly contradictory observations can apply to the ritual space focus in the same building. The role of ornamentation in aiding attention focus is obvious, but the role of hiding is less obvious. In all of the eight examples Hanks studied, the foci spend at least part of their time hidden by curtains or doors, hidden from view as a result of actions such as bowing or closing the eyes, or "hidden" by virtue of being an empty space. The decoration itself may be used to obscure or hide the object of the focus. Why? Hanks's research leads him to suggest that it adds to the *liminal* nature of the ritual space focus by rendering it both seen and unseen.

For many years, through his work in the theater, Barker (1977, 135–55) has tested the subtle qualities of space and the effects that these have on the mind and body.[3] One of his observations is that the strong focus of a space, created by the architecture, the furniture, and the actors, is both uncomfortable to stand in and uncomfortable to watch for very long, and that both audience and actors become physically restless. The strongest examples described by Barker were the theaters-in-the-round built in the 1960s, in which the center point was not used and was in fact deliberately weakened by set design, because the strong focal emphasis of the architecture created great difficulties. It is worth noting that two circular examples of space in Hanks's study, used by Druids and Baha'is, made little or no use of the center of the space. Such cases may suggest that, for physical reasons, the visitors to the space need some degree of rest from the strain of the ritual space focus. Grimes (1982, 43–44) notes that the liturgical mode of ritual "waits upon power" rather than wields it; in such a context it would be appropriate to avoid physically occupying or allowing prolonged observation of the point where the spatial/attentional power is at its strongest. Unlike other building types examined by Markus (1993), in the ritual spaces studied by Hanks the point of interface between the visitors and the inhabitants seems to occur at the deepest point of the building. Indeed, the way that the ritual space is used directly implies a focus beyond the space within the building. For Muslims, the focus points toward Mecca; in the case of the Sikh Gurdwara, it reaches toward the Golden Temple. For Hindus, the statues are "considered to be access routes through which spirits could enter and leave the world" (Mann 1993, 95). The ritual space implies a permeability beyond the limits of the building, toward a greater reality that worshippers might someday gain access to. There is therefore a perceived invisible extension to the structure of the building that leads elsewhere. The building is permeable by the divine through the gateway of the ritual focus. One could say it is half a building, physically incomplete just as the process of liturgical "waiting" is incomplete. This would seem to be a defining feature of liturgical ritual buildings.

Another part of a building's function is the exclusion of strangers, which plays a particular role in preventing disruption of liturgical ritual. None of the examples in Hanks's study has direct access from the outside to the main ritual space. Access is controlled by doors and bells, and is observed by cameras and windows. This increases the sense of separation from the ordinary world, in the same way that the ritual focus is also at the opposite end and at the deepest point in the permeability.

More generally, there is "restricted visual access" from the outside, as has also been observed by Nash (1997) at prehistoric sites. This discourages strangers from visiting. One cannot see in, and the activity within is not on display; this is in contrast to visitor centers with their large windows and wide-open reception areas.

It is significant that the eight buildings Hanks studied have little or no signage or publicity to encourage visiting by strangers. Access is limited to formal arrangements, such as school trips and Bristol Interfaith events, or as part of the national Open Doors Day scheme. Though theologically most religions take the position that they are open to all, in fact it appears that liturgical ritual space works to exclude strangers. Access is only on terms that will help preserve what occurs therein. The attentional focusing of the liturgical ritual is needed to draw attention away from the self, reducing self-awareness and any sense of separation from the group (Marshall 2002, 363). Outsiders may conflict with the sense of belonging engendered in ritual, and it may also be suggested that strangers make participants self-conscious—the sense of being observed by others may therefore reduce the attentional focus of the ritual. It is with this in mind that particular etiquette is advised for visitors, managing the nature and extent of their visibility.[4]

Incorporation and Exclusion: The Case of Monastic Architecture

We see, therefore, that the built environment can be manipulated to exclude or manage visitors to sacred spaces. Hanks's analysis of Bristol places of worship shows how architecture plays a role in shaping experience, and in this sense the spaces described are sites of incorporation, where individuals find themselves drawn into wider social and cosmological dynamics. Yet these are also spaces where such incorporation is managed. Access to the main ritual space is often restricted, with reception spaces creating an important zone of transition.

It is important to pay attention to these dynamics of inclusion and exclusion, and methods such as permeability mapping can provide a valuable tool for anthropologists and archaeologists attempting to understand these processes. Richardson (2003) has argued that understanding access restrictions can help us to understand hierarchies of use: for example, in the Bishop's Palace at Salisbury as it was arranged in the fifteenth century, we see "a tree-like route through a succession of rooms intended to filter out all but those of the highest rank"; this emphasized hierarchical distinctions between those allowed to proceed into the hall, those allowed into the parlor, and those allowed beyond into the bishop's private chambers, while reinforcing the preeminence of the bishop in society. In the context of sacred architecture, such restrictions of access can play an important role in drawing distinctions between ritual participants. Historically, such concerns have played a particularly important role in the use of Christian ritual space. For example, Duffy (1992) has described the role of rood screens in pre-Reformation English churches. These wooden or stone semipermeable screens stood as a boundary between the congregation in the main body of the church and the priest celebrating the ritual of the Mass at the altar in the east end of the church. "The screen itself was both a barrier and no barrier. It was not a wall but rather a set of windows" (Duffy 1992, 112); it obscured the view of the sacred action, preserving the mystery element, an important aspect of sacred architecture also in the Bristol sites studied by Hanks, as described in the preceding section. Yet as clergy and choir passed through the screen, leaving other worshippers in a position of restricted view, this could be interpreted as suggesting a hierarchy of access. Hall (2006), examining the significance of the rood screen in Italian monastic churches, argues that they played an important role in the division of space between laity and those who were members of religious or monastic orders, granting them a level of privacy and ritual segregation.

This theme is taken up later in this chapter in Richard Irvine's anthropological investigation of contemporary English Benedictine communities, which explores how monastic architecture defines and delineates the roles of those who use sacred space. Importantly, the study of monastic architecture also sheds light on the ways in which the behavior of worshippers may affect or even disrupt the effectiveness of the ritual space even as the architecture attempts to control it. The desire for separation is a particularly important aspect of Christian monasticism and is therefore a key point of inquiry for monastic archaeology. Aravecchia (2001) has used spatial analysis to examine access to hermitages of the fifth to seventh centuries in the Kellia, a monastic site in Lower Egypt. He suggests that "visitors probably went through different steps of selection" (2001, 30), with increasing levels of privacy moving through the courtyard, to the vestibule, along a corridor, and into the oratory—the monk's apartment, at an additional level of access from the exterior, is understood to be at an even further remove of privacy. Later additions to similar sites, however, show fewer levels of access required to reach the oratory, as well as the development of large halls apparently for shared eating and praying, which again are at fewer levels of access from the exterior. This analysis leads Aravecchia to suggest that the oratories of monastic apartments of later construction were more easily accessible from the courtyard, with the vestibule becoming integrated into the oratory itself, "thus seeming to lose its original function of separation between the courtyard and the sacred place of prayer of the monk" (2001, 32). Additionally, the development of halls for shared eating and prayer in later constructions, as well as the absence of kitchens specifically accessed from particular apartments, implies an increasing emphasis on communal life, with monks having a higher level of access to one another, and guests to the monastery having a higher level of access to the monks.

This kind of analysis is of great use in better understanding how monks manage processes of social contact and exclusion. Indeed, one of the important issues such an account raises is how monks managed contact with one another. Horn (1973) has outlined the historical development of the cloister, a shared passageway around a courtyard space that connects the living quarters of the monks with common areas for prayer, eating, and recreation. He traces the development away from scattered individual dwellings for monks, as in fifth-century Egypt and seventh- to eighth-century Ireland, and toward increasing connection. So the cloister, for Horn, is a clear indication of a move away from a monastic architecture in which individual monks' cells were separated and in which the primary concern is the maintenance of individual space, and toward a way of living that focuses on social interaction and leads to the creation of public space. This architectural arrangement comes to be indicated in the ninth-century Plan of St. Gall, which Horn has suggested is a "statement of policy of the leading bishops and abbots" prepared for reform synods held in Aachen in 816 and 817. Horn describes the plan as "paradigmatic" for monastic architecture; it sets out a pattern for a communal model based on shared and co-ordinated activity, such as that outlined in the *Rule of Saint Benedict*. This is a style of architecture that implies frequent interpersonal encounter.

In Irvine's ethnographic work with contemporary Catholic English Benedictine monasteries, focusing in particular on the community of St. Gregory the Great at Downside Abbey, Somerset, it is the cloister that provides the architectural frame for the ideology of *stability*, outlined in Chapter 58 of the *Rule of Saint Benedict* as one of the promises to be made when a monk joins the monastic community. Missionary work in England played an extremely large role in the early life of the English Benedictine Congregation, with life on the mission being the ultimate destination of the majority of those who entered the monastic life. The papal bull[5] *Plantata*, issued in 1633 by Pope Urban VIII, ratified the congregation's missionary mandate, confirming that the monks should, when making their profession, take a "Missionary Oath" through which they solemnly accepted the president of the congregation as having the sole authority to transfer them to or from the mission. Even after the community had relocated to England,[6] this commitment to leave the monasteries in order to carry out pastoral work continued. In the late nineteenth century, the function of the monastery as a training place for priests to work for the conversion of England was strongly emphasized by many English Benedictines who had moved on from the monasteries to work in parishes. However, we see that those who called for reform, and a shift in emphasis from the mission to the monastery, described stability as a "special essential" of the *Rule of Saint Benedict*. Francis Aiden Gasquet, the prior of the community when they commenced the building work in 1879, wrote that stability "is the key to the spirit of monasticism as interpreted in [Saint Benedict's] *Rule*, for by it the monastery is erected into a family, to which the monk binds himself forever" (1896, xiv).[7] To enter a Benedictine monastery is to become part of a corporate body, and to share in all aspects of life with that body, "acting only through it, sharing in all the joys and sorrows of its members, giving and receiving that help, comfort and strength which come from mutual counsel" (xii).

From this basis, it can be argued that monastic architecture should be understood as architecture of incorporation, through which members of the community find their life cycles incorporated into that of their new household. The reassertion of the commitment to stability is made visible in the architecture of the monastery. The entire monastic life cycle can be passed within the accommodation of the monastery; those at the early stages of their monastic development—postulants, novices, and juniors—have individual rooms in the novitiate section of the monastic accommodation, before moving to live in rooms in the main living quarters with the rest of the solemnly professed monks. The monastery also contains an infirmary, where sick and elderly monks live under the care of the infirmarian, an official appointed from within the community specifically to care for those who are ill. The infirmary has its own direct link to the Abbey Church, opening out into a gallery, enabling continual participation in the community's ritual life.

Below the infirmary and the rooms of the monks is the chapter house, where the monks meet together for chapters (meetings of all solemnly professed monks of the community) and conferences given by the abbot. There is also the calefactory,[8] a common room with chairs and newspapers where the monks spend periods of recreation and gather together after supper. These rooms, which form the ground floor of the west wing of the monastery, are linked to the Abbey Church and to the east wing of the monastery by a cloister. The east wing of the monastery contains the library, guest accommodation, and refectory.

So the monastery makes visible the commitment to stability (Irvine 2011). It does so primarily by connecting the different elements of the monks' daily life within the same complex: the sleeping quarters and the places for prayer, for study, for eating, and for relaxation. The cloister is therefore a site of frequent interpersonal encounter, as the monks pass through it regularly to reach the common areas of the Abbey Church (where they attend six communal services a day), refectory (where they join together in silence to eat three meals a day), chapter house, and calefactory. This is an architectural arrangement that stresses a life shared in common, not a life of isolated individuals.

One also sees stability made visible in the monastic cemetery. As Gilchrist and Sloane (2005) have shown in their archaeological study of graves in medieval monastic houses, the specific identity of monks is retained in their burials; they are buried as groups separated out from the laity, with habits and other tokens marking them out as members of a community. In the contemporary monastery at Downside, at the end of the life cycle, the monks are buried in grounds to the east of the monastery, next to the library, where row after row of black cast iron crosses form a massed community of the deceased. Even in death, the monks' bodies remain within the boundaries of the monastic family. Stability within the community continues even when the life of the individual monk is at an end.

Yet if the architectural arrangement of the monastery incorporates monks and their life cycles into a stable community, what about those beyond that community?

The Abbey Church is open to visitors and those who wish to attend services, and there is a bookstore and visitor center on the road leading to the Abbey Church. However, this is not merely a casual provision for outsiders: guests are in fact *built into* the structure of the monastery. The guest wing, providing room for around ten guests, occupies a floor above the monastic refectory and faces the living quarters of the monks across a courtyard. The guests' quarters in the east wing and the monks' quarters in the west wing are linked by the cloister, on which monks and guests converge in order to reach the refectory and Abbey Church where they eat and pray together (although they are seated separately). We therefore see that the built environment of the monastery assumes that there will be a near-constant presence of guests,[9] and the guest wing is an integral part of the monastic architecture. The scale of provision for hospitality varies from monastery to monastery. Shackley (2004) has shown how "spiritual tourism" has emerged as a significant commercial interest, and it is worth noting that some monasteries rely on income from guests as a primary means of sustaining themselves, although this is not the case at Downside Abbey.

Although the guest wing is included within the structure of the community, we can also see that it is held separate from the monks' accommodation. The simultaneous inclusion and exclusion of outsiders is outlined in the Constitutions of the English Benedictine Congregation, which instruct that there should be a central area, which must include the monks' sleeping quarters, which no outsiders should enter without the specific permission of the abbot. A wider area is then defined, including the refectory, library, and guest house, into which outsiders can be admitted but in conformance with norms established by the abbot. There is then an even wider area defined as the monastery grounds, which the monks may not leave without permission—although given the pastoral work that many of the monks are involved in, such movement beyond the monastery grounds is a regular occurrence. So there are layers within layers of enclosure, and so there are different layers of contact between monks and outsiders. So the Abbey Church, guest wing, and library are easily accessible from the exterior (the Abbey Church is the most accessible of the three, as permission is required to use the guest wing or library, but the church itself is open to all); however, additional layers of access (through locked doors, one of which is marked with a sign demanding SILENCE) are required to enter the cloister and reach the refectory; to pass through to the west wing of the monastery requires visitors to walk the full length of the north side of the cloister, something they would not ordinarily do, except on rare occasions when they might be invited to the common area of the calefactory. The private rooms of the monks are the most inaccessible part of the complex.

The importance of hospitality is a central concern of Benedictine life, as is clear from the history of guest provision; Kerr (2007) draws on documentary and archaeological sources to provide an account of monastic hospitality in medieval English monasteries. From the perspective of contemporary monasticism, Kevin Seasoltz, a liturgical scholar and a Benedictine of St. John's Abbey in the United States, writes,

"At the last judgement, Jesus will reveal to everyone the mystery of this hospitality. Through and in the visitor, Christ himself is welcomed or sent away, recognized or unrecognized, just as when he came unto his own people" (1974, 441). This care expresses the community's openness and awareness of God in others, and also offers an opportunity for contact and witness (Fortin 2003). Yet, in allowing this access, the monastery opens itself to the risk of disruption. The coming and going of guests can be disruptive to the stability through which monks commit to one place, and to the ordered *horarium* that punctuates the day, and while contact with guests is an important apostolate, it can jeopardize the very sense of recollection that brings guests to the monastery. For this reason, the outsider in the monastery is an ambivalent presence (Seasoltz 1974, 446). The presence of a guest provides an opportunity for an encounter that is understood as an encounter with Christ, and so an opportunity to serve the person of Christ. In addition, it provides an opportunity to communicate the monastery's values to the society beyond the cloister—yet the guest carries with him[10] a risk of disruption that could undermine those very values. It is for this reason that we see the simultaneous inclusion and exclusion of the outsider. He is granted access, but this access is limited. He is invited to participate in the life of the community, yet he is spatially separated from the monastic community in the Abbey Church, in the refectory, and in his sleeping quarters. The design of Christian monastic architecture is instrumental in achieving and maintaining a sort of division of labor between monks and laity, through which religious responsibilities may be carried out effectively—yet a theological focus on the spiritual goals of inclusion and participation complicates the achievement of this goal.

Ritual Change and Sacred Architecture

In analyzing these processes, it is important to recognize that sacred spaces are subject to change and are themselves the products of transformation of preexisting spaces. As we saw, the buildings studied by Hanks and referred to earlier have all been modified to varying degrees by the communities that use them, and this work on the buildings does not end; there are embellishments or extensions, ongoing repairs, and cleaning. It may be suggested that this process contributes to the aims of ritual. This "effortful behavior" is of itself "likely to produce a quasi-religious hardening of the initial or associated beliefs" (Marshall 2002, 369). The building itself, and its continuing adaptation, is part of the ritual process, not simply a frame for ritual activity or a shelter to house it.

Attitudes surrounding inclusion, exclusion, and proximity to the ritual space focus do not remain static over time, and the diachronic perspective of archaeology alerts us to the fact that changing use patterns in sacred architecture can signal shifts in attitude and changes in social relationships. Schachner (2001), for example, describes a shift in the ritual use of space in Pueblo society between 750 and 900 C.E. He notes reduced evidence of communal ritual in great kivas (ritual meeting spaces); older kivas were decommissioned, and as the population moved to new areas of settlement in 850–880 C.E., new great kivas were not constructed. Instead, ritual activity appears to have been focused on oversized pit structures. These were consistently smaller than the great kivas, thus physically limiting the number of participants in ritual. They exhibit a more formal layout, and their relationship with the surrounding domestic architecture implies that access could have been controlled. For Schachner, this indicates increased control of communal ritual by particular segments within the villages, which may have had important political implications, as ritual control would have provided justification for access to productive land. This shift in ritual process did not endure, however, possibly because of the resistance of those disenfranchised by the change.

The history of Christian architecture is also indicative of shifts in ritual process. As Spicer (2000) has argued, the fundamental architectural impact of the Reformation was an emphasis on the primacy of the Word of God; hence, the pulpit replaces the altar as the focal point. Davies (1982) suggests that the form of the nave in Romanesque and Gothic Christian architecture creates a path toward the chancel at the east end of the church: "its very shape beckons forward." In this way, the form of the church leads the participant toward the altar and tabernacle, the foci of devotion to the Eucharist and the sacrament of Christ's Last Supper. Yet following the Reformation, there was a distinct change of emphasis, and churches "served to enhance the visibility and audibility of the preacher by ensuring a central position for the pulpit." Indeed, in some Scottish churches, such as Aberdeen and Brechin Cathedrals, this led to the chancel, the part of the church where the altar had formerly been located, becoming redundant and abandoned.

This perspective on ritual change helps us to interpret contemporary Christian architecture. The monastic churches of the Catholic English Benedictine Congregation, which we discussed in the preceding as the context for Irvine's ethnographic work, are illustrative of changes in attitudes to ritual. Downside Abbey, in Somerset, was built in several phases between 1880, when Dunn and Hansom began work, through to the construction of the choir by Thomas Garner around 1900, and the completion of the nave by Giles Gilbert Scott in 1925.[11] The church is built in the Gothic style and is deliberately imitative of medieval architecture, copying various details from medieval abbey churches (the choir stalls, for example, are copies of those in Chester Cathedral, formerly a Benedictine monastery). "It is not a medieval church. . . . And yet to the perceptive stranger visiting it to-day, there is no doubt that it possesses the atmosphere of a medieval church" (James 1961, 6). We approach the Abbey Church, then, with the recognition that it evokes a particular past and attempts to bring it into the present. The church is arranged on a clear axis leading toward the tabernacle, with laity seated in the west end and monks seated in the east end of the church. The church contains numerous small chapels, radiating from an ambulatory around the east end. These chapels provided a route for patronage of the monastery, with wealthy laypeople paying for their decoration and dedicating them to particular saints to whom they had a devotion (James 1961, 27–33). They also performed an important function for the community, providing a location for each of the monks who was ordained priest to say their daily Mass. In a monastic community, this created a demand for a high number of additional altars. Ampleforth Abbey, Yorkshire, completed in 1961 by Scott, also contains a large number of small chapels for this purpose; these chapels are located under the Abbey Church in the crypt (Corbould 1961).

The churches of more recent monastic foundations demonstrate rather different attitudes to ritual. The monastic community of St. Louis, Missouri, in the United States was founded by English Benedictines from the Ampleforth community in 1955. In contrast to earlier English Benedictine churches, which retain some imitation of the Gothic past and are orientated on a horizontal axis, the church at St. Louis, designed by Gyo Obata and completed in 1962, was built in a modern style, featuring three tiers of parabolic arches, to a circular plan in which the congregation gathers around a central altar. The monks' choir stalls might be seen as part of this collective gathering, with the site of the ritual of the Mass as the continual focal point. Similarly, the Abbey Church at Worth, a community founded by monks from Downside Abbey, was built from 1964 on (consecrated in 1975) to a design by Francis Pollen (Powers 1999, 52–65); here once again, the plan is circular, with the roof styled in a flying saucer shape that quite possibly takes its inspiration from science fiction (Powers 1999, 60). The central altar is once again a focal point, with the congregation gathered around, although it should be noted that the monastic community is marked out as a separate unit, seated on a distinct raised platform behind the altar. In contrast to the many side chapels featured in previous Benedictine churches, here there are only two additional chapels in the body of the church, tucked away behind "snail like walls of brick" (Powers 1999, 56). Whereas side chapels had performed an important function in churches such as Downside, and therefore have architectural prominence, the focus at Worth is very much on the communal Mass celebrated around the shared altar. These changes reflect wider shifts in the ritual attitudes of the Catholic Church; we see a greater focus on communality and the involvement of the laity following the Second Vatican Council of the 1960s, summarized in the call for "fully conscious and active participation"[12] and embodied in a new form for the Mass, using the vernacular language and emphasizing the togetherness of priest and people, with the priest facing the congregation rather than turning away from them, for example. Architectural styles have responded to these changes by creating new spaces and adapting old ones in keeping with the reforms (Schloeder 1998).

Sacred Architecture as a Site of Experience

So far, we have considered sacred buildings as locations of inclusion and exclusion, and examined them as structures that are enmeshed in processes of change. They are sites of social action—but our comprehension of this social action is limited if we are unable to look beyond a formal analysis of the space. If we are to understand sacred architecture, we must appreciate the sensory dimensions of the experiences that take place within the built environment and give it its particular character. Ethnography can play an important role in bringing this sensory aspect to life (Pink 2009), and, in particular, autoethnographic description allows us to draw on the researcher's own sensory responses to better understand the scene being described; for example, Hammoudi's (2006) account of the hajj to Mecca draws on the sights, smells, and sounds experienced in order to give a sense of what it is like to be on pilgrimage.

Candace Weddle's work on the role of the senses in ancient Greek and Roman sacrificial practice suggests one way in which the study of more ephemeral aspects of religious spaces may increase our understanding of the functions of religious architecture. The relationship of worshippers to the divine is articulated not only in the form and use of religious spaces but also in the sensory elements that are produced as a part of ritual. The sights, sounds, and smells of worship, working on the full range of human senses, punctuate the practice of worship, in some instances signal the physical extent of ritual space, and often allow for the signature of worship to be carried over into other social spaces. The rite of sacrifice in ancient Greece and Rome, two cultures that shared many common traits, provides an excellent example of the use of sensory elements to define, delineate, and activate sacred space. Unfortunately, our ability to analyze these elements is hampered by the ephemeral nature of sensory evidence. However, archaeological and literary evidence provides a starting point, and an ethnographic approach may enrich our understanding of how the sensory experience of sacrifices affected Greek and Roman spaces of worship.

When the Greeks and Romans sacrificed to their gods, the sights, sounds, and smells of the rites permeated the city. The smoke from altars filled the air with incense, voices were raised in song to the accompaniment of flutes and drums, and prayers were intoned. If the offering included live victims, the smells of slaughtering and butchering the beasts and roasting flesh and hides on wood fires were notable. Though the act of sacrifice was not limited to architectural spaces specifically designed for ritual use, such locations were important loci for public sacrifice. Considering the sensory effects of the rites carried out on temple grounds raises important questions about the use of such spaces and their relationship to their surroundings.

The most obvious approach to recovering ephemeral sensory elements of ancient sacrifices is to consider related evidence in archaeological and literary sources. Although somewhat sterile, this approach yields much information. Sacrificial scenes are well represented in surviving Greek and Roman art, and we rely heavily on artistic representations of the rites for our understanding of what worshippers would have witnessed, smelled, and heard.[13]

Visual representations of Greco-Roman sacrifices include explicit references to multiple senses that were consciously activated during the rites. A representative example is a relief (Figure 6.3) depicting the emperor Marcus Aurelius

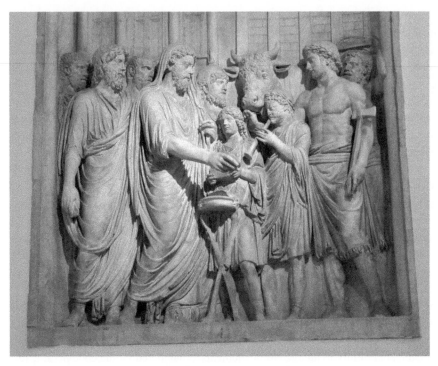

Figure 6.3 Detail of a relief from an honorary monument to Marcus Aurelius: sacrifice to Capitoline Jupiter (Rome, 176–180 C.E., Capitoline Museum). Photo: John Pollini.

(r. 161–80 C.E.) with covered head, pouring a liquid offering onto the fire of a portable brazier (*foculus*). That this is a pre-sacrificial act (*praefatio*) is indicated by the presence of an ox, the eventual victim, peering over the heads of the men. We may observe the ritual costumes of the various actors and imagine the further sensory impact of their actions. Adding to the scent rising from the offered liquid (perhaps water but more likely wine to which spices have been added), the emperor will burn a few lumps of costly aromatics, taken from the open incense box (*acerra*) held by a youthful attendant. These actions are accompanied by the music of a flute player (*tibicinus*).[14]

The relief is at once both informative about the sensory experience of the sacrifice and limited in what it can communicate. Consider, for example, one of the sources of smell depicted in the image. Reliefs such as this that show the offering of incense provide evidence for *how* the act was performed, but this does nothing to suggest the actual scent.[15] For that, we turn to ancient descriptions of burning incense, often described as a "sweet" smell.[16] As evocative as some ancient descriptions of incense may be, they fall far short of communicating the experience of smelling that incense. The same holds true for the flute player's tune. In the absence of the elements themselves, lost to the intervening centuries, we use such important but lacking sources as evidence for the sensory aspects of sacrifice.[17]

Given such methodological difficulties, it is important to consider alternative approaches that allow us to arrive at less "senseless" examinations of Greek and Roman sacrifice. Once we achieve a measure of success, we may consider specific sacrificial locations and imagine more fully the sensory effects of a sacrifice.

It is difficult for scholars to conceive of the sensory impact of the ancient sacrificial spectacle because none of us has experienced it firsthand. We do, however, have the opportunity to experience modern sacrificial rites, and our understanding of ancient sacrifice may benefit from a judiciously applied autoethnographic analysis of such rites. The following abbreviated description of Islamic sacrifices is autoethnographic in the most basic sense in that it is based on the personal experience of contemporary Muslim sacrifice by one of the co-authors; here, Weddle takes the role not of the ethnographer as dissociated outsider but rather of an individual experiencing the rites through the same sensory processes as the other observers. (The autoethnographic character of the following section is reflected in the use of the first person to refer to Weddle's own experience.) This is not an attempt to imply any direct comparison between modern sacrifices and the ancient practice of cult. Rather, the goal is to gain an awareness of the sensory experience of sacrificial slaughter in order to stimulate important questions about the sights, sounds, and smells of ancient Greek and Roman sacrifice, and about data that may persist in the archaeological record that could elucidate the sensory effects of those rites.[18]

* * *

The Sensory Experience of Sacrifice: An Autoethnographic Investigation of Modern Rites[19]

I attended the Kurban Bayramı sacrifices on December 8, 2008, in the Halıçıoğlu neighborhood of Istanbul. Kurban Bayram is a Muslim religious holiday that commemorates the intended sacrifice of Ishmael by Abraham, and a similar event in which the father of Mohammed was almost sacrificed by *his* father.[20] The sacrificial area I visited was designated for the slaughter of large animals (that is, cows and bulls), which allows me to make the best suggestions about ancient sacrifices of adult bovines. The sacrificial location was an open lot in which stations for dealing with the animals had been set up; the entire area of the lot was approximately fifteen by thirty feet (five by ten meters).

There had been a number of animals sacrificed before I arrived (the fourth or fifth animal I saw slaughtered was announced in Turkish as *doksan*, or ninety), and the number waiting remained steady while I was there. Contrary to my expectations, the animals were extremely docile. The smells of the slaughtering did not agitate them, they were unbothered by the activity around them, and they made only the normal sounds of animals in proximity to one another; the people made much more noise than the animals.

An enclosed trailer about the size and height of a standard twenty-foot shipping container had been brought into the area, and the slaughter was being carried out at one open end. The trailer was equipped with a makeshift drainage system composed of a PVC pipe carrying blood from the floor of the trailer into a refuse pit. I was standing about seven feet (two meters) from the end of the trailer where the animals were being killed, directly next to the refuse pit. It was about eight feet (two and a half meters) deep and served as a receptacle for the blood drained from the floor of the trailer, as well as for waste portions of the animals' bodies (Figure 6.4).

The only portions of the bodies that were being discarded regularly were hooves and tails; the majority of the waste in the pit was the contents of the animals' digestive systems. As the stomachs and intestines were removed, they were carried to the edge of the pit. Two women cut the organs open, removed the waste from them, and pushed it into the pit, then set the viscera aside for later consumption or other use.[21] The concrete wall forming one side of the pit was covered in blood and fecal and intestinal matter. The smell of the offal, excrement, and contents of the animals' stomachs greatly overpowered the scent of the blood. In fact, the fresh blood coming

Figure 6.4 Refuse pit at the Istanbul Kurban Bayram sacrifice area, containing entrails, hooves, blood, and waste. Photo: Candace Weddle.

from the animals had very little scent, but presumably as it sat in the open air in the pit or on the ground around the sacrificial area, the smell would increase, exponentially on days with warmer temperatures.

The process of sacrifice was as follows: The animal was led up a ramp to the floor of the trailer. In order to force the cattle into a prone position, a chain attached to a hydraulic mechanism was looped around one back leg and the animal was lifted into the air, then lowered to the ground on its side, with its neck pointing away from the crowd. An assistant grasped the head of the animal and pulled it back to expose the throat. The man carrying out the sacrifices, a trained butcher, used a sharp knife to slice the neck deeply. The sacrificer's goal, as stipulated by Islamic regulations, is to sever both main arteries in the neck, as well as the gullet and windpipe (Siddiqi 1978, 39). This symbolically destroys the means of breath, of ingestion, and of circulation. More pragmatically, it also results in a quick death, and for this reason it is safe to assume that the same practice was common in Greek and Roman rites, in which any unexpected action of a panicked animal at the moment of sacrifice could invalidate the entire ritual.

In most cases the animal struggled very little. The severing of the neck arteries creates a massive amount of blood, which is thicker and of a more vibrant red color than I had expected. Again, the smell of the blood was minimal, but the *sound* of it was something that I was not prepared for. Because of the height of the trailer, the flowing blood pouring down through the PVC pipe and also off the back of the trailer sounded like falling water and was quite striking (Figure 6.5). We may assume that a similar sound was created by the blood of victims falling to the pavement of an ancient altar platform. Though the image of the bright blood of a dying animal may be the most immediate sensory marker of a sacrifice, the sound of that blood should not be underestimated as a rich and evocative element of the proceedings. Each animal was left to bleed for about twenty seconds before the butchering process was begun.

I returned to the sacrificial site on January 27, 2009, fifty days after the sacrifices. My first impression was that the site was much smaller than I had believed; the presence of the animals, the trailer, the butchering tables, the people, and the activity had lent a false sense of size to the area. By the time of my return to the site, the refuse pit had been filled in with dirt and chunks of concrete. Despite this, the smells of the animals did linger; it was not offensive, but was definitely noticeable. The strongest smell was manure, due in part to the fact that some of the waste the animals produced while waiting had not been cleared away. However, when I walked to the area of the covered refuse pit I could smell the slightly metallic scent of blood. The odor was most clearly distinguishable in the vicinity of the concrete retaining wall, despite the fact that it had been thoroughly cleaned.

* * *

Though there is not space to consider here all of the implications of the sensory elements of sacrifice noted by the researcher, it is possible to suggest a few examples

Figure 6.5 Blood falling from the Kurban Bayram trailer platform following slaughter of a bull. The pipe routing most of the blood to the refuse pit can be seen below the trailer. Photo: Candace Weddle.

of how such an experience can advance our understanding of the use of ritual space in antiquity. The experience of the space itself may lead us to reconsider the spatial experience of Greek and Roman temple areas. To apply this observation to a specific location, we may consider the so-called Temple of Domitian, a Roman imperial-period temple in the important city of Ephesus, located in modern-day Turkey.[22] This temple provides an excellent case study because its location in the center of an urban area allows us to suggest the impact of sensory elements of sacrifice on the surrounding neighborhood. Further, the discovery of the altar in situ in 1931, decorated with a relief of a sacrificial bull or ox, allows us to say with certainty that blood sacrifice of bovines was carried out there.

The grounds of the Temple of Domitian are located on top of an artificial three-story terrace much larger in area than the Bayram sacrificial site, at approximately 200 by 300 feet (sixty by ninety meters), but even such a sizable area seems a limited space in which to conduct large-scale sacrifices involving multiple bovine victims, human worshippers, and attendants. The space was occupied by a now-absent temple building and an altar located (as per the standard Greek and Roman arrangement) in front of the temple. In addition, a colonnade ringed the north, south, and west sides, taking up some of the space that is now open and imparting a sense of enclosure to the area that is lacking today. It seems reasonable to conclude that those structures would have made the space of the temple terrace seem even more cramped. However, given the described experience of the Bayram site both during and after the rituals performed there, we should consider the possibility that the ritual buildings and activities may actually have *increased* the impression of the size of the space.

Based on the autoethnographic exercise, we may also make suggestions regarding the smells of sacrifice, an important ritual aspect only hinted at in primary ancient evidence. The observation that the scent of blood lingered most strongly in the concrete of the wall adjacent to the refuse pit suggests that that smell may persist quite some time in certain surfaces. This has interesting implications for ancient altars comprised of marble, a very porous stone that would have soaked up and retained all types of sacrificial liquid. Even if altars were cleaned assiduously, it seems likely that the smells of sacrifice would have been in evidence near those structures long after the slaughter.

Our thinking on the smells of sacrifice may perhaps be challenged in a more fundamental way as well. Before witnessing the Bayram sacrifices, the researcher had considered the smell of waste products only in terms of the manure produced by the animals prior to sacrifice. The experience caused her to recognize that the disposal of the waste in the stomach and intestines of the animals, which must have been an important and immediate part of ancient sacrifice as well, is by far the overpowering source of smell. In contrast, the scent of the blood at the sacrifices was much less than anticipated. Further, considering the disposal of this type of refuse, which in the Bayram example was introduced into a pit and promptly covered over, raises questions about ancient sacrificial practice and the experience of sacred architecture that may in some cases be answered definitively by archaeological evidence. The deposition of manure, even for a short period of time, leaves an archaeologically recoverable chemical signature in the soil. The inspection of ancient sacrificial sites for traces of manure deposits could yield suggestive evidence for the handling of sacrificial waste in antiquity. The recognition of a significant source of scent that is addressed only in passing in our primary sources may lead to a new use for archaeological data from ancient temple sites.[23]

Furthermore, the persistence of scent at the site of the modern sacrifices may aid us in suggesting the effects ancient sacrificial sites had on their surroundings. Observations drawn from this autoethnographic exercise make us aware that the sensory experience of ancient cult included not only things seen, heard, smelled, tasted, and touched during the active practice of cult, but also ways in which the sacrificial spaces impacted their surroundings even in periods devoid of active sacrifice. Repeated use of the same sacrificial spot over and over again, year after year, would have had a great and lasting impact on the cult spaces, an impact that would have spilled over into the surrounding urban area. Consideration of ancient holy places based on careful scrutiny of modern rites comparable to the ones carried out there, rather than solely on the impact of the sites as experienced many years after their functional life has ended, may lead to a fuller understanding of how the sense elements of worship would have extended beyond the boundaries of religious spaces and affected the surrounding land- or cityscape.

In Greek and Roman antiquity, the meaning of religious architecture lay in its use. This is explicit in the fact that a location could be considered holy in the absence of structures, based solely on demarcation accomplished through ritual. In order to truly understand an ancient Greek or Roman religious space, we must understand what went on in it; the senses were an extremely important part of that. Though their traces are ephemeral, we can combat the austerity of the archaeological remains by judiciously applying experience of comparable modern rites to ancient evidence for how the spaces were utilized and affected, and for how they in turn affected worshippers and others who experienced them.

Toward a Deeper Understanding of Sacred Architecture: The Possibilities for a Dialogue between Archaeology and Anthropology

We have set out to show the possibilities that emerge from a conversation between archaeology and anthropology. As scholars attempting to better understand the sacred architecture we encounter in our work, we have found that this is an area of common concern between our disciplines and that our disciplines have much to offer one another methodologically and theoretically. Archaeologists are able to benefit from ethnographic insights to envisage how buildings are used, while anthropologists are able to benefit from the archaeologists' diachronic perspective and awareness of the material form of the places where people gather.

We have seen how methods used by archaeologists for assessing access within and movement around built structures can aid our understanding of the interaction between sacred space and the people using that space. Permeability mapping has been discussed as a flexible and easily applicable method to use as part of the ethnographic process, aiding both specific analysis and cross-cultural comparison. It gets below the surface details of the decoration and iconography and becomes a map of social knowledge, revealing restrictions on the movement of the users of the building, and so the users' hierarchies and exclusions. It makes vital interactions of people and space tangible and so can deepen our understanding of the ritual process. Yet an analysis of such processes also requires an awareness of the experience of ritual, including its sensory aspects, and it is here that autoethnographic methods are of benefit in helping us to grasp the intangible qualities of space that may not be visible in the material record.

This is an ongoing conversation but one that shows much promise. As archaeologists and anthropologists encounter sacred architecture, we share a common concern with the question of how buildings are inhabited: we seek to understand the interaction between human activity and architectural form. Through dialogue between our disciplines, we can deepen this understanding.

Notes

1. These Bristol sites are located at 8 Church Road, 163b Church Road, and 71–75 Fishponds Road, respectively.
2. Per standard U.S. convention, "second floor" here refers to the first floor above ground level, while "first floor" will be used for the floor at ground level.
3. Hanks has experienced Barker's methods firsthand through attendance at his drama workshops.
4. Weller (2003) outlines appropriate visiting etiquette across a range of religions in the United Kingdom.
5. A papal bull is an official decree issued by the pope.
6. Their monastery was founded in Douai, then a notable center for Catholic exiles (Bossy 1975, 12–17), as a house from which to send monks for the mission in England. They remained on the continent until policies suppressing monastic orders in France, as well as the events of the French Revolution and the declaration of war against Britain by the French revolutionary government, made it unsustainable to continue English Benedictine life there; they returned to England in 1794 and settled at their current site in 1814.
7. With regards to Gasquet's authorship of these words, it is worth noting that Knowles (1963, 252) writes, "It seems certain that [Gasquet's introduction to] *Monks of the West* . . . was almost entirely the work of two 'ghosts', Edmund Bishop and Dom Elphege Cody"; in addition to this, we see very similar words in pamphlets authored by others. It could be argued that this demonstrates the extent to which such views were held and agreed on as the collective opinion of a group of monks in the community at this time.
8. From the Latin *calefacere*, "to warm"; the name is retained from that traditionally given in Benedictine monasteries to the room with the fire where the monks would have gone to warm themselves.
9. The guest wing is closed to visitors only for a period during the summer, around the time when the monks are making their own annual retreat.
10. Since 2007 the monastery's policy is to allow only male guests; although the guest wing itself is not a gender-marked space, the refectory is, and the difficulty of providing meals in a place apart from the community is often cited as a reason for this restriction of female guests.
11. See James 1961 for a history of Downside Abbey Church.
12. This widely cited phrase is drawn from Article 14 of *Sacrosanctum Concilium*, the Constitution on the Liturgy promulgated in 1963 during the Second Vatican Council.

13. The sense of taste is less often alluded to in the corpus of sacrificial imagery. It was most obviously activated at the ritual banquets following the slaughter, at which the meat of the victims was consumed. Our primary sources of evidence for these feasts are textual. See, for example, Linders 1994 for "menus" of items served at the sacrificial banquets of the Posideia and Eileithyaia on the island of Delos in the early second century B.C.E.

14. Cult musicians are common in Roman sacrificial scenes, indicating their ritual importance.

15. The smell of incense was certainly not the only, nor perhaps even the most important, smell produced during the practice of Greek and Roman sacrifice, but it is a scent that very specifically invoked the presence of deities and provided a means of communication with them.

16. For example, Olympos, the dwelling place of the gods, is described as sweet-smelling (θυώδεος), a term that can even be translated as "smelling of incense" (*Homeric Hymn to Hermes* 4.322).

17. In addition to such investigations of ancient art and literature, some more experimental procedures for studying ancient sensory elements have been employed with varying degrees of success. Notably, there have been limited attempts to play archaeologically recovered ancient instruments (this approach must be applied with the greatest caution since it inevitably damages the object) and to construct modern functional facsimiles. Though there are clear positive applications of these techniques, the difficulties inherent in such projects are equally clear: Reproduced objects, precise as they may be, are not the original objects, and the sounds they produce are not the original sounds. Further, it is impossible to know whether the sounds that modern musicians elicit from ancient instruments, or from reproductions of ancient instruments, bear *any* resemblance to the sounds the Greeks and Romans heard. Two thousand years of development in the history and technique of music stand between us and the ability to produce a Roman melody on a Roman *tibia*. On reconstruction and preservation of Greek and Roman instruments (and the problems inherent in such projects), see Ersoy 2002 and Tamboer 2002. Tamboer considers the difference between creating reconstructions for educational use as opposed to for purposes of experimental archaeological research. On potential applications of archaeomusicology to the field of music history, see de Geer 1988.

18. Due to space constraints, we will consider only the impact of the actual sacrificial slaughter, omitting discussion of the butchering process and distribution of meat, though those activities were an important part of ancient sacrificial processes as well.

19. Portions of this section were first published in expanded form in "The Sensory Experience of Blood Sacrifice in the Roman Imperial Cult" (in Day forthcoming).

20. In Islamic tradition, it is the "true firstborn" of Abraham (that is, Ishmael, his son by his handmaiden Hagar) who is the intended sacrifice, not Isaac as in the biblical narrative.
21. Some stomachs and entrails were being discarded, but a significant number were salvaged.
22. Excavations were first conducted on the temple during the Austrian Archaeological Institute's campaigns in 1930–31 and 1960–61. As a result of the most recent seasons of excavation and geophysical research by that institute in 2009–11, identification of the building as the imperial cult temple in honor of the emperor Domitian is in question.
23. For discussion of ancient guidelines for disposing of manure produced by sacrificial animals, see especially Dillon 1997 and Németh 1994.

References

Aravecchia, Nicola. 2001. "Hermitages and spatial analysis: Uses of space at the Kellia." In *Shaping community: The art and archaeology of monasticism*, ed. Sheila McNally, 29–38. Oxford: Archaeopress.

Barker, Clive. 1977. *Theatre games: A new approach to drama training*. London: Methuen.

Bossy, John. 1975. *The English Catholic community, 1570–1850*. London: Darton, Longman and Todd.

Corbould, Edward. 1961. "Ampleforth Abbey Church." *Ampleforth Journal* 66: 163–81.

Davies, J.G. 1982. *Temples, churches and mosques: A guide to the appreciation of religious architecture*. Bath, UK: Pitman Press.

Day, J., ed. Forthcoming. *Making senses of the past: Toward a sensory archaeology* (working title). Center for Archaeological Investigations Occasional Paper, no. 40. Carbondale, IL: Center for Archaeological Investigations.

de Geer, Ingrid. 1988. "Music archaeology in music history writing: A case study." In *The archaeology of early music cultures: 3rd International Meeting of the ICTM Study Group on Music Archaeology*, ed. Ellen Hickmann and David W. Hughes, 275–87. Bonn: Verlag für Systematische Musikwissenschaft.

Dillon, Matthew P.J. 1997. "The ecology of the Greek sanctuary." *Zeitschrift für Papyrologie und Epigraphik* 118: 113–27.

Duffy, Eamon. 1992. *The stripping of the altars: Traditional religion in England, 1400–1580*. New Haven, CT: Yale University Press.

Durkheim, Émile. 1915. *The elementary forms of the religious life*, trans. Joseph Ward Swain. London: George Allen and Unwin.

Ersoy, Hande Kökten. 2002. "Primary condition report and proposals for the conservation of a Roman tibia." In *The archaeology of sound: Origin and organisa-*

tion. *Papers from the 2nd Symposium of the International Study Group on Music Archaeology at Monastery Michaelstein, 17–23 September 2000*, ed. Ellen Hickmann, Anne Draffkorn Kilmer, and Ricardo Eichmann, 211–13. Rahden, Germany: Verlag Marie Leidorf.

Fortin, John R. 2003. "The reaffirmation of monastic hospitality." *Downside Review* 121: 105–18.

Gasquet, Francis Aidan. 1896. "Sketch of monastic constitutional history." Introduction to *The monks of the West from St. Benedict to St. Bernard* by Charles Forbes, comte de Montalembert. London: J.C. Nimmo.

Gilchrist, Roberta, and Barney Sloane. 2005. *Requiem: The medieval monastic cemetery in Britain*. London: Museum of London Archaeological Service.

Gould, Shane. 1999. "Planning, development and social archaeology." In *The familiar past? Archaeologies of later historical Britain*, ed. S. Tarlow and S. West, 140–54. London: Routledge.

Grimes, Ronald L. 1982. *Beginnings in ritual studies*. Lanham, MD: United Press of America.

Hall, Marcia B. 2006. "The tramezzo in the Italian Renaissance, revisited." In *Thresholds of the sacred: Architectural, art historical, liturgical, and theological perspectives on religious screens, East and West*, ed. Sharon E.J. Gerstel, 215–25. Washington, DC: Dumbarton Oaks Research Library and Collection.

Hammoudi, Abdhella. 2006. *A season in Mecca: Narrative of a pilgrimage*, trans. Pascale Ghazaleh. Cambridge, UK: Polity.

Hillier, B., and J. Hanson. 1984. *The social logic of space*. Cambridge: Cambridge University Press.

Horn, Walter. 1973. "On the origins of the medieval cloister." *Gesta* 12 (1/2): 13–52.

Irvine, R.D.G. 2011. "The architecture of stability: Monasteries and the importance of place in a world of non-places." *Etnofoor* 23 (1): 29–49.

James, Augustine. 1961. *The story of Downside Abbey Church*. Stratton-on-the-Fosse, UK: Downside Abbey Press.

Kerr, Julie. 2007. *Monastic hospitality: The Benedictines in England, c.1070–c.1250*. Woodbridge, UK: Boydell.

Knowles, David. 1963. *The historian and character and other essays*. Cambridge: Cambridge University Press.

Linders, Tullia. 1994. "Sacred menus on Delos." In *Ancient Greek cult practice from the epigraphical evidence: Proceedings of the Second International Seminar on Ancient Greek Cult*, ed. Robin Hägg, 71–79. Stockholm: Svenska Institutet i Athen.

Mann, A.T. 1993. *Sacred architecture*. Shaftesbury, UK: Element Books.

Markus, Thomas A. 1993. *Buildings and power: Freedom and control in the origin of modern building types*. London: Routledge.

Marshall, Douglas A. 2002. "Behavior, belonging and belief: A theory of ritual practice." *Sociological Theory* 20 (3): 360–80.

Nash, George, ed. 1997. *The semiotics of landscape: The archaeology of the mind.* Oxford: Archaeopress.

Németh, G. 1994. "Μεδ' ὄνθον ἐγβαλεν: Regulations concerning everyday life in a Greek temenos." In *Ancient Greek cult practice from the epigraphical evidence: Proceedings of the Second International Seminar on Ancient Greek Cult,* ed. Robin Hägg, 59–64. Stockholm: Svenska Institutet i Athen.

Pink, Sarah. 2009. *Doing sensory ethnography.* London: Sage.

Powers, Francis. 1999. *Francis Pollen: Architect, 1926–1987.* Oxford: Robert Dugdale.

Renfrew, C., and E. Bahn. 2000. *Archaeology: Theories, methods and practice.* 3rd ed. London: Thames and Hudson.

Richardson, Amanda. 2003. "Corridors of power: A case study in access analysis from medieval England." *Antiquity* 77 (296): 373–84.

Scarry, Elaine. 1985. *The body in pain: The making and unmaking of the world.* Oxford: Oxford University Press.

Schachner, Gregson. 2001. "Ritual control and transformation in middle-range societies: An example from the American Southwest." *Journal of Anthropological Archaeology* 20: 168–94.

Schloeder, Steven J. 1998. *Architecture in communion: Implementing the Second Vatican Council through liturgy and architecture.* San Francisco: Ignatius Press.

Seasoltz, R. Kevin. 1974. "Monastic hospitality." *American Benedictine Review* 25: 427–51.

Shackley, Myra. 2004. "Accommodating the spiritual tourist: The case of religious retreat houses." In *Small firms in tourism: International perspectives,* ed. Rhodri Thomas, 225–38. Oxford: Elsevier.

Siddiqi, Muhammad Iqbal. 1978. *The ritual of animal sacrifice in Islam.* Lahore: Kazi.

Spicer, Andrew. 2000. "Architecture." In *The Reformation world,* ed. Andrew Pettegree, 505–20. London: Routledge.

Tamboer, Annemies. 2002. "Excavated sounds: Reconstructions of lyre, hornpipe and other archaeological instruments for education and research." In *The archaeology of sound: Origin and organisation. Papers from the 2nd Symposium of the International Study Group on Music Archaeology at Monastery Michaelstein, 17–23 September 2000,* ed. Ellen Hickmann, Anne Draffkorn Kilmer, and Ricardo Eichmann, 237–47. Rahden, Germany: Verlag Marie Leidorf.

Turner, Victor. 1969. *The ritual process: Structure and anti-structure.* Chicago: Aldine.

Weller, Paul, ed. 2003. *Religions in the UK: Directory 2001–03.* Derby, UK: The Multi-Faith Centre at the University of Derby and the Inter Faith Network for the United Kingdom.

West, Susie. 1999. "Social space and the English country house." In *The familiar past? Archaeologies of later historical Britain,* ed. S. Tarlow and S. West, 103–22. London: Routledge.

–7–

Life with Things: Archaeology and Materiality

Rosemary A. Joyce

The recent reemergence of materiality as a key topic for social scientists and humanists (e.g., Alder 2007; Alexander 2008; Arnold, Shepherd, and Gibbs 2008; Bennett 2004; Dezeuze 2008; Gieryn 2002; Hitchings 2004; Meyer 2008), including social anthropologists (Miller 2005; Myers 2001), has at times seemed to be taking place without substantively engaging archaeology, a set of disciplinary approaches founded fundamentally on the proposition that we can talk about the lives people led in the past through the things that have persisted from that past to our present. This is not to say that archaeologists have remained silent in debates about "the social lives of things," "object agency," or even actor network theory (Gosden 2005; Gosden and Marshall 1999; Knappett 2005; Martin 2005; Normark 2010; Olsen 2003, 2007; Shanks 2007; Witmore 2007). Yet just when discussions of materiality are yielding a productive blurring of lines that sees ethnographers studying ancient Moche pots (Weismantel 2004) and archaeologists looking at the way that Las Vegas recycles Egyptica (Meskell 2004), it nonetheless seems that often we archaeologists are talking past our interlocutors.

We archaeologists claim a specific expert position in discussions based on our long history of grounding *in* materiality, even as the status of matter *as* grounding is being called into question. More than a decade ago, it was suggested that "archaeologists take what's materially left of the past and work on it intellectually and physically to produce knowledge" through the crafting of representational media (Shanks and McGuire 1996, 76). Archaeologist practitioners share language, including terms of craft we understand because they have historically circulated in the dialogues that bind us together (Joyce 2002). As we use the terms of craft that we have tested and come to trust over generations, we may fail to adequately account for the complex models of circulation of things that our terminologies index, bringing into our contemporary discussions conceptual baggage we think we have left behind.

In order to explore ways to reframe the understandings of materiality that archaeology provides that may be obscured by our ways of talking about things, I draw on case studies from research I have conducted independently and collaboratively in the Ulua River valley of Caribbean coastal Honduras. Extending from life in the earliest villages yet known, settled before 1600 B.C.E., to colonial and Republican-era history and archaeology (ca. 1750–1930 C.E.), what unites these studies is my understanding of archaeology as a tracing of the continual assembling of networks in which materialities that served as mediators in the past persist and are available for us to incorporate in our accounts (after Latour 2005). This is a way of thinking about lives with things in no way limited to the practice of archaeology. It needs only to be placed in dialogue with questions being debated across the social sciences and humanities, including in social anthropology.

I offer this analysis as an anthropologist, trained in the tradition of the United States that encompasses archaeology, with a perspective inseparable from the history of that tradition (see Wylie 2002). That perspective has particular implications for my understanding of how archaeology has and can contribute to understanding the materiality of social life. It is thus worth recapitulating some key points of that history. In the common project of twentieth-century American anthropology, archaeology was originally charged to understand the past through the study of excavated sites and the "material culture" embedded in them. Material culture studies in the 1930s and 1940s challenged the concept of cultural production as an automatic reflection of group identity. Employing older museum collections as the basis for interviews with members of the communities from which they had been collected, museum anthropologists established roles for individual preferences, learning, and particularistic experiences on the forms of ethnographic material culture (Schevill 1992). By the 1950s, fierce debates raged in American archaeology about whether similarities in form used to group things recovered in excavations had natural and unequivocal causes in such things as group identification, "norms," or "culture" in general, of which material culture was a problematic mirror, subset, or extension, depending on which models were in use. Definition of terminologies to allow archaeologists to draw equivalences between the things excavated in one place and social facts such as kinship, economy, politics, religion, and the like that might have existed at the same location some time in the past (Willey and Phillips 1958), did not resolve these debates.

The "new archaeology" of the 1960s and 1970s called for a reinvention of anthropological archaeology as the study of generalizable processes, using scientific methods often expressed in the language of hypothesis testing and falsification. While this approach began with the bold claim that nothing in human life was outside the scope of archaeology (Binford 1962), in practice, the focus rapidly narrowed to those aspects of social life that were considered more basic: the behaviors involved in provisioning society and exploiting environments, the social structures that were considered most likely to exist in societies of particular scales with particular economies in specific environments, and, to a limited degree, the external expression of social identities for largely functional purposes. The resulting environmental determinism, reductionism, and methodological focus of processual archaeology facilitated the emergence in American archaeology in the 1980s and into the 1990s of a number of archaeological critiques (Preucel 1995). While actually quite varied, these critical archaeologies shared concerns with subjectivity, agency, relations of power, questions of representation, and history as a product of archaeological research (Brumfiel 1992). In these reconceptualizations of American anthropological archaeology, "material culture" underwent transformations as well. Once understood as expressions of a fundamentally ideational "culture," a means by which people could signal their identities more or less consciously, things became more active, "constituting," "materializing," "embodying," or otherwise causing specific forms of social relations to take shape. Yet even as our archaeological understanding has shifted from a static material culture to an active materiality, we have maintained a practice of talking about "what's materially left of the past" (Shanks and McGuire 1996, 76) as if that materiality persisted unchanged, allowing our interlocutors to misconstrue what we actually mean and how we actually do materiality in archaeology.

Materializing Practices, Historicizing Practice

As we understand archaeology as founded on the idea that we can talk about the lives people led in the past through *traces* of past action perceptible in our present, our attention should be directed to the ways archaeologists rematerialize traces of practices in the past, traces of materialities that in their time themselves materialized practice. The relationship between our materializing practices and those of the past is not, in any sense, simple recapitulation or reiteration but, rather, attests to the movement of things along their continuing itineraries.

Consider a ubiquitous archaeological trace: a postmold, the ghost of a posthole (Pauketat and Alt 2005). A series of such traces makes up the evidence I use to argue that, at a place today called Puerto Escondido, Honduras, a series of houses were built, inhabited, demolished, and replaced between 1600 and 900 B.C.E. (Joyce 2007a). My own materializing practice begins with the conventional, albeit counterfactual, statement that the color and texture of the superimposed sediments that my troweling makes appear on a flat surface "are" a posthole. In this pattern of color and texture that is all that remains to hint at a hole dug 3,000 years ago, from which a post was removed and into which by-products of later human existence trickled, we are not seeing the placement of the post, or the digging of the hole. Rather, we are seeing the latest state of a dynamic history that continues today as we intervene and reconstitute color and texture as material evidence of a chain of past practices (Joyce 2008a).

That is, the physical practices of archaeology today are literally historicizing practices, the constitution of material histories. These we index through representational strategies that have become so much taken for granted that we may literally fail to see the lack of identity between our use of *posthole* for soil texture and color variability, and what anyone digging posts today or in the past would have imagined by this term. Our use of conventionalizations like these is an inevitable outcome of the formation of a discipline through ongoing dialogic exchanges that employ internal languages recognized by others within the group (Joyce 2002). Yet conventionalized language like this undoubtedly obscures for those outside the disciplinary circle our understanding that the trace we recognize is a sign of history, not a thing recaptured from a past lived experience and revived in our present circumstances. Archaeologists trace complex histories of deposition registered in meters-deep sequences of different soil colors and textures, within which we can isolate some planes as points of contact between ancient inhabitation and our modern redescription of traces of postholes and pits, "features" that stand for and stand as the elements of houses long disappeared (Joyce and Pollard 2010). This understanding of materiality as historicized gives archaeologists the potential to contribute a necessary temporal dimension to understanding materiality. To do that, though, there are internal obstacles we must overcome.

I have argued that in order to bring archaeological representations in line with our actual ways of thinking about people's lives with things we need to abandon a number of residual approaches to understanding materiality that simply do not work. Among these is a simplistic model of signification in which things stand as representatives of some sort of social whole, for example, pots for peoples. The controversy about whether "the Olmec" spread from the Gulf Coast of Mexico to other areas of Central America, based on identifying pots with particular design characteristics as likely made in the Gulf Coast, is a case in point (Joyce 2008b). The materials science involved is precise and does indicate the likelihood that the pots were made from clays developed from uniform source rock. When pots with that common composition differ from others used in a particular place, the conclusion that the rarer pots were imported is not particularly difficult to explain even to noncombatants. But the slippage that raises the temperature of this debate is the one that moves us from pots with particular shapes, surface colors, and incised designs to the people such pots are understood to index—the Olmec. Here, our theory of representation is simply inadequate to allow us to understand these materialities in anything like a contemporary anthropological sense.

In common with a number of other contemporary archaeologists, I have suggested that we need to address our task with a theory of meaning that treats the material dimension of signification as active, rather than the quasi-linguistic model that sustained archaeology for most of the twentieth century. I and others find the resources we need in a Peircean semiotics (Bauer 2002; Joyce 2007b, 2008a; Knappett 2002, 2005; Lele 2006; Preucel 2005; Preucel and Bauer 2001). Preucel and Bauer (2001, 87) describe a critical shift in archaeological practice when we substitute the triadic relation of sign, object, and interpretant in the Peircean sign for the dyadic relation of signifier and signified in the Saussurean sign. The third term demands we consider the activity of the interpreter (Preucel and Bauer 2001, 91–92). The inclusion of the relation of preexisting objects and an active interpreter shifts analysis from a more restricted model of meanings contained in vehicles that is evident in the equation of pots with peoples, to one of meaning-making, as the creation of relations among people and objects unfolding in time. The more complex spectrum of interacting indexical, iconic, and symbolic relations between signs and their objects introduced through a Peircean semiotic engagement has also been identified as critical to contemporary understanding of materiality and meaning (Knappett 2002, 102–3). As products of specific histories, Peircean symbols are far from arbitrary. Indexical signs register "an existential relation" between a sign and its referent that is particularly important for archaeologists trying to identify how pots might be connected to people, even if they do not stand simply as signs of peoples (Preucel and Bauer 2001, 88). Preucel and Bauer cite Richard Parmentier's discussion of a traditional archaeological analysis of a pottery style as an example (p. 90). Parmentier suggested we understand pottery styles as indexical signs incorporating iconic signs. Each pot recognizable as in a specific style indexes the set of repeated traits that make up the style. So in the example of identifying different pots across Mexico as Olmec, the visible features of shape, surface color, and incised design are legible as the same due to their mutual resemblance, or iconicity. The identification of "resemblance" clearly requires an act of interpretation, one in which modern archaeologists attempt to stand in the place of past makers, users, and viewers of these pots.

Preucel and Bauer (2001, 93) argue that this perspective reinstates the flow of engagements—with things, with signs—that we intersect when we analyze archaeological materialities as histories. Those histories, already conceived of as the "social lives" or "cultural biographies" of things (Appadurai 1986; Hoskins 1998; Kopytoff 1986) have immense potential to bridge archaeological and other ways of thinking. Yet to achieve a connection between archaeological understandings of things and ethnographic accounts, I suggest we need to take another step and consider whether a focus on the lives of objects entirely captures how we think about things from the traces of their passage through time.

Social Lives of Things: Object Biographies and Object Itineraries

The challenge for archaeologists is to maintain a simultaneous focus on traces as evidence of pragmatic engagement in the world, and of meaningful links among human actors, without reducing things to sketchy outlines without weight or sensory qualities. When I say that the variability in soil color and texture that I sense as I excavate "is" a posthole, I violate this ideal. If I instead talk about these same characteristics as traces of the pragmatic ends of building, the ongoing history of dwelling, and the meaning-filled engagement with buildings and their environs by human beings who create them as sites of activity and in turn are shaped by them, I come closer to doing something recognizable by other kinds of anthropologists. We can talk about the "use lives" and "cultural biographies" of houses and find ourselves talking to each other, instead of past each other (Gerritsen 1999; Tringham 1991, 2000; Waterson 2000).

Nonetheless, object biography is a challenging concept that does not entirely fit the archaeological, or indeed sociological, situation of everydayness. Archaeologists have as often used the notion of object biographies to discuss whole classes of things as to trace the lives of specific things (Dant 2001). Biographies are supposed to have distinct beginnings and ends. But objects actually move in and out of relationships, from treasure to trash and back again (Thompson 1979). What archaeologists do is follow the entire chain of movement and transformation, beginning before there is an object as such with enlistment of raw materiality and continuing after discard through the physical alteration of some thing into other things.

I suggest that a more natural concept for archaeology to explore is the itinerary of things, evident in the traces of their passage (Joyce forthcoming). Many archaeological terms of reference for distinctive things, the kind that are the natural subjects of object biographies, actually index geographic locations. For example, specific carved stone vessels manufactured in Honduras between 500 and 1000 c.e. are called Ulua marble vases. These are objects whose biographies are actually best considered in terms of movement and place (Luke 2010; Luke and Tykot 2007). The geographic name indexes the specificity of place, and not just any place, but the place where we understand these things to have been crafted into their original form. That place, in this case, the lower Ulua River valley, is one point on the itinerary of these objects. But it is not the last point on their journey, nor even necessarily the place where archaeological practice encountered these things. Yet wherever they traveled, in antiquity reaching as far south as Costa Rica and as far north as the lowlands of Guatemala, and, in more than a century of modern art collecting, expanding their reach throughout the museums of Europe and the Americas, Ulua marble vases carried with them a trace of the place where they originated.

When archaeologists talk about objects, we routinely use the term *provenience* to single out the unique location where a specific object—not just the generic or categorical class of objects—was found by the archaeologist. The privilege accorded this one stop on its itinerary neither exhausts what is of interest nor actually portrays how archaeologists think about the places things occupied. The complete itinerary—closer to what the art historical term *provenance* references—is what a sense of things as historicized traces of practices requires us to examine.

To return to the example of Ulua marble vases: As their name indicates, they are understood as products of the same workshops along the Ulua River, at sites like Travesia (Luke and Tykot 2007). Material science analyses give a basis for this claim, by linking the chemical composition of the marble of known vases to the compositions of identified quarries across the landscape of the Ulua valley. The results point toward a concentration of vessel production related to a single quarry but also demonstrate variability among these products that must be understood in terms of the waxing and waning of workshops over time. The circulation of products from the same marble resource does not simply point back to a deferred and somehow more authentic original origin point. It is the passage of marble from the quarry to the workshop, and of vases from the workshop to a succession of users, and ultimately into the museums and archaeological research collections where they are found today, that is of interest, not simply the thing itself, even if it is conceived of as the subject of a biography. As marble from the main quarry near Santa Rita was carved, probably in or near the town of Travesia thirty-five to forty-five miles (sixty to seventy kilometers) away, and vases were sent out from the workshop town to more distant locales, the provenance each accrued—its history of circulation—mediated specific connections among human beings. The geological and stylistic features we discern serve as contemporary but only partial traces of this itinerary, and it is the itinerary that provides us a way to think about the cultural production and social relationships in which these things were entangled.

Struggling with the Memory of Things

We struggle with the reality that our improving ability to trace the itineraries of things makes our understandings more, not less, complex. Nor is it enough to trace the circulation of things. We also need to understand the circulation of references to things, references that served as precedents of action. Memory—social, cultural, or individual—has thus come to be figured as a rich topic in contemporary archaeology of materiality, where materialities are understood as forms through which memory work may take place (Mills and Walker 2008).

Let me offer for consideration another trace: a fragment of a green marble vase excavated in a secure archaeological provenience in the midst of the Ulua River valley, at a site called Mantecales (Joyce and Pollard 2010, 299–303). This vessel fragment was not simply placed in space, where it was encountered on a buried surface on a low earthen platform that developed through generations of habitation over hundreds of years. It was placed in time, around 850 c.e., by the thousands of fragments from dozens of shallow dishes, broken and discarded at the same time—the same event—that saw the marble vase fragment abandoned.

Transcribed as a moment in time by archaeological conventions, the destruction and discard of these bowls was the culminating moment in a series of actions that took place over a period of at least 150 years and that left as traces the pile of broken pottery that buried a single fragment of one green marble bowl. Standard culture-historical descriptions fail to completely capture the capacity of the things in this place to orient, compel, foster, give meaning to, inform, and enrich the actions that followed.

In the beginning, what would become an enduring orientation of action was set in motion by the placement of three fragmented vessels: the neck from a large jar, flanked by two lids that were used to place over buckets of burning tree resins. Once established, this focal point in a terrain with widely distributed traces of incense burning persisted as an axis, materially marked by what ultimately would be seven superimposed jar necks, around which fragmented portions of other specialized vessels for burning incense were repeatedly deposited. Because this axis of action was enclosed in a rectangle of built stone walls, which we excavated completely, we can say that in no case were all the fragments of any vessels left here. The deliberate separation of fragments left bodies of human and animal figures while abstracting the heads. The sole human figure included, about one-third life size and complete only from midbody down, was found with a separately modeled effigy of the kind of bag that would have contained resin to burn. This pottery replica was pierced for suspension from the figure's hand, a hand that was missing from this place. Jar necks placed after this were flanked by lids with feline figures, again lacking the head and face.

The repetition and layering of material traces, residues of actions in which these things were used, and to which the human figure makes reflexive reference in its truncated gesture, culminated in the shaping of a space containing not simply material, but memory, underlying both literally and historically the placement on the final paved surface of a stone vessel fragment. Again, the complete excavation of the deposit allows us to affirm that the remaining pieces were not left here. This is the kind of decomposition that Küchler (1999, 68) suggests can be a "source for future recollections of what was rendered absent." The archaeological trace consists not just of what was found, but of what was not found, what was brought elsewhere in another part of the itinerary of this thing.

Persons and Possessions

Traces archaeologists once would have regarded as trash are now central to our understanding of the itineraries of things that form the assemblages through which we historicize practices (Joyce and Pollard 2010). We understand the circulation across space of fragments as creating networks of connections between persons and things (Chapman 2000). This understanding implies a kind of enduring identity between people and the things they make and use, a question of possession, not merely use and discard (Hendon 2000; Joyce and Hendon 2008).

Consider another green marble fragment: the base from a second vessel, deposited at about the same time as the events at Mantecales, about six miles (ten kilometers) south at the hilltop town, Cerro Palenque (Hendon 2010). This marble fragment was placed, along with two spiny oyster shells, under an inverted bowl, buried during the construction of a terrace to one side of a low platform. As at Mantecales, this fragment of a vessel was curated and interred separately from any other pieces of the original vessel to which it belonged.

The courtyard where this fragment was carefully placed was a rich site for think-ing about the biographies of things (Hendon 2010). Across the courtyard, a trench was dug and filled with fragments of dozens of smashed pottery bowls. Some were distinctively marked with impressed designs, produced by molds also broken and disposed of in the same location. Immediately adjacent to this trench were the traces of firing facilities appropriate to produce such objects, in the form of fired clay and burned carbon, all that was left of the collapse of these small kilns. The assemblage of traces described here points to a series of events, in-gatherings of human beings who intersected relatively short-lived things, made, used, and discarded under the authority of those who lived in this place. We might, following Kockelman (2007), want to consider the making and breaking of these things in relation to expanding and contracting the scope of the person by acquiring and giving up "possessions." That requires us to ask *where* the other fragments of things like those curated near the political and social center of the town of Cerro Palenque traveled.

Fragments of distinctive mold-made vessels recovered from the trench at Cerro Palenque mimic the much larger marble vases that were in contemporary use. The stone vases have been found clustered in the central part of the Ulua River valley, especially near the large town of Travesia, or were found at the town closest to the most commonly used quarry. The smaller clay effigies extended out beyond this core zone. Ceramic effigies originated in many of the towns in the core area where stone vases were also used, the only sites where the molds to make the effigies in clay have been found. Carried away from the places where they were made, they conveyed with them connections both to other things and also to human beings whose person-hood was constituted as much in engagements with things as in engagements with other human actors. Indeed, we may want to question the productivity of maintaining a strict boundary that purports to separate persons, places, and things, when these are so tightly bound by the circulation of materialities.

Person-like objects already had a long history in the Ulua River valley when the people of Mantecales, Travesia, and Cerro Palenque engaged with each other in the ninth century C.E. The application of human features to vessels was already hundreds of years old in 800 B.C.E., when potters at Playa de los Muertos, on the river between Cerro Palenque and Travesia, gave bottles human forms, turning them into personi-fied containers of the same kinds of things that filled the bodies of human beings (Joyce 2008c). Both human beings and the shaped fired clay images we call figurines were worked, decomposed, and circulated (Joyce 2003). Human skeletal elements were abstracted from burials or concentrated together in cave ossuaries, while figur-ine limbs and heads were broken and often separated into different refuse deposits. Personified objects literally served to compose socialized bodies, hung as amulets or pendants around the neck (Joyce 2003, 2007b, 2008c). Personified objects semi-otically served to compose socialized bodies, singling out as topics of comment life stages from infancy to young adulthood to old age. The extraordinary details incorporated in these small personified objects require, demand, compel handling.

Their material construction, with inner armatures covered by layers of clay flesh and a thin cap of fine clay skin, make their crafting like in kind to human crafting. At the same time, the marking of these person-like objects with geometric patterns, and the contemporary marking of human bodies with patterns made possible by use of stamps and seals, identified humans and figurines with other less iconic objects, like the bowls used and disposed of mingled with human bones in burials.

Concluding Thoughts

It is appropriate in a paper encouraging an explicit shift to talking about things in motion that I leave this discussion somewhat open. I have made what I think is a simple argument, that archaeological perspectives on materiality provide a necessary disrupting of other ways of seeing things. What Michael Shanks calls an "archaeological sensibility" is informed by our very long time frame and respect for the substances from which things are constituted and to which they decompose:

> The archaeological sensibility says that we only ever have fragments to work upon, that every locale is a potential scene of crime where anything could be relevant, that there remains too much to be discovered beneath the surface of things, and much that we will not like, because the stories we have been told are meant to console and quieten us. (Shanks, cited in Gónzalez-Ruibal 2006, 179)

In particular, I argue that archaeological practice is not actually best described as a kind of cataloguing of things, even if the original stasis of categorization is replaced by a more supple narration of lives of things. What we archaeologists actually engage with in our contemporary craft practice are not things as such, but things as traces. What we do in retracing itineraries of things is a form of reassembly of social networks in the specific sense described by Latour (2005), that is, the construction of a new network that extends to connect us and now to there and then. Even when we deal with what seem archetypal things, like the marble vases that are collected today as prized artworks around the world, delimiting our task as that of telling the biography of such things presents an intolerable misconstrual of how we actually tease out the connections of things with people and other things.

Central to archaeological engagement with things are two concepts that demand reparsings of materiality, as traces and assemblages. Archaeological interest in itineraries of things does not end when the unity of the thing is compromised, just as it does not begin when the thing exists as a fully crafted whole. Archaeological traces and the things whose histories they point to form part of assemblages that are distributed across space and time, connecting persons and things in networks across which the ability to act is distributed. These networks are both pragmatic and signifying.

There should be nothing here that sounds unfamiliar to social anthropologists. That our craft as archaeologists involves physical engagement with soil and water, stone and bone, may dispose us to see things where others might not. But we see things as others in the broad domain we form part of also do: as part of the material world within which humans are engaged, by which they are shaped, and which they continuously reshape, albeit not always (or perhaps even often) with full control of what they do. What we bring to an understanding of life with things is a sense of material in constant motion, in transit from hand to hand and place to place, blurring the boundaries of person, place, and thing.

References

Alder, K. 2007. "Introduction to focus: Thick things." *Isis* 98: 80–83.

Alexander, J. C. 2008. "Iconic consciousness: The material feel of meaning." *Environment and Planning D: Society and Space* 26: 782–94.

Appadurai, A. 1986. "Introduction: Commodities and the politics of value." In *The social life of things*, ed. A. Appadurai, 3–63. Cambridge: Cambridge University Press.

Arnold, M., C. Shepherd, and M. Gibbs. 2008. "Remembering things." *Information Society* 24: 47–53.

Bauer, A. 2002. "Is what you see what you get? Recognizing meaning in archaeology." *Journal of Social Archaeology* 2: 37–52.

Bennett, J. 2004. "The force of things: Steps toward an ecology of matter." *Political Theory* 32: 347–72.

Binford, L. 1962. "Archaeology as anthropology." *American Antiquity* 28: 217–25.

Brumfiel, E. 1992. "Breaking and entering the ecosystem: Gender, class and faction steal the show." *American Anthropologist* 94: 551–67.

Chapman, J. 2000. *Fragmentation in archaeology: People, places and broken objects in the prehistory of south eastern Europe*. London: Routledge.

Dant, T. 2001. "Fruitbox/toolbox: Biography and objects." *Auto/Biography* 9: 11–20.

Dezeuze, A. 2008. "Assemblage, bricolage, and the practice of everyday life." *Art Journal* 67: 31–37.

Gerritsen, F. 1999. "To build and to abandon." *Archaeological Dialogues* 6: 78–97.

Gieryn, T. F. 2002. "What buildings do." *Theory and Society* 31: 35–74.

Gónzalez-Ruibal, A. 2006. "The dream of reason: An archaeology of the failures of modernity in Ethiopia." *Journal of Social Archaeology* 6: 175–201.

Gosden, C. 2005. "What do objects want?" *Journal of Archaeological Method and Theory* 12: 193–211.

Gosden, C., and Y. Marshall. 1999. "The cultural biography of objects." *World Archaeology* 31: 169–78.

Hendon, J. A. 2000. "Having and holding: Storage, memory, knowledge, and social relations." *American Anthropologist* 102: 43–53.

Hendon, J.A. 2010. *Houses in a landscape: Memory and everyday life in Meso-america*. Durham, NC: Duke University Press.

Hitchings, R. 2004. "At home with someone nonhuman." *Home Cultures* 1: 169–86.

Hoskins, J. 1998. *Biographical objects*. New York: Routledge.

Joyce, R.A. 2002. *The languages of archaeology: Dialogue, narrative, and writing*. Oxford: Blackwell.

Joyce, R.A. 2003. "Making something of herself: Embodiment in life and death at Playa de los Muertos, Honduras." *Cambridge Archaeological Journal* 13: 248–61.

Joyce, R.A. 2007a. "Building houses: The materialization of lasting identity in formative Mesoamerica." In *The durable house: House society models in archaeology*, ed. R. Beck, 53–72. Carbondale: Southern Illinois University.

Joyce, R.A. 2007b. "Figurines, meaning, and meaning-making in early Mesoamerica." In *Material beginnings: A global prehistory of figurative representation*, ed. C. Renfrew and I. Morley, 107–16. Cambridge: McDonald Institute for Archaeological Research.

Joyce, R.A. 2008a. "Practice in and as deposition." In Mills and Walker 2008, 25–39.

Joyce, R.A. 2008b. "Speaking for absent subjects: Responsibility in archaeological discourse." In *Mixtec writing and society/escritura de nuu dzaui*, ed. M.E.R.G.N. Jansen and L.N.K. van Broekhoven, 15–26. Amsterdam: Royal Netherlands Academy of Arts and Sciences.

Joyce, R.A. 2008c. "When the flesh is solid but the person is hollow inside: Formal variation in hand-modeled figurines from formative Mesoamerica." In *Past bodies*, ed. D. Boric and J. Robb, 37–45. Oxford: Oxbow Books.

Joyce, R.A. Forthcoming. "From place to place: Provenience, provenance, and archaeology." In *Provenance: History of art and ownership*, ed. G. Feigenbaum and I. Reist. Los Angeles: Getty Research Institute.

Joyce, R.A., and J.A. Hendon. 2008. "Persons and possessions: Archaeological approaches to thinking about things." Paper presented at the 73rd annual meeting of the Society for American Archaeology, Vancouver, BC, Canada.

Joyce, R.A., and J. Pollard. 2010. "Archaeological assemblages and practices of deposition." In *Oxford handbook of material culture studies*, ed. D. Hicks and M. Beaudry, 289–304. Oxford: Oxford University Press.

Knappett, C. 2002. "Photographs, skeumorphs and marionettes: Some thoughts on mind, agency and object." *Journal of Material Culture* 7: 97–117.

Knappett, C. 2005. *Thinking through material culture*. Philadelphia: University of Pennsylvania Press.

Kockelman, P. 2007. "Inalienable possession and personhood." *Language in Society* 36: 343–69.

Kopytoff, I. 1986. "The cultural biography of things: Commoditization as process." In *The social life of things*, ed. A. Appadurai, 64–91. Cambridge: Cambridge University Press.

Küchler, S. 1999. "The place of memory." In *The art of forgetting*, ed. A. Forty and S. Küchler, 53–72. Oxford: Berg.

Latour, B. 2005. *Reassembling the social*. Oxford: Oxford University Press.

Lele, V. P. 2006. "Material habits, identity, semeiotic." *Journal of Social Archaeology* 6: 48–70.

Luke, C. 2010. "Ulua marble vases abroad: Contextualizing social networks between the Maya world and lower Central America." In *Trade and exchange: Archaeological studies from history and prehistory*, ed. C. D. Dillian and C. L. White, 37–58. New York: Springer.

Luke, C., and R. Tykot. 2007. "Celebrating place through luxury craft production: Travesia and Ulua style marble vases." *Ancient Mesoamerica* 18: 315–28.

Martin, A. 2005. "Agents in inter-action: Bruno Latour and agency." *Journal of Archaeological Method and Theory* 12: 283–311.

Meskell, L. 2004. *Object worlds in ancient Egypt: Material biographies past and present*. Malden, MA: Blackwell.

Meyer, B. 2008. "Media and the senses in the making of religious experience: An introduction." *Material Religion* 4: 124–35.

Miller, D., ed. 2005. *Materiality*. Durham, NC: Duke University Press.

Mills, B., and W. Walker, eds. 2008. *Memory work: Archaeologies of material practices*. Santa Fe, NM: School for Advanced Research Press.

Myers, F., ed. 2001. *The empire of things: Regimes of value and material culture*. Santa Fe, NM: School of American Research Press.

Normark, J. 2010. "Involutions of materiality: Operationalizing a neo-materialist perspective through the causeways at Ichmul and Yo'okop." *Journal of Archaeological Method and Theory* 17: 132–73.

Olsen, B. 2003. "Material culture after text: Re-membering things." *Norwegian Archaeological Review* 36: 87–104.

Olsen, B. 2007. "Keeping things at arm's length: A genealogy of asymmetry." *World Archaeology* 39: 579–88.

Pauketat, T. R., and S. M. Alt. 2005. "Agency in a postmold? Physicality and the archaeology of culture-making." *Journal of Archaeological Method and Theory* 12: 213–37.

Preucel, R. W. 1995. "The postprocessual condition." *Journal of Archaeological Research* 3: 147–75.

Preucel, R. W. 2005. *Archaeological semiotics*. Malden, MA: Blackwell.

Preucel, R. W., and A. A. Bauer. 2001. "Archaeological pragmatics." *Norwegian Archaeological Review* 34: 85–96.

Schevill, M. B. 1992. "Lila Morris O'Neale: Ethnoaesthetics and the Yurok-Karok basket weavers of northwestern California." In *The early years of Native American art history*, ed. J. C. Berlo, 162–90. Seattle: University of Washington Press.

Shanks, M. 2007. "Symmetrical archaeology." *World Archaeology* 39: 589–96.

Shanks, M., and R. McGuire. 1996. "The craft of archaeology." *American Antiquity* 61: 75–88.

Thompson, M. 1979. *Rubbish theory: The creation and destruction of value*. New York: Oxford University Press.

Tringham, R. E. 1991. "Households with faces: The challenge of gender in prehistoric architectural remains." In *Engendering archaeology: Women and prehistory*, ed. J. Gero and M. Conkey, 93–131. Oxford: Basil Blackwell.

Tringham, R. E. 2000. "The continuous house: A view from the deep past." In *Beyond kinship: Social and material reproduction in house societies*, ed. R. A. Joyce and S. D. Gillespie, 115–34. Philadelphia: University of Pennsylvania Press.

Waterson, R. 2000. "House, place and memory in Tana Toraja Indonesia." In *Beyond kinship: Social and material reproduction in house societies*, ed. R. A. Joyce and S. D. Gillespie, 161–76. Philadelphia: University of Pennsylvania Press.

Weismantel, M. 2004. "Moche sex pots: Reproduction and temporality in ancient South America." *American Anthropologist* 106: 495–505.

Willey, G. R., and P. Phillips. 1958. *Method and theory in American archaeology*. Chicago: University of Chicago Press.

Witmore, C. L. 2007. "Symmetrical archaeology: Excerpts of a manifesto." *World Archaeology* 39: 546–62.

Wylie, A. 2002. *Thinking from things: Essays in the philosophy of archaeology*. Berkeley: University of California Press.

Archaeological Ethnography: Materiality, Heritage, and Hybrid Methodologies

Lynn Meskell

Shared literatures and shared intellectual concerns between archaeology and anthropology are not new, certainly not in Britain. In fact, social archaeology in Britain from at least the 1980s on borrowed heavily from anthropologists in reconfiguring our ideas about landscapes, aesthetics, gender and embodiment, and subject–object relations. British and European archaeologies certainly outstripped their American counterpart when it came to theoretical innovation and savvy during those decades. Yet, obviously, reading and integrating anthropological accounts is not tantamount to conducting ethnographic work. I would argue that methodological innovation that incorporates both field practices represents a more recent endeavor over the last few years (Byrne 2007; Colwell-Chanthaphonh and Ferguson 2007; Ferguson and Colwell-Chanthaphonh 2006; Lafrenz Samuels 2009; Meskell 2005, 2009c; Mortensen and Hollowell 2009; Weiss 2007). For instance, U.S.-based scholars are navigating between different kinds of research now, due to their specific historical and geopolitical embedding. One might conclude that America's troubles at home—and abroad—not only have spurred on a new ethic of practice but also have opened up a new suite of possibilities and methodologies.

If I recall my graduate training in Cambridge in the mid-1990s, despite the fact that no actual courses were taught, it is notable that there was little engagement with social anthropologists. The Downing Street divide was certainly not acrimonious but rather ambivalent. Archaeologists read the work of their colleagues perhaps, but I very much doubt that the reverse was true. What continues to be striking on reflection, however, was the serious time lag between departments in the adoption of theoretical approaches. Take one salient example, debates over gender and sexuality. Most feminist archaeologists in the late 1990s were satisfied to read social anthropologists writing in the 1980s (or even 1970s) rather than incorporating contemporary research by colleagues including Henrietta Moore or Marilyn Strathern. This slippage resulted in outmoded scholarship, the reproduction of certain essentialisms, and a political refusal to consider other dimensions of difference—put simply, to privilege women and to erase other modes of exclusion and inequality. While archaeology and anthropology were part of an undergraduate tripos, the notion of integrated disciplines, or even sustained conversations, was the exception, not the rule.

That being said, scholars like Henrietta Moore (1982, 1987), Danny Miller (1985), and later Victor Buchli (2000) conducted ethnographic work as archaeology students but then moved fairly smartly into social anthropology and material culture studies. Archaeologists might selfishly lament that loss, yet it provided the bedrock for an exciting new field of material culture studies, for which we are collectively the richer. And while all these scholars might retain varying degrees of archaeological solidarity, particularly with the work of Michael Rowlands (2005), Chris Tilley (2004), and Victor Buchli (2002; also Buchli and Lucas 2001), the institutional apparatus in Britain tends to divide rather than integrate. The new combined BA degree at University College London is certainly one step toward providing education in both disciplines, but perhaps that is the very point. New programs have to be invented at this juncture to forge a methodological meeting ground, whereas the institutional structure in the United States already exists and a growing number of departments are producing graduates who are trained in both archaeological and ethnographic methodologies.

New developments in American archaeology over the past decade have brought to fruition what British archaeologists have long proposed—that data collection, theoretical interpretation, and heritage development are no longer discrete practices. American archaeologists now routinely venture into other social domains, in part because of geopolitics, not incidentally the particular North and South American histories of colonization, genocide, and indigenous movements (e.g., Colwell-Chanthaphonh and Ferguson 2004; Daehnke 2007; Dongoske, Aldenderfer, and Doehner 2000; Edgar et al. 2007; Fine-Dare 2005; Watkins 2001; Watkins et al. 2008). These developments have spurred on new and compelling field projects and insights that are, in turn, producing more rigorous accounts and generating innovative interpretations that move the discipline forward. Tim Pauketat and I (2010) have recently argued that it is this particular positioning, and the generative nature of debates involving Native American materials, histories, and collaborations, that has situated North American archaeology somewhat differently from its British counterpart. From the British perspective, the historical redress of political encounters tends to take place elsewhere, rather than negotiating with indigenous communities at home at the very intersection of archaeological practice. In fact, recent developments in English heritage strongly suggest a desire to emulate the North American context of recognition, repatriation, and collaboration, even though theirs are not indigenous claimants but rather Druids. Here I am referring to recent developments around pagan petitioning for reburial of human remains at Avebury on the grounds of ancestry, and the public consultation that followed (see Thackery and Payne 2008). I will not comment on the content but rather draw attention to the implementation of recognition ethics as a process. Perhaps it is the realization of these rich potentials in the United States, derived from dialogue and collaboration across a range of stakeholder communities, starting from a position of hostility and moving toward rapprochement, which marks the real turning point and coming of age for American archaeology.

I want to turn now to a more concrete instantiation of these developments and outline one mode of a hybrid practice I refer to as archaeological ethnography—a traversing of these two distinct, but necessarily enmeshed, subfields. Since anthropology in the United States institutionally combines archaeological and ethnographic enterprises, our undergraduate and graduate students can, and often do, migrate across those domains during their doctoral training. It seems, then, a very obvious transition to undertake work that combines the field practices of respective traditions, archaeological and ethnographic, in relevant contexts. Since 2003 my own work in South Africa has been an archaeological ethnography, by which I mean a holistic anthropology that is improvisational and context dependent (Meskell 2005, 2006; Meskell and Masuku Van Damme 2007; Meskell and Scheermeyer 2008). Archaeological ethnography might encompass a mosaic of traditional forms including archaeological practice and museum or representational analysis, as well as long-term involvement, participant observation, interviews, and archival work. In my own work in Kruger National Park I took an interdisciplinary team to work at the Iron Age site of Thulamela to conduct digital scanning of its architecture and features, and to gather materials for visualizations of the site, including the three-dimensional recording of objects (Meskell 2007). This work also entailed museum consultation, site visits, interviews, and archival work, as well as sustained interaction with numerous stakeholders both inside the park and outside its boundaries. Through a hybrid set of practices, drawing on archaeology and ethnography, I was attempting to address multiple understandings of the site, now and in the past, without privileging one "ethnic" group, by encouraging numerous people to speak about the site, in various languages and from varied perspectives. While the crux of those discussions was the archaeological past, it is not possible to parse out heritage from other issues of ancestral land, forced dislocation, landscape, power, oppression, and recent histories, among other matters. Rather than diluting archaeology, this hybridity enriches it significantly and recenters it in contemporary cosmopolitan societies.

Here it is important to underline that there is a difference between a serious ethnographic engagement and the more casual encounters many archaeologists experience in the field when simply talking to various stakeholders or seeking information to aid their research. Importantly, what I propose here diverges markedly from ethnoarchaeology and is not intended to be extractive or to model past behavior from contemporary lifeworlds. What I am describing recalls Strathern's classic discussion of the ethnographic moment, and in archaeological ethnography that fieldwork encompasses multiple techniques and field situations, which happen simultaneously in the field, the lab, and the museum and also in the framing and writing of our projects. True to long-standing recognition in archaeological theory, writing the past and writing the present occur synchronously—and quite literally in the case of ethnographic interventions.

While the ethnography of archaeological enterprises and heritage deployments has been the subject of anthropological field studies largely from the United States (Abu el-Haj 2001; Benavides 2005; Breglia 2006; Herzfeld 1991, 2009; Wynn 2007), I would suggest there might be a difference when archaeologists conduct their own ethnographic work. This is not to say our accounts are implicitly better, but they are grounded in different ways. Like Sally Merry's (2006, 2009) deterritorialized ethnography, we might ask how archaeological subjects and objects travel internationally and how transnational issues and priorities are remade in local terms. From these shifting vantage points, archaeologists are engaged in modes of cultural translation, where we scale up and down, traversing registers, with archaeologists being practitioners, students, experts, working with communities and learning from them, examining organizations and structures and sometimes working within them. Simultaneously, this forms part of our larger disciplinary accountability. Obviously, we already have the requisite insider expertise, we benefit from our knowledge of the craft and its results, and thus one initial stage of our training has already been achieved. Such reflexive research can similarly be positioned as the ethnography of us, of what we do as practitioners, thus lessening the exotic patina and keeping our work closely aligned to an "anthropology at home." We have a knowledge of the field, a deep experiential understanding, yet that, too, is challenged by engaging with other stakeholders and the modalities through which we come to take their accounts seriously, namely, through encounters and interviews. The seemingly discrete positions of insider and outsider become more permeable, and that porosity undoubtedly operates as an ethical check on our interpretations and our politics more broadly.

Yet where this work diverges from mainstream ethnography is with the foregrounding of the past's materiality, specifically those traces of the past that have residual afterlives in living communities, that are often considered spiritually significant, and that invite a kind of governmental monitoring and control that many indigenous communities and archaeologists increasingly find problematic. It is not simply about the ethnographic study of extensive field projects and practitioners abroad, nor is it a kind of discourse analysis or exposé of fieldwork. In the main, archaeological ethnography often entails collaborating with, rather than studying, the people with whom we work in the heritage sphere.

Archaeological ethnography also converges with broader cosmopolitan concerns to empower local communities and effect change at higher levels of power structuring. It links closely to new forms of collaborative archaeology currently being undertaken in postcolonial contexts like Australia and North America (Colwell-Chanthaphonh and Ferguson 2007; Lilley 2009; Lilley and Williams 2005; Stoffle, Zedeno, and Halmo 2001). It profitably dialogues across hybrid excavations of the archive and the museum, thus linking the field again to history, material culture studies, and museum anthropology. Ultimately this is an outgrowth of an ethical archaeology, one that takes as its project the contemporary relevance of archaeological heritage and claims responsibility for our participation. The notion that archaeology's subjects are dead is slowly moving from a position of orthodoxy to an outmoded and unethical stance few could validate.

Archaeological Ethnography in South Africa

My own South African fieldwork was conducted primarily in Kruger National Park, although I worked for some time at Mapungubwe National Park, the Rock Art Research Institute at the University of the Witwatersrand, and Conservation Corporation Africa Lodges around Kruger and Mkhuze parks and conducted interviews in different parts of the country over the years. Kruger holds a special attraction for a host of very different reasons: it is the jewel in the crown of African national parks, it is attempting to shed its brutal Afrikaner nationalist image, and a new African National Congress black leadership encourages black participation and visitation. Today, the organization boasts successes in social transformation, and the park is much touted as a key driver for black economic empowerment and uplift. Kruger faces enormous challenges resulting from its racist and repressive history (Carruthers 1995), itself refracted in the impoverished conditions of those descendent communities forcibly removed from their settlements and now bordering the park, as well as the specter of successful land claims and restitution.

Kruger is also home to well over 1,000 archaeological sites within its two million hectares, from early hominid sites to those of the recent past. Under the new dispensation the long-ignored cultural past of San and black South Africans could be finally showcased and appreciated. For such an illustrious park, there has been a dearth of published ethnographic work. The reasons for this must be considered historical and political. Central to my research was the state of the archaeological past and the views of various stakeholders toward revitalizing ancestral and cultural sites, including resident scientific researchers, international scholars, and those evicted from the park. Yet the priorities of the past have been rather precariously interpolated within an overwhelming focus on biodiversity conservation, so that Kruger serves as a lens through which to examine the larger framings of nature-based tourism and conservation in South Africa. The park is also a parastatal agency, thus reflecting the tensions between state and nonstate actors pertaining to economic growth and social inclusion in the arenas of employment, tourism, and conservation. For these and other reasons—largely that people were so incredibly open to this research—I found Kruger captivating and felt very privileged to have been included and welcomed into the various communities. Over the years I was based at Skukuza, Kruger's research station, and had sustained interactions and interviews with park managers, research scientists and technicians, ecologists, service workers, rangers, heritage officers, and those forced from the park during previous regimes. Taken together this forms a densely textured account of the place of the past in one of South Africa's most important and celebrated landscapes.

The questions that drove the early work revolved around past mastering: In particular, how might the depredations of the colonial and apartheid eras be ameliorated? Given the erasures, what did people know of their past in the park—specifically their ancestral sites? What was the role of archaeology and archaeologists in the programmatics of the new nation, and how exactly would heritage pay? The idea that the poverty and fragility of life that I witnessed in communities on the park's western border could be addressed by a recuperation of the past seemed unlikely; even the invidious notion of creating cultural villages and showcasing the imagined and ossified identities of the past for tourist revenues seemed impossible. How exactly could the archaeological past provide any form of therapeutic benefit, whether economic, social, or psychical? In many of my conversations it became clear that heritage and dwelling on the past were luxuries that people like myself could entertain. Certainly, almost every elder interviewed could recount stories from the past and, when pressed, shared their opinions on sites, archaeologists, museums, and Kruger, but clearly these were not central concerns. Other imperatives occupied their thoughts and our conversations: compensation for the loss of their land and cattle, employment in the park for their families, developing international tourism in their villages, remuneration for destruction of their crops by animals escaping from Kruger, government aid and making good on electoral promises. These concerns were repeated endlessly from the far north at Pafuri to the southern region around Mthetamusha. For my research to privilege the archaeological past and gloss over contemporary matters seemed disingenuous. If anything, reconfiguring the research to consider archaeological heritage within the broader categories of histories and pasts, and interpolating something called "heritage" into more encompassing or compelling constructions such as governmentality and environmentality, biodiversity and conservation, black economic empowerment, and development and sustainability, might prove both more comprehensive and illuminating. The very use of the word *heritage* raises a problematic in South Africa as in the public arena it tends to specify more recent contemporary culture and tribal configurations of music, art, dance, performance, and the like. Moreover, heritage (particularly historic sites and museums) has been deemed the terrain of historians rather than archaeologists in the eyes of both the government and the general public. As prior scholarship reveals, the status of archaeology remains rather low due to the political profile of the discipline under apartheid, coupled with archaeologists' ambivalence and unwillingness to embrace the sociopolitical dimensionality of their work, while historians have traditionally been more celebrated for their ethical engagements.

Discourses of biodiversity form the backdrop to the archaeological present, specifically its global success and ability to outstrip cultural heritage on national and international agendas. These discourses privilege nature over culture and typically sacrifice historical recognition and restitution for the "greater good" of conservation. Irrespective of leadership or regime change, in South African national parks, state power continues to devalue the archaeological past and its human histories. Narratives of *terra nullius*, or "empty lands," have resurfaced in dangerous and familiar ways. The now-discredited discourse erases indigenous histories and is perilously hitched to the celebratory discourses of conservation and biodiversity, since both espouse global desires for pristine wilderness, minimal human intensification, the erasure of anthropogenic landscapes, the primacy of nonhuman species, sustainability, and so on (Meskell 2009c). There is a denial of indigenous presence, irrespective of the documented rock art, prehistoric sites, and Iron Age remains. Without recognition of the complex and continued human history in Kruger's landscapes there is little chance of historical justice and restitution for indigenous South Africans in these regions. Archaeologists have played no small part in this erasure, certainly during the apartheid years, and their racialized narratives, and even their silences, have had a tremendous residual force to this day for black South Africans (Hall 1988; Shepherd 2003). Cultural heritage is seen as divisive and particular, whereas natural heritage is global and encompassing, entreating us all to subscribe to its world-making project.

Here, an archaeological ethnography provides a suite of hybrid methods to uncover the archaeological past and present. It is situated firmly within broader cosmopolitan dispositions and practices. Increasingly, archaeologists are examining the ways in which local and national heritage politics are made and unmade through international discourses and regulations, and how transnational bodies and organizations such as UNESCO, the World Bank, and conservation and funding agencies are curiously brought into play in local arenas (Arantes 2007; Lafrenz Samuels 2009). Balancing appeals to universalism with those of cultural diversity remains a critical tension that underlines much of the existing literature on heritage and our engagements as practitioners. These strange proximities and multiplicities are experienced in particular regions and locales in distinct ways, even though the organizational directives might aspire to a presumed universality and neutrality. More important, salvage politics are often united by incentives of common goods; they are promise based and future driven and depend on networks of participation, discipline, and sacrifice (see Hayden 2003) that discursively create desirable heritage citizens. In an Orwellian tone, interventionist policies that control the past also serve to predict future outcomes, promising sustainable development, betterment, and socioeconomic uplift. What must be sublated in the present will be recouped in the future by coming generations, while international elites and the adequately resourced will be able to enjoy the spoils of heritage and conservation in the present in the form of cultural and ecological tourism and research. Such promissory strategies tend to deprivilege indigenous and minority communities, often disempowered constituencies whose land, livelihood, and legacies are threatened.

Increasingly, a new generation of archaeologists is uncovering the intellectual foundations and political economies of "heritage," the legal, political, and ethical strata that underlie implicit tensions over access, preservation, and control of the material past in a volatile present. They are questioning the translatability of such terms and practices across a wide array of sites and locations. My own position, informed by cosmopolitanism (Meskell 2009a, 2009b), has considered the discursive production, consumption, and governing of other people's pasts through examination of the participants, organizations, stakeholders, beneficiaries, and victims. Hybrid modes of research enable us to question how different black communities living on the edge of a celebrated national park envision the global. The communities bordering Kruger National Park draw on the networks of indigenous rights, international law, and expert international researchers to craft a particular identity and stake in the reclaiming of the natural commons. And even so-called national parks are ipso facto transnational bodies comprised of American funders, European aid agencies, nongovernmental organizations, government officials, impoverished park workers, and foreign research scientists. Identifying competing conceptions of the common good, and the practices by which new and emergent social realities come into being, is very much at issue here.

Readers may ask why archaeologists should be interested in the logics of conservation, biodiversity, sustainability, or development. Moreover, does an archaeological ethnography have anything to offer scholars and practitioners working in these other fields? One answer is that archaeologists need to recognize more fully our epistemic genealogies and the interwoven threads binding understandings of natural resources and nature conservation to cultural resources, landscapes, and values (Lowenthal 1997, 2006). Resource use and sustainability inform, to a large degree, cultural heritage concerns about site usage, occupation, and lived traditions: often undervaluing them when it comes to indigenous owners and stakeholders (Byrne 1991, 1995). Land use legacies and human histories can easily be erased in the productions of place forged through ecological narratives. Many heritage managers tend to view the past as both raw material and finite resource, a "fossil fuels" template of the world that wants to restrict utilization and save our stocks for future generations. Conservation is seen very much as a global good for a common humanity: whether natural or cultural. In that equation human interventions are destructive, dangerous, and undesirable. Just as some of my colleagues in Kruger National Park are concerned that any sort of natural resource utilization is the beginning of the end and refuse to allow sustainable harvesting of flora and fauna, heritage agencies the world over typically struggle with the realities of human occupation, encroachment, ongoing traditional practices, visitation, and appropriation in and around significant sites. These are struggles over diverse spiritual materialities, specifically variant philosophies of heritage and materiality.

Just as animals, plants, and landscapes have been deemed part of the national estate for moral and scientific uplift from the Victorian era on (Ritvo 1987), archaeological and historic sites are often wrested from their immediate inheritors for the benefit of others, all in the name of the global good. The convergences of both natural and cultural protection and management undoubtedly culminated throughout the colonial occupations of Africa, Asia, Australia, and so on by British and other European empires. Today, nature-based tourism, increasingly popular in southern Africa

(Keitumetse 2009; Segobye 2006; Witz, Rassool, and Minkley 2001), allows for the possibility of thriving "tribal cultures," and we onlookers remain enthralled by their specifically indigenous abilities to promote and preserve that beauty and ethnic diversity in a colorful, feathered, beaded sort of way. In contemporary South Africa, a new populism and ethnic revitalization has led to hostility and violence against citizens and foreigners alike. A willing ignorance of past connections, precolonial histories, and colonial indirect rule has rebounded once again to turn victims into killers (Mamdani 2002). We ignore these genealogies and conflations at our own peril, but more seriously at the expense of those individuals who have already suffered grave historical injustice.

In closing, it is important to note that the Bristol Association of Social Anthropologists conference effectively crystallizes the interconnectedness between British social archaeology and anthropology. Hopefully it represents an ongoing development rather than just a timely reflection. Perhaps it is no coincidence that many of the invited speakers are based in the United States and are already bridging these disciplinary divides, as described at the outset of the paper. One particular forum for these hybrid methodologies in the United States is the annual American Anthropological Association conference that brings archaeologists and anthropologists together, increasingly in the same sessions, talking about intersecting interests. Materiality, heritage politics, and international and cosmopolitan obligations, as well as human rights—areas in which there is a burgeoning interest—are some of the most productive domains for disciplinary exchange. One could say that the objects of archaeology are changing, archaeologists' traditional remit is expanding, and archaeologists have broadened the epistemic and ontological scope of their disciplinary project.

References

Abu el-Haj, N. 2001. *Facts on the ground: Archaeological practice and territorial self-fashioning in Israeli society*. Chicago: University of Chicago Press.

Arantes, A.A. 2007. "Diversity, heritage and cultural politics." *Theory, Culture and Society* 24: 290–96.

Benavides, O.H. 2005. *Making Ecuadorian histories*. Austin: University of Texas Press.

Breglia, L.C. 2006. *Monumental ambivalence*. Austin: University of Texas Press.

Buchli, V. 2000. *An archaeology of socialism*. Oxford: Berg.

Buchli, V., ed. 2002. *The material culture reader*. Oxford: Berg.

Buchli, V., and G. Lucas, eds. 2001. *Archaeologies of the contemporary past*. London: Routledge.

Byrne, D. 1991. "Western hegemony in archaeological heritage management." *History and Anthropology* 5: 269–76.

Byrne, D. 1995. "Buddhist stupa and Thai social practice." *World Archaeology* 27: 266–81.

Byrne, D. 2007. *Surface collection: Archaeological travels in Southeast Asia*. Walnut Creek, CA: AltaMira.

Carruthers, J. 1995. *The Kruger National Park: A social and political history*. Pietermaritzburg, South Africa: University of Natal Press.

Colwell-Chanthaphonh, C., and T. J. Ferguson. 2004. "Virtue ethics and the practice of history: Native Americans and archaeologists along the San Pedro Valley of Arizona." *Journal of Social Archaeology* 4: 5–27.

Colwell-Chanthaphonh, C., and T. J. Ferguson, eds. 2007. *The collaborative continuum: Archaeological engagements with descendent communities*. Thousand Oaks, CA: AltaMira.

Daehnke, J. D. 2007. "A 'strange multiplicity' of voices: Heritage stewardship, contested sites and colonial legacies on the Columbia River." *Journal of Social Archaeology* 7: 250–75.

Dongoske, K. E., M. Aldenderfer, and K. Doehner, eds. 2000. *Working together: Native Americans and archaeologists*. Washington, DC: Society for American Archaeology.

Edgar, H. J. H., E. A. Jolie, J. F. Powell, and J. E. Watkins. 2007. "Contextual issues in Paleoindian repatriation: Spirit Cave Man as a case study." *Journal of Social Archaeology* 7: 101–22.

Ferguson, T. J., and C. Colwell-Chanthaphonh. 2006. *History is in the land: Multivocal tribal traditions in Arizona's San Pedro Valley*. Tucson: University of Arizona Press.

Fine-Dare, K. S. 2005. "Anthropological suspicion, public interest and NAGPRA." *Journal of Social Archaeology* 5: 171–92.

Hall, M. 1988. "Archaeology under apartheid." *Archaeology* 41: 62–64.

Hayden, C. 2003. *When nature goes public: The making and unmaking of bioprospecting in Mexico*. Princeton, NJ: Princeton University Press.

Herzfeld, M. 1991. *A place in history: Social and monumental time in a Cretan town*. Princeton, NJ: Princeton University Press.

Herzfeld, M. 2009. *Evicted from eternity: The restructuring of modern Rome*. Chicago: University of Chicago Press.

Keitumetse, S. O. 2009. "The eco-tourism of cultural heritage management (ECT-CHM): Linking heritage and 'environment' in the Okavango Delta regions of Botswana." *International Journal of Heritage Studies* 15: 223–44.

Lafrenz Samuels, K. 2009. "Trajectories of development: International heritage management of archaeology in the Middle East and North Africa." *Archaeologies* 5: 68–91.

Lilley, I. 2009. "Strangers and brothers? Heritage, human rights, and cosmopolitan archaeology in Oceania." In Meskell 2009a, 48–67.

Lilley, I., and M. Williams. 2005. "Archaeological and indigenous significance: A view from Australia." In *Heritage of value, archaeology of renown: Reshaping archaeological assessment and significance*, ed. C. Mathers, T. Darvill, and B. Little, 227–47. Gainesville: University of Florida Press.

Lowenthal, D. 1997. "Environment as heritage." In *Culture, landscape, and the environment: The Linacre lectures, 1997*, ed. K. Flint and H. Morphy, 197–217. Oxford: Oxford University Press.

Lowenthal, D. 2006. "Natural and cultural heritage." In *The nature of cultural heritage and the culture of natural heritage: Northern perspectives on a contested patrimony*, ed. K. R. Olwig and D. Lowenthal, 79–90. London: Routledge.

Mamdani, M. 2002. *When victims become killers: Colonialism, nativism and the genocide in Rwanda*. Princeton, NJ, and Oxford: Princeton University Press.

Merry, S. E. 2006. "Anthropology and international law." *Annual Review of Anthropology* 35: 99–116.

Merry, S. E. 2009. "Legal transplants and cultural translation: Making human rights in the vernacular." In *Human rights: An anthropological reader*, ed. M. Goodale, 265–302. Malden, MA: Wiley-Blackwell.

Meskell, L. M. 2005. "Archaeological ethnography: Conversations around Kruger National Park." *Archaeologies: Journal of the World Archaeology Congress* 1: 83–102.

Meskell, L. M. 2006. "Deep past, divided present: South Africa's heritage at the frontier." *Western Humanities Review* 60: 110–16.

Meskell, L. M. 2007. "Falling walls and mending fences: Archaeological ethnography in the Limpopo." *Journal of Southern African Studies* 33: 383–400.

Meskell, L. M., ed. 2009a. *Cosmopolitan archaeologies*. Durham, NC: Duke University Press.

Meskell, L. M. 2009b. "Cosmopolitan heritage ethics." In Meskell 2009a, 1–27.

Meskell, L. M. 2009c. "The nature of culture in Kruger National Park." In Meskell 2009a, 89–112.

Meskell, L. M., and L. S. Masuku Van Damme. 2007. "Heritage ethics and descendent communities." In Colwell-Chanthaphonh and Ferguson 2007, 131–50.

Meskell, L. M., and C. Scheermeyer. 2008. "Heritage as therapy: Set pieces from the new South Africa." *Journal of Material Culture* 13: 153–73.

Miller, D. 1985. *Artefacts as categories: A study of ceramic variability in central India*. Cambridge: Cambridge University Press.

Moore, H. L. 1982. "The interpretation of spatial patterning in settlement residues." In *Symbolic and structural archaeology*, ed. I. Hodder, 74–79. Cambridge: Cambridge University Press.

Moore, H. L. 1987. "Problems in the analysis of change: An example from the Marakwet." In *Archaeology as long term history*, ed. I. Hodder, 88–104. Cambridge: Cambridge University Press.

Mortensen, L., and J. Hollowell, eds. 2009. *Ethnographies and archaeologies: Iterations of the past*. Gainesville: University Press of Florida.

Pauketat, T., and L. M. Meskell. 2010. "Changing theoretical perspectives in Americanist archaeology." In *Voices in American archaeology*, ed. W. Ashmore, D. D. Lippert, and B. Mills, 193–219. Washington, DC: Society for American Archaeology.

Ritvo, H. 1987. *The animal estate*. Cambridge, MA: Harvard University Press.

Rowlands, M. 2005. "A materialist approach to materiality." In *Materiality*, ed. D. Miller, 72–87. Durham, NC: Duke University Press.

Segobye, A. K. 2006. "Divided commons: The political economy of southern Africa's cultural heritage landscapes—Observations of the central Kalahari game reserve, Botswana." *Archaeologies* 2: 52–72.

Shepherd, N. 2003. "State of the discipline: Science, culture and identity in South African archaeology, 1870–2003." *Journal of Southern African Studies* 29: 823–44.

Stoffle, R. W., M. N. Zedeno, and D. B. Halmo, eds. 2001. *American Indians and the Nevada test site: A model of research and consultation*. Washington, DC: U.S. Government Printing Office.

Thackery, D., and S. Payne. 2008. "Draft report on the request for reburial of human remains from the Alexander Keiller Museum at Avebury." Available online: http://www.english-heritage.org.uk/server/show/nav.19819.

Tilley, C. 2004. *The materiality of stone: Explorations in landscape phenomenology*. Oxford: Berg.

Watkins, J. 2001. *Indigenous archaeology*. Walnut Creek, CA: AltaMira.

Watkins, J. E., L. J. Zimmerman, H. Burke, and C. Smith, eds. 2008. *Kennewick man: Perspectives on the ancient one*. Thousand Oaks, CA: AltaMira.

Weiss, L. M. 2007. "Heritage making and political identity." *Journal of Social Archaeology* 7: 413–31.

Witz, L., C. Rassool, and G. Minkley. 2001. "Repackaging the past or South African tourism." *Daedalus* 130: 277–96.

Wynn, L. L. 2007. *Pyramids and nightclubs: A travel ethnography of Arab and Western imaginations of Egypt, from King Tut and a colony of Atlantis to rumors of sex orgies, urban legends about a marauding prince, and blonde belly dancers*. Austin: University of Texas Press.

–9–

The Anthropological Imagination and British Iron Age Society

Paul Sillitoe

Tribal people value liberty and equality highly. That is my experience, confirmed by a wide reading of ethnography on stateless orders worldwide. It is an observation that has informed my attempts to understand Highland New Guinea society, in the face of some fierce criticism.[1] (I am leaving to one side the challenge that the focus on the individual poses for the French-derived collectivist social philosophy approach that dominates social anthropology.)

But I am puzzled. In Britain we also espouse a high regard for freedom and fairness; indeed, for many of us these are core British values. According to some commentators, they are a preoccupation of English academics. One characterization of national traditions informing anthropology notes that "anthropologists themselves, recognizing that they take their own culture's obsessions into the field, have identified the solipsistic element in their work: . . . the British explore the limits of individual liberty and equality in the face of the obligations of citizenship" (Kuklick 1991, 279). Another comments that "the Anglo-Saxons . . . may be reproached . . . for seeing everywhere individuals in the modern sense of the term, people imbued with the values of liberty and equality" (Dumont 1975, 338–39). It is not only us British, of course; Americans also espouse these values, going so far as to carry guns to defend their rights and freedom; their interest in equality is, as one observer puts it, a "civic religion" (Salzman 1999, 56). Furthermore, the political egalitarianism, individual sovereignty, and reciprocal relations that I see so prominent in New Guinea Highland life have intriguing parallels with the values expressed in the French Revolution slogan of "equality, liberty, and fraternity."

What puzzles me is where our high estimation of liberty and equality comes from. After all, we live in a state that markedly curtails our individual sovereignty, increasingly and worryingly so with the so-called War on Terror, as politicians use this as a reason to put in place ever more sophisticated Big Brother surveillance technology. And our society is grossly unequal, with some persons claiming absurdly high incomes, having resources to gamble on the stock exchange, for instance, while others scrape by on the minimum wage, welfare benefits, or less, such that some households are obscenely wealthy while others live in abject poverty. How is it that we have such a contradictory state of affairs, espousing certain values while apparently ignoring them—unlike tribal people, who live by what they espouse?

An Archaeology of Values

One possibility is that love of liberty and equality are deeply embedded cultural values from previous times, when our ancestors lived in a more egalitarian society. It is arguable that we hear an echo of our tribal past in today's values. We might otherwise expect the British, as heirs to a hierarchical order of many generations, to accept unquestioningly the moral blandishments that have evolved to justify their society's constraining and unequal arrangements, such as others do—like those of the South Asian region. Yet there is a long and honorable tradition of challenging the dictate that you should "know and accept your place." I set out to review what archaeology tells us about our ancestors, on the assumption that it may indicate the origin of our contradictory belief that liberty and equality are core British qualities. In other words, I seek evidence of a "tribal footprint" from a period when our ancestors lived in stateless orders that gave them priority.

This paper seeks to go beyond piecemeal ethnographic analogy focusing on a particular class of related artifacts or whatever, by looking for comparisons with stateless political-economic ideology that are consistent with the broad sweep of the archaeological and literary evidence. In drawing on the ethnographic record to illuminate and help interpret the excavated assemblage, evidence of settlement, burial remains and so on, and associated literary references to Iron Age life, this chapter aims to reveal plausible social arrangements informed by acephalous egalitarian principles, to tease out credible indications of these, and assess associated values and implications for understanding the Celtic social order.

The results of preliminary investigations, as I returned to undergraduate notes and consulted some recommended texts, were not encouraging. After the Neolithic (from 7000 B.C.E. on), archaeological interpretations bear no relation to what I know about tribal political economy, although they feature the word "tribe." It seems that our ancestors have lived in hierarchically organized societies since the Bronze Age (1300 to 700 B.C.E.) and possibly earlier in the Neolithic, too, improbably long ago for tribal values to leave any impression (just as they apparently have not in South Asia, where hierarchical states date from similar distant times). Certainly by the Iron Age (from 2,600 years ago), the British were apparently ruled by chiefdoms and kingdoms. Archaeologists describe ranked societies led by an aristocratic warrior elite occupying hillforts, uncannily reminiscent of the much later knights-in-armor castle-dominated medieval era. They even give us an early example of the "golden triangle" syndrome, portraying the home counties in the cultural vanguard with royal dynasties first adopting civilized ways there (Cunliffe 1991, 203).

But further research revealed that some archaeologists increasingly think that the evidence challenges the orthodox warrior aristocracy view of Celtic society. They argue that egalitarian tribal orders continued well beyond the Neolithic "revolution" into the Iron Age, up to the Roman invasion and beyond in some regions.[2] According to this time frame, our puzzling Janus-faced relationship with liberty and equality started only two millennia ago and in some parts of the British Isles even more recently. This agrees with the proposition that it accounts for these values continuing to feature prominently in our worldview, or else we might expect readier acceptance of hierarchy and inequality, as is evident, as noted, under the caste system, where religion has evolved to convince people that it is the natural order for a few to be on top and many at the bottom of a social pyramid.

The revisionist archaeological view calls to me as an anthropologist reviewing the evidence in the light of many years' experience of tribal life, being more in agreement with political-economic logic as it applies to stateless orders. It suggests that the emphasis on classical scholarship in British education over many generations may have resulted in too ready an acceptance of the Roman and Greek authors' accounts. This intimates the problems that we face with evidence, which comes from two principal sources, archaeological and literary, each with its strengths and weaknesses (see Piggott 1965, 226–27). Archaeological evidence is limited with regard to those aspects of culture that leave scant material record, such as social organization, behavior patterns, values, and beliefs. The classical literary evidence is heavily biased by Roman and Greek worldviews and cultural judgments, and political motivations, as is the medieval Irish evidence, as the monks framed their accounts according to their medieval world with its kings, courts, and bishops, again distorting it ethnocentrically with hierarchical assumptions about the nature of society.

Territorial Organization

The revision toward a more stateless view is not entirely new, however, for archaeologists have long suggested that Iron Age society had acephalous features, regularly using the word *tribe*, for instance (evidence, of course, of the ambiguity of this much used and abused term), but somehow mixed up with a hierarchical order, resulting in some contradictory representations.[3] It is not necessarily evidence of woolly thinking but of another problem with the evidence, namely, its variability between regions and through time. We see this variability clearly in the archaeological record.

It is evident in the variety of settlement patterns across Britain with scattered enclosed and open farmsteads featuring variable numbers of round houses that differ in size and construction. According to Tacitus, the German Celts "never live in cities, and will not even have their houses set close together" (Mattingly 1967, 114). The scattered pattern strongly suggests an uncentralized tribal order. It is difficult to envisage any central power exerting authority over such a dispersed population, especially with limited and difficult communications.

Many of the settlements are defended, ranging from ditch and earth bank rampart to palisaded enclosures, and from house platforms erected in lakes to impressive "broch" stone towers.[4] This further implies a fractious and uncentralized socio-political environment. The comment by Tacitus about "a people, hitherto scattered, uncivilised and therefore prone to fight" (Mattingly 1967, 72) lends support to this view. It is not that people were necessarily engaged in fighting constantly but that the possibility of armed aggression was ever present, as seen in more densely populated tribal societies. The reports of Celts as boisterous and bragging people complies with this interpretation, ethnographic reports of such behavior being evidence of people ready to defend their interests.[5] According to the Greek author Poseidonius, they were "moved by chance remarks to wordy disputes . . . [as] boasters and threateners given to bombastic self-dramatisation," which, combined with "the frankness and high-spiritedness of their temperament," made violent encounters likely (Laing 1979, 32; Laing and Laing 1995, 23).[6]

It is necessary to take care in generalizing about the Celtic world, which, as noted, varied between regions across the British Isles and through the several centuries of the Iron Age. It is possible that people spoke separate languages in different regions,[7] which complies with the factious tribal image. On the continent, Caesar reports three different languages and associated variation in customs (Hanford 1967, 29). And archaeologists today identify different cultural traditions, such as Hallstatt and La Tène, on the basis of material remains. Also, there were considerable differences depending on the extent of contact, indirect and direct, with, and subsequent domination by, the Roman Empire (Cunliffe 1991, 528–48; Darvill 1990, 166–82). Whatever the extent of the variation, and it is considerable, we have to engage in a certain amount of generalization, given the scanty nature of the evidence, if we are going to depict Iron Age political economy at all, aiming here for a sketch locating the general principles.

We are particularly interested in the pre-Roman tribal period. In this respect, it is noteworthy that stateless Iron Age life continued for longer in northern Britain, even persisting in some places throughout the Roman occupation, and we might take certain evidence from there to be indicative of acephalous arrangements elsewhere across the country previously (Harding 2004, 291–92, 301–4; Ralston and Ashmore 2007, 229–36). The persistence of Celtic life in these regions furthermore lends support to my contention about a contemporary tribal footprint. It is arguable that socialism is more strongly rooted in Scotland and Wales today because tribal orders existed there more recently than in England; as a more recent aspect of people's cultural history, they have stronger affinity to the values of fairness and freedom that underpin socialist ideals.[8] The Scottish Parliament and Welsh Assembly regularly challenge the centralizing tendency of the Whitehall establishment, for instance, spurning the capitalist line that concerns about equality reduce economic efficiency to the cost of all.

Subsistence Regime

The Iron Age subsistence regime further complies with an uncentralized political economy. Comparative ethnography indicates that political economies fall somewhere on two intersecting continua (arranged graph-like at right angles). One axis is egalitarian-stateless versus hierarchical-state polity (the latter implies centralized government), and the other axis is subsistence-independent versus subsistence-interdependent domestic groups (the latter implies some sort of market). The archaeological evidence suggests that Celtic settlements, which featured a mixed farming regime (see, for example, Barker 1985; Fowler 1983), were independent subsistence units with some passage of produce and goods between them. While not a sufficient condition on its own to ensure their equal liberty, for we know of many subsistence-independent peasant households subjugated by powerful elites, this arrangement is a significant aspect of stateless orders, ensuring that no one section of society can control the livelihood needs of another and so neutralizing the threat of feudal-cum-Marxist-like domination.

Similarly, and equally important with respect to independence, settlements were able to supply their various other material needs. The technology was accessible to all. While localities were self-sufficient, there was some movement of things between regions (see Cunliffe 1991, 444, 470; Sharples 2007, 176–77). The archaeological distribution of some objects shows that people with access to certain limited resources produced more goods than they needed locally, as they are found dispersed beyond their regions. It is possible that households produced objects beyond their needs with a view to exchanging them for goods from elsewhere, or, alternatively, wider demand prompted it as there was willy-nilly a constant need of things. The motivation may have been equally social and material, leading to periodic sociable interaction between communities.

There was possibly incipient labor specialization—for example, in metalwork, pottery, and so on—based on access to raw materials. However, the livelihoods of communities with access to such resources did not depend on their exploitation. Likewise, particularly skilled and experienced individuals did not live by manufacturing things for sale, as demand was too small. They were farmers like everyone else, albeit they may have spent more time engaged in crafts for which they had particular aptitudes. We see the talents of some of these unknown craftsmen in some of the beautiful objects in the archaeological record. It is probable, in view of contemporary tribal evidence, that both farming and craftwork featured a certain sexual division of labor, with men undertaking heavier tasks such as land clearance, plowing, carpentry, and metal forging, while women were responsible for weeding and harvesting, winnowing and storing crops, spinning wool, and weaving clothing.

Access to Land

It is probable that the scattered settlements claimed rights to surrounding territory, a pattern that suggests an equitable distribution of land, equal access to resources being another feature of uncentralized orders. There is no evidence of land shortage leading to unequal holdings. Even if we take the highest population estimates, pressure on land would have been minimal to judge from demographic growth in the coming centuries under a similar farming regime, which proved capable of supporting several times the Iron Age numbers. Further evidence comes from Caesar, who states that among the Gauls, "No one possesses any definite amount of land as private property"; instead, communities "annually assign a holding to clans and groups of kinsmen or others living together, fixing its size and position," and then "the following year make them move on somewhere else" (Hanford 1967, 36; see also Bradley and Yates 2007, 100; Harding 2004, 295–96).[9]

The reasons that Caesar gives for this communal land tenure system conjure up a stateless order. They include ensuring that persons do not become "anxious to acquire large estates, and the strong be tempted to dispossess the weak" and also keeping "people contented and quiet by letting every man see that even the most powerful are no better off than himself" (Hanford 1967, 36). It appears that whatever economists' contemporary arguments about private ownership improving efficiency and the Marxist critique, our ancestors saw the dangers of concentrating resources in the hands of a few over two millennia ago, and subsequent history has proved them correct with the repeated impoverishment of the majority and unjust inequalities—witness the Enclosure Acts.

Social Organization

Kinship probably defined access to land. The size of settlements revealed in archaeological excavation is consistent with kin group occupation, most likely extended families. A ramifying network of extensive kin relations likely linked homesteads in any region. Kinship as an aspect of political-economic arrangements is another feature of stateless orders. The classical sources use a variety of terms for relatives and kin groups, including *cognationes*, *propinquus*, *familia*, *domus*, and *gens*, which are open to wide interpretation, encompassing kinsman, descendant, relations, family, kindred, household, clan, people, and so on, and are sometimes used interchangeably. The Irish sources refer to the *derbfine*, defined as an extended family group comprising four generations that traces descent agnatically back to a common great-grandfather

(Gibson 1988, 50; Harding 2004, 295–96; Laing 1979, 20; Laing and Laing 1995, 19). The *derbfine* claimed rights to land collectively and controlled stock in common, too. While the Irish sources are suggestive, their focus on judicial rules gives little idea about actual human behavior (Wailes 1988, 221).

Some authors argue for agnatic descent arrangements after the segmentary model, with corporations holding territory in common, acting politically to maintain peace internally, and uniting to protect members from external threats and engage in armed encounters (Meinhard 1975, 1–29). The existence of subgroups called *gelfine* within *derbfine* (reminiscent of minimal lineages), and the aggregation of several *derbfine* that trace descent patrilineally back to a common ancestor into larger groups called *túath* (frequently glossed as "tribes"[10]), also imply segmentary arrangements. The four-generation definition of *derbfine* further suggests fission along segmentary lines: with each new generation, the previous great-grandfather figure's sons, as foci of new *derbfine*, would become the point of division.

On the other hand, descent orders, with their ancestor focus, often prompt an interest in burial. But few regions evidence such a concern in the Iron Age, disposal of human remains during this era most often featuring cremation. Archaeologists, routinely on the lookout for burials as a source of remains and evidence of human activity, think that the majority died without leaving any trace (human remains do not match settlement evidence for numbers of people). While it is possible that patrilineal groups played some part in Iron Age social organization, it is difficult to specify in what way, for the role of descent can vary widely between communities. The debacle over the nature of descent in the New Guinea highlands indicates the complexity of the issues (Sillitoe 2010, 45–46). If such confusion can occur where ethnographers can talk to the actors, we can appreciate the care that we need to exercise in speculating on the arrangements peculiar to our Celtic ancestors.

Ethnographic Analogy

We are better informed about armed hostilities, from which we might glean something about Iron Age social arrangements. The archaeological record gives us the weapons used and structures built for defense, some of considerable size, plus forensic evidence of violent wounds from human remains. And the literary sources focus heavily on fighting, the classical authors such as Caesar and Tacitus giving details of military campaigns and the Irish epics full of the heroic deeds of warrior champions. They not only give some indication of how the Celts organized themselves to prosecute hostilities, and hence a glimpse of their political organization, but also invite comparison with the ethnographic record. There are some suggestive parallels with certain parts of the Polynesian Pacific, notably Aotearoa and Fiji, in the weapons used, defensive constructions, wounds suffered, and accounts of military engagements. Furthermore, with regard to the character of Celtic descent concepts, some see parallels with the Polynesian *ramage*, which is a social group founded on kin connections thought of genealogically but flexible with respect to membership (Gibson 1988, 5).

While ethnographic analogy opens another line of thought on Celtic society and political relations, it too has its limitations. The convincingness and force of any analogy vary with time, place, and culture. Although we can never be sure of their appropriateness, they are better than nothing. Analogies may open the range of possibilities considerably. In considering an extinct stateless-subsistence political economy, reviewing evidence from similar contemporary orders is more likely to throw up useful pointers to interpretation than relying on our own imaginations, conditioned by a state-ordered market existence quite alien to that of our ancestors two millennia ago. While we are unavoidably biased culturally, as my opening quotations affirm and the postmodern critique points out, ethnographic analogies help us confront our assumptions by presenting us with alternatives, lessening our projection of our own inappropriate cultural experiences. The past is another culture too, and analogy may help us detect echoes from these distant times that not only help make sense of our ancient forebears' ways but also relate to current concerns about liberty and equality.

Hillforts

The political features of certain near-contemporary Polynesian cultures parallel to some extent, and so may illuminate, as noted, what the archaeological and literary evidence suggests for Iron Age Britain. The Maori *pa* and the Celtic *dunum* are strikingly similar, although situated on opposite sides of the world and separated by some two millennia (Best 1927). The parallels, so conspicuous, have long attracted comparison and serve as a classic example of ethnographic analogy. In 1927, in the first issue of the archaeological journal *Antiquity*, the editor comments, "We cannot see the men who built and defended the hilltop settlements of Wessex; but we can learn much from living people who inhabit similar sites . . . from traditional accounts of Maori forts we learn, by comparison, to understand the dumb language of prehistoric earthworks" (Crawford 1927, 3). In both cultures the evidence suggests that populations lived in scattered homesteads, using forts as citadels in times of stress, when threatened by attack.

The hillforts of both Europe and Polynesia occur on sites that are naturally easily defended such as hilltops, ridges, cliffs, and so on. They vary in size and internal arrangements, from large (such as Maiden Castle and Auckland) to small. They commonly include human-made barriers of varying extent, sometimes around the entire perimeter and others at vulnerable points. These vary in construction and include earth banks and fosse of varying dimensions, stone revetted embankments, wooden palisade arrangements, and various stone wall structures. It is possible that they had several uses (Cunliffe 1991, 285, 346–56). It is plausible that they originated as straightforward stock pens to defend animals from rustling, particularly during times of unrest, and subsequently evolved into more elaborate citadels, serving as visual statements of a community's standing and ability to defend itself and its livestock, used not only in times of hostilities but also at others to host periodic gatherings such as fairs and festivals.[11]

When we look at hillforts today, especially the massive ones, we imagine that large numbers of persons must have worked on them, challenging the stateless interpretation of Iron Age society: For how could so many people organize themselves in an acephalous context? The problem resolves itself when we think that the remains we see today are the result of community efforts extending over several generations and centuries. It is not necessary that they imply the organization of many people at one time to build them. Excavation evidence shows communities extending hillforts over considerable intervals from fairly small enclosures to larger ones. The Maori ethnography shows how it was possible for modest numbers of people working over a considerable time to erect quite startling defenses with a modest technology of digging sticks, paddle-like implements, and flax bags to carry the spoil (see Firth 1927, 66–78; Groube 1970, 133–64).

The Polynesian ethnography also suggests some possible unexpected features regarding the construction and evolution of such structures. On Fiji, for instance, attackers sometimes erected their own defenses of ditches and fences around an enemy's position (Clunie 1977, 25), which, renewed and added to whenever new hostilities broke out, could become established features (which archaeologists would likely interpret as evidence of an initial line of defense erected by the defenders). The Polynesian ethnography further illuminates the internal arrangements of hillforts (see, for example, Cunliffe 1984, 1991, 312–70; Guilbert 1981; Harding 1976; Jesson and Hill 1971; Wheeler 1943). Arrays of postholes are among the most prominent features, occurring singly and in pairs, threes, and fours. Descriptions of Maori *pa* suggest that they could be the remains of watchtowers (Ellison and Drewett 1971, 183–94). There is documentary evidence for this interpretation, too, Caesar noting that during his siege of Avaricum in France the Gauls "equipped the whole circuit of the wall with towers, furnished with platforms and protected by hides" (Hanford 1967, 192–93)—although it is possible that they were copying Roman tactics to repel Caesar's attack (Norton-Taylor 1974, 124–25).

Some circles of postholes match the dimensions of houses excavated elsewhere in farmsteads and suggest that sometimes people resided within hillforts, for periods anyway. The Maori likewise sometimes had houses within defended *pa*. Another, equally plausible interpretation of some postholes, which again has Maori parallels, is that they supported storage structures (for food, weapons, possessions, and so on, protecting them from the elements, vermin, stock, etc.). The Maori also built roofed structures sunk into the ground, called *rua*, to store sweet potato tubers and other foodstuffs (Bellwood 1971, 56–95). Indeed, pits are the other principal feature within British hillforts. Some hillforts had considerable storage capacity to judge from the density of holes, largely storage of grain in wicker-lined pits (similar to farmsteads). These suggest that in times of unrest surrounding homesteads might stockpile supplies there not only to ensure food during defense but also to prevent enemies from destroying stocks or helping themselves, thus ensuring that they could not stay long as they soon had food-supply problems; we know that securing supplies was a significant issue that cut short Fijian assaults (Clunie 1977, 30–31). According to Tacitus, the German Celts had "the habit of hollowing out caves underground and heaping masses of refuse on the top. In these they can . . . store their produce . . . and should an invader come, he ravages the open country, but the secret and buried stores may pass altogether unnoticed or escape detection, simply because they have to be looked for" (Mattingly 1967, 114). The Fijians stored fermented vegetable food in such pits to use in time of hostilities (Clunie 1977, 19).

The existence of clay-lined pits for water suggests that water supply was an issue too (Darvill 1990, 139). We know that this was the weakness of many Maori *pa*, as they occupied elevated and easily defended locations that rarely had natural water sources (such as springs) within their environs. Again, the Polynesian ethnography gives an intriguing alternative use for pits. The Fijians dug some pits, called *lovosa*, as mantraps, both inside and outside their earthworks, putting sharpened stakes in the bottom and camouflaging over them carefully so that unwary enemy fell into them (Clunie 1977, 18). This brings us to the tactics of armed engagements and how people organized themselves to fight. The position with food and water resources suggests that attacks featured brief engagements. The problem of supplying strongholds on top of steep-sided hills suggests that communities retreated to them only briefly for defense, while their foes were in the vicinity, knowing that they would likely leave after an engagement, taking whatever spoils they could grab (Ralston 1981, 80).

Armed Hostilities

The image we have is of women, children, and stock taking refuge in the hillfort while men defended the perimeter, which was pretty much impregnable if the attackers were fewer in number or equally matched, as seems likely. It is what Caesar conveys when he writes that "the Britons apply the term 'strongholds' to densely wooded spots fortified with a rampart and trench, to which they retire in order to escape the attacks of invaders" (Hanford 1967, 139). The serious engagements occurred when the defenders made forays out to engage the enemy in skirmish-like battles or perhaps set pieces that showed each side could match the other. This again is the image Caesar gives, describing how "scattered parties made skirmishing attacks out of the woods, trying to prevent the Romans from penetrating their defences" (p. 134). The horsemanship of the Celts and use of chariots, combining "the mobility of cavalry with the staying-power of infantry" (p. 126), further corroborates this interpretation of fighting irregular encounters and forays, not military engagements in the sense of disciplined Roman troop formations with a command hierarchy. The ramparts of hillforts would also have hindered rapid, surprise horse-mounted and chariot strikes of the sort that Celtic tactics favored. The Polynesian ethnography gives a similar image. Among the Maori the feint attack and ambuscade were used by defenders to precipitate an engagement before the invaders were ready.

The weaponry supports this interpretation. While their arsenals were somewhat different, they favored weapons with similar functions. The only projectile-firing weapon used by both Celts and Polynesians was the sling.[12] They favored close-contact weapons of the sort used in hand-to-hand combat. In Celtic Britain they were swords, daggers, battle axes, and stabbing spears,[13] and in Maori Aotearoa a range of clubs, from bludgeons to axe-like clubs (Te Awekotuku 1996, 37–38). The slash and chop wounds on human remains further testify to close combat. This weaponry indicates that hostilities were unlikely to feature drawn-out sieges. The evidence points to hillforts as almost impregnable strongholds unless faced by a state-ordered army, instead of a tribally organized fighting force, which resorted to alien tactics—that is, did not follow the expected rules of engagement. The response of the Celts to the Roman invasion of their territories, as reported by Caesar, confirms this view, with people retreating to their hillforts and sallying forth to engage legionnaires; we can only speculate on their dismay at the relentless Roman siege tactics.

The Romans in their turn found Celtic tactics perplexing (Cunliffe 1991, 120). We can almost hear Caesar's exasperation: "In chariot fighting the Britons begin by driving all over the field hurling javelins, and generally the terror inspired by the horses and the noise of the wheels are sufficient to throw the opponents' ranks into disorder" (Hanford 1967, 126), or at least those of unaccustomed Roman troops who expect to face a regimented foe. Descriptions of Celtic engagements suggest they were disorganized affairs. According to Caesar, "they never fought in close order, but in very open formation" (p. 137). Irish literary sources confirm the desultory nature of fighting, which was more often " 'heroic', with larger-scale engagements limited to raids, ambushes and, by later standards, short-lived battles" (Ralston 1981, 79). The escapades of that wonderful character Asterix and his cartoon-strip sidekick Obelix capture nicely the apparent mayhem of Celtic fighting. Similarly, "traditional Maori warfare—fighting technique, military strategy and leadership structures—puzzled Western observers and ethnographers. They judged the Maori at war as lacking effective and visible command, capricious and poorly organised. . . . highly mobile, compact units of warriors engaged the enemy in short, fast skirmishes, attacking by surprise. . . . Attack, engagement and hasty withdrawal formed the most common field strategy" (Te Awekotuku 1996, 35–36).[14] The overall impression is of stateless-style encounters, which, lacking any command or agreed-on strategy, appear chaotic to outsiders.

What are the implications of these apparently disorganized armed hostilities for our understanding of political life? This question moves us from the level of direct comparison, of one trait with another, to the level of conditional analogy, standing back from specifics to look for plausible common principles. The evidence for short-term engagements and standoffs suggests more-or-less equally matched forces. It was unlikely that one side could overpower the other; indeed, the idea of defeat was probably alien—until the Romans invaded, that is, with the aim of conquest. Similarly, the conquest campaign of the British colonial forces confused the Maori, who were also familiar with relatively balanced sides engaging in tit-for-tat encounters, not one defeating the other—although some of today's exaggerated oratory refers to devastating routs, the Maori concept of honor contradicts it, stopping the crushing of a vulnerable enemy.

The literary evidence further conveys the impression of balanced forces. The showmanship that accompanied Celtic engagements suggests two sides squaring up and displaying their strength and ability to match one another, as in Caesar's impressed account of their equestrian gymnastics: "They can run along the chariot pole, stand on the yoke, and get back into the chariot as quick as lightening" (Hanford 1967, 126). In addition, there were the battle cries intended to intimidate the enemy further, accompanied by the roaring of long-neck carnyx trumpets. The parallels are striking with the *haka* war dances of the Maori, made famous by the All Blacks rugby team, and the *pūkāea* war horns blown to intimidate and confuse the enemy. The occurrence of duels between evenly matched warriors, among both the Celts and Maori, also complies with idea of balance (Cunliffe 1991, 496), as celebrated in the Celtic "heroic tradition."

A balance of forces brings to mind the opposed segmentary arrangements that are a feature of stateless orders structured according to descent principles. When put alongside *derbfine* seen as agnatically recruited groups, these indications of equilibrium again suggest something along descent-organized lines. The chance that hostilities also featured the rustling of stock is a further parallel, as the raiding of cattle or camels is a prominent feature in fighting between descent-ordered pastoralists. For instance, Caesar refers to a raiding party seizing "a quantity of cattle—a prize much sought after by these Barbarians" (Hanford 1967, 173). Such a fractious political environment is characteristic of acephalous orders where varying groups of kinsmen oppose one another on different occasions.

Disputes

That Iron Age communities did not aim to defeat one another in armed hostilities—as reflected in them being largely evenly matched—complies with what we know of stateless orders. The idea of engaging in wars of conquest makes sense only in state contexts, where one nation wishes to extend political power over another and its resources. There is, by definition, no authority to exert such control in acephalous contexts. It is more likely that disputes that turned violent started armed conflict in these circumstances, when persons infringed others' rights and they sought to protect these. People have to be ready to defend their interests with no central authority to appeal to, and a readiness to resort to violence if necessary is common in higher-density stateless populations. We catch a glimpse of these attitudes in Strabo's observation that "the whole race is madly fond of war, high-spirited and quick to do battle. When they are stirred up, they assemble in their bands for battle quite openly" (Norton-Taylor 1974, 14). And it complies with Poseidonius's and Tacitus's comments cited earlier about "bombastic" behavior and being "prone to fight," "hands twitching to sword-hilt at the imagined hint of an insult" (Piggott 1965, 229). In their readiness to stand up for themselves and fight if necessary, we see people willing to defend their individual rights and those of relatives, a focal stateless concern.

The Irish texts indicate some reasons for disputes. Many concerned rights to farmland and damage to and trespass on others' fields (Wailes 1988, 223). Rights to livestock were also a lively source of differences. The rustling of stock possibly caused armed conflicts and was also a consequence, with communities engaged in hostilities taking any opportunity to make off with animals in retaliation. We can imagine that theft, marital discord, infidelity,[15] and defaults on obligations such as various payments were a source of differences, as elsewhere. While some classical texts, such as Caesar, refer to Druids—soothsayer priests—acting as arbitrators, this is difficult to square with stateless arrangements (Hanford 1967, 32). It is possible that Druids fulfilled a role similar to persons with supernatural faculties in some tribal societies, such as Nuer leopard-skin priests, serving as go-betweens in the negotiation of a settlement, possibly endorsing agreements mystically. It is hard to envisage how these were finally enforced other than by the wronged party taking some action if necessary, maybe backed up by the threat of a supernaturally sanctioned curse.

When disputes became deadlocked, violence was possible. Again, as in other stateless contexts, if an aggressive dispute led to a fatality this might precipitate armed hostilities. When one side incurred a death debt, the revenge ethic would kick in, and a conflict possibly erupted. The "blood-feud was an integral part of retribution" (Laing 1979, 21), and as Tacitus tells us, "A man is bound to take up the feuds as well as the friendships of father or kinsman" (Mattingly 1967, 118). We do not know the likely composition of such feuding groups, but his reference to kin (*propinquus*) suggests a body larger than a single-household extended family (Meinhard 1975, 5). The old Irish tracts further make it clear that Celtic lore held entire families responsible for their members' wrongdoings (Norton-Taylor 1974, 87), which suggests that all relatives could be targeted in revenge, which is common in tribal hostilities. We can interpret this as the ultimate safeguard of liberty. If one party resorted to violence, in other words, sought physically to coerce the other to do something, and this resulted in loss of life, a group mobilized immediately seeking to balance the score.

The idea of achieving a balance of affairs is again evident. When people had differences they would have sought parity and redress, following stateless logic generally, not justice and punishment. Their aim would have been to effect a balance in relations disturbed by any wrongdoing, probably through recompense. In this respect it is interesting to note that the Maori, who also engaged in feuds, used the term *utu* for violent retribution, which literally means a reciprocal return for something, here the avenging of a wrong (Te Awekotuku 1996, 35). The payment of compensation featured in the settlement of Celtic disputes and violent episodes,[16] serving to restore, as in other acephalous orders, the disturbed balance. According to Tacitus, "feuds do not continue unreconciled. Even homicide can be atoned for by a fixed number of cattle or sheep, and the satisfaction is received by the whole family. This is much to the advantage of the community, for private feuds are peculiarly dangerous side by side with liberty" (Mattingly 1967, 118). This is reminiscent of other stateless orders, such as those of African pastoralists who pay blood-cattle. Here again "whole family" (*universa domus*) likely refers to an extended body of kin, possibly constituted along descent lines (Meinhard 1975, 5). Also, the last phrase about "feuds being dangerous alongside liberty" suggests the apparently precarious, even paradoxical (to those of us used to central authority) balance stateless tribal orders achieve between social order and political freedom.

While kin were responsible for contributing to and sharing out compensation, the role they played in effecting settlements is unclear. The ties between kin in different communities were probably significant in arranging settlements, particularly in times of armed conflict. The comment by Tacitus about a man's influence relating to the extent of his affinal network strongly suggests this: "The larger a man's kin and the greater the number of his relations by marriage, the stronger is his influence" (Mattingly 1967, 118). So does his previous comment about the importance of the mother's brothers and sister's son relationship: "The sons of sisters are as highly honoured by their uncles as by their own fathers. Some even go so far as to regard this tie of blood as peculiarly close and sacred" (pp. 117–18). This also possibly hints again at some agnatic ideology informing relations, patrilineal systems often singling out this relationship as particularly significant—albeit it could equally reflect Roman patriarchal ethnocentric bias. Whatever the composition of local groups in reality, whether jurally lineal or cognatic, cross-cutting links between relatives would have been important in facilitating settlement of disputes and violence between communities, by affording connections that could help communication and allow some trust. The support of kin would have been vital to personal security and central to the process of negotiating settlements such as exchange of compensation, possibly guaranteed by druidical approval.

Marriage

A man could extend his affinal network and hence his influence by marrying more than one woman, although according to Tacitus polygyny was uncommon, Celts being "almost unique among barbarians in being satisfied with one wife" (Mattingly 1967, 115). They also, according to other reports, practiced polyandry, women some-times having more than one partner; as Caesar commented, "Wives are shared be-tween groups of ten or twelve men, especially between brothers and between fathers and sons; but the offspring of these unions are counted as the children of the man with whom a particular woman cohabited first" (Hanford 1967, 136n). It is hard to know what to make of such conflicting reports, indicative of the problems that attend reading the literature on Celtic life. It is possible that people living in one region or era largely practiced monogamy while others practiced polygyny and yet others polyandry.

If, as suggested, connections established between communities through marriage were important in regulating their relations, kin would have had a vested interest in any union, which concerned not only the couple but also their respective social networks. While kin would likely have been involved in arranging a marriage, it is noteworthy that no woman could be forced against her wishes to marry any man; she was free to choose her partner. Again, as Tacitus notes, "Girls . . . are not hurried into marriage" (Mattingly 1967, 117). Consequently, women were key parties to the cross-cutting ties between communities, if contemporary stateless orders are any guide, particularly if there was an agnatic ideology featuring a preference for patri-local residence; occupying such bridging positions between communities would have given women some influence in neighborhood affairs.

The exchange of wealth between the bride's and groom's kin further indicates their interest and involvement in the arrangement of a marriage. The reports are again confusing about the transactions, with reference to both bridewealth and dowry. According to Tacitus, the wealth "is brought by husband to wife. . . . Parents and kinsmen attend and approve of the gifts, gifts not chosen to please a woman's whim or gaily deck a young bride, but oxen, horse with reins, shield, spear and sword. For such gifts a man gets his wife, and she in her turn brings some present of arms to her husband. In this interchange of gifts they recognize the supreme bond . . . of marriage" (Mattingly 1967, 115–16). Caesar puts emphasis on the dowry: "When a Gaul marries, he adds to the dowry that his wife brings with her a portion of his own property estimated to be of equal value" (Hanford 1967, 34). The Irish texts, however, talk about women being "valued in cattle," which suggests bridewealth.

Exchange

The Celts, it appears, had exchange institutions analogous to those reported in the ethnographic literature for other stateless political economies. They set up series of reciprocal transactions that confirmed otherwise informal social networks (Sharples 2007, 174–84). In addition to bridewealth and compensation transactions, they en-gaged in exchanges that involved "client" arrangements (see Gibson 1988, 51–52; Norton-Taylor 1974, 70–73). It is difficult to know what to make of them. According to the Irish texts persons contracted others as clients by giving them animals called *raith*; the recipients were obliged to make return payments of calves and milk. A would-be patron gave the "surplus of his cattle, of his cows, his sheep, that his own land cannot bear . . . in capital to acquire clients" (MacNeill 1924, 293). The more clients a person had, the higher his social status. Apparently clients were obliged to accept such gifts. The patron's gift was pegged to the client's *dire*, "honor price." All individuals had such a price, which reflected their social standing and wealth. (The reference to honor price is suspiciously reminiscent of the Anglo-Saxon notion of wergild that regulated compensation paid for homicide and other crimes according to the price put on persons in respect of their rank—a further hint of ethnocentricity in the Irish texts, written by monks who probably could not conceive of tribal exchange as opposed to feudal transactions.)

Exchange relates to the movement of objects around Iron Age Britain generally. Some things traveled over considerable distances, sometimes hundreds of miles—for example, pottery and metalwork. There is a tendency to think of this movement taking place through trade—either with trading parties visiting regions and buying things, or with people selling them on from hand to hand across regions. Trade implies purchase and sale in market-like contexts, prompted largely by material need or demand. It is not the only interpretation possible. If sociopolitical exchange was a feature of life, which seems probable given the evidence and what we know about nonmarket orders elsewhere, then many things may have moved in transactions motivated by social and political concerns, not economic and resource ones, which would have conditioned their flow in critical regards.

If what we know of other tribal contexts is any guide, it is probable that *raith* stock transactions were reciprocal exchanges of a quite different nature to business-like patron–client dealings. We can shift the emphasis from hierarchy and commercial-like assumptions to more neutral contexts that allow for equality and social consider-ations, if instead of talking about patrons and clients we refer to exchange partners. The ethnographic literature on the exchange of animals gives us some idea of the possible complexion of these transactions between partners, such as the exchange of pigs between relatives in New Guinea, which subsequently demands a reciprocal payment, and of cattle in Africa, where transactions have a strong moral component; obligations can link families across generations, and not giving is shameful and can provoke persons to utter curses (see Maybury-Lewis 1992, 81–85).

The *raith* stock partnerships suggest similar complex arrangements for raising animals that served as wealth.[17] They possibly intimate the sort of arrangements that occur in egalitarian orders and prevent certain persons from controlling production of things transacted in sociopolitical exchanges, such as bridewealth and compensa-tion, and becoming richer than others. While it is rash to suggest arrangements akin to spheres of exchange,[18] it is suggestive that homesteads were largely independent regarding subsistence. The ornate objects found in the archaeological record, regu-larly interpreted as the possessions of ruling aristocrats, may have served as highly valued wealth objects transacted in exchanges. They were produced in limited numbers and possibly acquired high values through time with use in exchange. They may have passed elsewhere, becoming valuables not produced locally but obtainable only through exchange, so cutting the link with their manufacture. In this respect it is possible that people ascribed particular value to imports from other regions. And to continue drawing analogies with contemporary ethnography, the destruction of some such objects found in archaeological contexts (e.g., at La Tène) may be evidence of competition, such as in the *potlatch* exchange institution of the Northwest Coast peoples, as opposed to the breaking of captured enemies' weapons or those of admired warriors and their deposition in water to propitiate spirits, which is the interpretation popular with archaeologists.

The Celts' love of feasting might also reflect such reciprocal competition, again similar to *potlatch* feasting where people try to outdo rivals. According to Tacitus, "No nation abandons itself more completely to banqueting and entertainment than the German. It is accounted a sin to turn any man away from your door. . . . As the guest takes his leave, it is usual to let him have anything he asks for; the host, too, is no more shy in asking. They take delight in presents. . . . Drinking bouts, lasting a day and a night, are not considered in any way disgraceful. . . . For drink they extract a juice from barley or grain, which is fermented" (Mattingly 1967, 118–20). The consumption of alcohol clearly featured prominently at feasts, in which elaborate drinking vessels figured, and when wine became available with the expansion of the Roman Empire northwards, the Celts drank it in considerable quantities to judge from amphorae unearthed by archaeologists. Again, wine would have had a particular value in reciprocal feasting contexts as it was not produced locally. Another medium of exchange to arrive with the Roman Empire was money, which, spreading across the nearby continent, makes an appearance in southern Britain toward the end of Iron Age.[19]

It is improbable that people used coins much as currency in market dealings before the Roman conquest. In order to function as a standard store of wealth transferable against fixed—priced—amounts of goods, it is necessary to have a central authority to control minting and guarantee value. It is possible that when people learned that the powerful invaders valued these metal tokens and that they could be redeemed with foreign traders against their valued imports such as wine, they gradually adopted them as wealth transactable in their own sociopolitical contexts. Again, they could not produce Roman coins locally but only obtain them from others, ensuring the all-important separation from manufacture. But locally minted money makes an appearance in the archaeological record. While it clearly imitates Roman currency, it is different. The coins found have variable compositions of valuable metals (notably gold, bronze, and silver) and differ widely in size and design, as we might expect with no authority to control minting. Perhaps those who accumulated sufficient precious metals manufactured coins, somewhat in the manner of gold torques and finely wrought ironwork and bronze ware previously.

Leadership and Hierarchy

The classical and later sources suggest that the emergence of a social class–like hierarchy was not down entirely to the arrival of the Romans with their military and money. They refer to a ranked society, for example, the patron–client arrangements mentioned earlier, some accounts of which report two classes of clients—"free" and "base," the latter almost depicted as serfs (Norton-Taylor 1974, 72–73). And according to Caesar, Celtic society comprised three ranks: "the common people," who "are treated almost as slaves," and "the two privileged classes," who "are the Druids and the Knights" (Hanford 1967, 31). Both sources refer to rulers, *rí* ("kings"), who in the Irish texts reign over *túath* ("tribes"), with the powerful acting as the overlords of weaker neighbors to create kingdoms (Norton-Taylor 1974, 68–73).[20]

These accounts are difficult to evaluate. They doubtless reflect to some extent the tendency of Roman authors and medieval scribes to see aspects of their own social experiences in what they heard and observed of Celtic life. The ethnocentric tendency of invaders to identify "rulers" with whom they can "reach agreements" is evident some two millennia later with European colonialists' recognizing of "kings" and "queens" among subjugated peoples. The British gave insignia, such as neck pendants engraved "king" and "princess," to those so identified among the Australian Aborigines, as they supposedly negotiated the confiscation of their land and birthrights. If such misunderstanding of hunter-gatherers who have the most egalitarian and informal polities on record is possible, it is understandable that the Romans reported a social hierarchy similar to that in Italy on conquering the Iron Age farmers of northern Europe.

Until recently, as noted, archaeologists went along with this hierarchical depiction of Celtic society, their interpretations reminiscent of medieval barons and knights dominating the surrounding population from their castle keep (Cunliffe 1991, 141; Harding 2004, 292–96; Piggott 1965, 227). But the hillfort evidence scarcely confirms occupation by rulers; no grand structures are identifiable from the posthole record. Some have identified the period's few elaborate graves, such as those in the Arras cemetery of Yorkshire that feature chariots and associated harness with weapons and some rich personal effects, as those of the powerful elite. But graves are modest in most regions, often containing nothing more than cremated remains, as noted earlier. We could interpret these idiosyncratic inhumations in many other ways, such as the culmination of climactic exchange sequences featuring the disposal of valued goods to mark the unexpected deaths of esteemed kinspersons. Analysis of skeletal remains from a Slovenian cemetery of the Hallstatt period, where graves contained different amounts of goods, further questions the idea that these mark differences in social status, as there is no evidence of variation in nutritional status; all persons apparently enjoyed much the same diet (Murray and Schoeninger 1988, 155–76). Whatever the hierarchy, it had no medieval parallel.

It is difficult to disentangle the effects of the northward expansion of the Roman Empire from what pertained previously in Celtic society. It is indisputable that Roman contact and subsequent conquest played a significant part in shaping the hierarchical social order described by the classical authors (Millett 1990), who reported not only on what they expected to see but also on the effects of their state's expansion. We know from more recent colonial and neocolonial contexts that an invading nation-state can soon impose an authoritative hierarchy on a population; some of the subjugated come to occupy offices through chance, astuteness, connivance, thuggery, and so on and then, with vested interests, support the system. It is even possible that a society will develop such hierarchical features as it seeks to match and repel such an invader. The later changes in hillfort structures way beyond stock-defending pens could be evidence of such transformation, although any pre-invasion shift toward a more ranked order was not particularly effective militarily, as the Romans soon conquered the Celts.

It is possible that some of the confusion in the literature between egalitarian and hierarchical arrangements results from the conflation of different historical periods during a time of rapid social change. It is hard to envisage how, as Caesar describes, feuding parties were persuaded to gather peaceably at a central place for Druids to pass judgment on disputes, and what authority ensured compliance with their deliberations. It is also a mystery how the Germans accepted an elected leadership in time of conflict while at other times they recognized no common authority. For, according to Caesar, "When a tribe is attacked or intends to attack another, officers are chosen to conduct the campaign and invested with powers of life and death. In peace-time there is no central magistracy" (Hanford 1967, 36). It flies in the face of realpolitik to imagine those with authority subsequently relinquishing it. Such contradictory observations suggest that any rank arrangements had features unfamiliar to the authors.

Indeed, the existence of some sort of social class–like hierarchy in Celtic society poses something of a conundrum, which we cannot ignore as all the literary sources recount such an arrangement. It flies in the face of egalitarian tribal arrangements, which much of the evidence, as interpreted above, otherwise evokes. Comments by the classical authors on freedom, for instance, suggest a high estimation of liberty such as we find in stateless orders. According to Caesar, the Celts thought that "it was better to die in battle than to resign themselves to the loss of . . . the liberty inherited from their ancestors" (Hanford 1967, 179). The Gallic leader Dumnorix starkly expressed these values when cut down on Caesar's orders by a Roman cavalry troop, reportedly crying out, "I am a free man in a free state" (Norton-Taylor 1974, 121). The "Caledonian leader" Calgacus also graphically expressed it when rallying men to fight the Romans with the words "to a man you are free. . . . We, the last men on earth, the last of the free" (Mattingly 1967, 79–80). While these references to liberty could be interpreted to express a wish for freedom from the Roman yoke, they nonetheless express the idea of being free of any superior authority. They indicate a particular Celtic attitude to any hierarchy that may have been emergent in their cultural order.

Whatever the sociopolitical arrangement, it had to accord with a more-or-less stateless environment, if tribal ways were prominent, as argued here. The idea of social ranking that does not conflict with egalitarian values seems like a paradox. The ethnography of Polynesia is again suggestive. It indicates the possible contours of leadership and rank in British Iron Age society, combining an element of hierarchy with an ethic of equality. The Maori and Fijians, together with other Western Polynesians such as the Samoans, live in hierarchical cultures where ethnographers have identified "chiefs." They are nonetheless open and democratic, belying the idea that liberty and equality are compromised for those who live in such orders.

A Polynesian Hierarchy

The political economy of Samoa illustrates such arrangements.[21] The *matai*, sometimes called "father," is head of the household. He holds a formal title identified as "chiefly" and has responsibilities for those who live with him. The *matai* title is the property of the household's *aiga* ("extended family"); all households have an associated title. The responsibilities of the *matai* include custody of family land, coordination of household activities and responsibility for ensuring that all share equally in the results of their cooperative endeavors, promotion of family unity and standing, settlement of disputes between kin, representation of the family at village meetings, and coordination of activities necessary to meet family social obligations. The *matai* works the land and fishes like any other family member and has no privileges. He is unable to make unreasonable demands on members. The Samoan household is democratic. The freedom persons have to choose their place of residence means that no *matai* can force his wishes on them—if he tries they can move away. The more persons resident, the larger the political influence of the household and *matai* titleholder.

An *aiga* may comprise a number of branches called *faletama* (in a manner reminiscent of the Celtic *derbfine* kin groups and segmentary descent). When a *matai* dies, the various branches come together to deliberate and elect a successor. Male branch members are more eligible. The principal qualifications are family service and age, a reputation for competence, and knowledge of ceremonial protocol. There are possible parallels here with ancient Celtic society where, Tacitus tells us, "councils" among the Germans "elected the chiefs"; the Irish texts talk about the election of Celtic "kings" by their peers (Mattingly 1967, 106, 111; Norton-Taylor 1974, 68). Similar considerations seem to have exercised them in making their selection, with Tacitus telling us that "as for the leaders, it is their example rather than their authority that wins them special admiration—for their energy, distinction." Discussions can be protracted in Samoa, as each *faletama* branch has its own contender. This is a further parallel with ancient Celtic society where, according to Caesar, "In Gaul, not only every tribe, canton and subdivision of a canton, but almost every family, is divided into rival factions" (Hanford 1967, 30). All have a chance to express an opinion. Men predominantly succeed to *matai* titles, women only occasionally. The Celts apparently were more even-handed; some females wore the *bracae* ("trousers") in their families, occupying designated offices and presumably representing their kin at community meetings; for, according to Tacitus, "Britons make no distinction of sex in their leaders" (Mattingly 1967, 66). The most notable example is Boudica, who featured in the Iceni tribe uprising against the Romans.

A *matai* title is either *ali'i* or *tulafale*, glossed "chief" or "talking chief." There are three categories of each. These parallel the different ranks of chief described in the early Irish literature, which also numbered three, from lowest to highest: the *aighe fine*, *ri*, and *ri ruirech* (Gibson 1988, 51). These differ significantly from Samoan title classes that all equate with a similar-sized extended family, as the Celtic titles equated with descent groups of increasing size, from the *derbfine* ("lineage") to the *túath* ("tribe") and *mor túath* ("great tribe"). The *matai* meet in the *fono* ("council house"), where the community conducts its formal affairs. In an archaeological context it would likely be identified as the chief's house, as the largest structure in the region. The places where *matai* sit, adjacent to particular house posts, reflect the rank of their titles and the order in which they take part in ceremonial activities. The rank order is largely ceremonial and confers no particular political authority.

In *fono* debates, when they discuss village issues, all have an equal right to speak. The weight of what they have to say depends not on their title but on knowledge of the issue. Samoans subscribe to the view that decisions are reached only after spirited debate. Each *matai* canvases and represents the thoughts of his *aiga* on the matter. There are again parallels with classical accounts of Celtic society. After mentioning factions led by men of prestige, Caesar maintains that this arrangement ensures that "all the common people should have protection against the strong; for each leader sees that no one gets the better of his supporters by force or by cunning—or, if he fails to do so, is utterly discredited." Subsequently, he tells us that "the discussion of politics is forbidden except in a public assembly" (Hanford 1967, 30, 35). Young untitled men may also act like a police force to enforce Samoan village council decisions. There is even an echo of such arrangements in the classical literature, where Tacitus tells us that among the Germans "dignity and power alike consist in being continually attended by a corps of chosen youths" (Mattingly 1967, 112).

The aim at *fono* meetings is to reach a decision that is agreeable to all those present regardless of rank. People acknowledge that only decisions to which the entire village, or a good majority, agree are likely to meet with compliance. They are keen to demonstrate village unity through the solidarity of the council. There is no voting; the mood emerges during discussion. Those involved may discuss an issue informally first and seek common ground before initiating a *fono* council discussion, being cautious of speaking out publicly in support of some action before they know what their fellows think about it. Likewise, Tacitus tells us that among the Germans "on matters of minor importance only the chiefs debate, on major affairs the whole community; but even where the commons have the decision, the case is carefully considered in advance by the chiefs." And he proceeds later to describe the conduct of a meeting: "It is a defect of their freedom that they do not assemble at once or in obedience to orders, but waste two or three days in their dilatory gathering. When the mass so decide, they take their seats fully armed. . . . Then such hearing is given to the king or chief as age, rank, military distinction or eloquence can secure; but rather it is their prestige as councillors than their authority that tells. If a proposal displeases them, the people roar out their dissent; if they approve, they clash their spears. No form of approval can carry more honour than praise expressed by arms" (Mattingly 1967, 106, 110). It is a democratic arrangement that combines a genuine regard for liberty and equality within a nominally hierarchical system.

On ceremonial occasions, on the other hand, Samoans greatly admire oratorical skill and treat public speaking as an art. Speeches follow prescribed procedures and conform to conventional structures committed to memory. This is reminiscent of the Druids of Iron Age Britain, who committed sagas and genealogies to memory and recited them at public events such as feasts. According to Caesar, "pupils have to memorize a great number of verses—so many, that some of them spend twenty years at their studies. The Druids believe that their religion forbids them to commit their teaching to writing" (Hanford 1967, 32). The Samoan orators are expected to show a firm grasp of formal protocol and cleverly allude to legendary events, and to display wisdom in turning a phrase appropriate to an occasion. The persuasive skills of experienced "talking chiefs" can be such that few oppose them, particularly when they express the views of the council, for example, in settling disputes or directing community events. Again this may illuminate the references in the classical texts such as Caesar to the involvement of Druids in the settlement of disputes, which as mentioned previously are otherwise difficult to comprehend. Their role may have been formally to declare and sanction the decision of some collective.

Conclusion

There is an intellectual tradition of looking back to our Celtic ancestors to under-stand something about current issues. While I am unaware of any previous attempts to assess the possible acephalous origins of our concerns for freedom and fairness, there has long been an interest in Celtic pagan beliefs, particularly as informing our continued interests in Mother Nature, often expressed in a secular way today through the green movement and environmental activism. Indeed, conjecture about these beliefs and their significance inspired much early anthropology—notably seeing the origins of religion in people's animistic beliefs and concern for fertility—albeit long eschewed because of associations with bogus cultural evolutionary theory (see, for example, Frazer 1922; Jevons 1896). This interest extends to contemporary Druid romanticism and cultural reinvention of Druidic lore, dating from Victorian times and before, which reminds us to take care not to fall into the trap of overromanticizing Iron Age life, after the Celtic revivalists (Carruthers and Rawes 2003b). We need to avoid the reverse, too, also dating from Victorian times, of seeing tribal life as degraded, after the evolutionary theorists. We need to plot a middle way between these two extremes.

In the light of the fragmentary and opaque evidence, how much faith can we have in the proposition that the current high, albeit contrary, regard that we British espouse for liberty and equality has its roots in our past, that it descends from tribal times to the present day, as our current society is so patently unfair and restrictive of freedoms? It is necessary to realize that we are not talking about specific evidence but rather the possible presence of an ethic—the suggestion of cultural arrangements that indicate the centrality of these values to social life—as the ethnographic evidence shows they are generally for stateless tribal orders. The archaeological data suggest that our ancestors lived in such tribal orders up to the time of the Roman invasion and beyond. Nonetheless, this is to go back some two millennia. Is it tenable to suppose these values persisted from then to now? It is not so improbable when we recall that for the majority of our history we have lived in tribal contexts. If we date the emergence of modern humans to 100,000 years ago and the end of the British tribal order to the Roman invasion 2,000 years ago, we have been subject to a hierarchical state for a mere 2 percent of our existence. We have a tribal heritage, which may well have consequences for our current attitudes to freedom and equality.

Notes

1. These comments are informed by a recent introspective review of my research in New Guinea (Sillitoe 2010).
2. See, for example, on this revised view Harding 2004, 294; Hill 1995a, 1995b; James 2007, 160; and Ralston and Ashmore 2007, 230.
3. For example, see the work of Jacquetta and Christopher Hawkes (1962), who refer in one place to "the yeoman cultivator, who could turn warrior at will," living in a society where there was "little evidence for a disproportionately wealthy exploiting class" (p. 101), and then elsewhere talk about invaders who "forced themselves by conquest upon the natives" using "great forts, just as the Norman conquerors" to secure "their rule" (p. 128), leaving the reader thoroughly puzzled.
4. See Darvill 1990, 139–53; and Cunliffe 1991, 213–311 for a review of settlement patterns.
5. Edward E. Evans-Pritchard's account of Nuer behavior is a widely cited example (see Evans-Pritchard 1940).

6. In phrases matching the flamboyant behavior, Laing (1979, 23) describes the Celt as "a swaggering braggart, his hand twitching for his sword, alert for insult, intended or accidental."

7. In this event, Celtic comprised a family of closely related languages, evident today in the Goidelic southern group of Welsh, Cornish, and Breton, and the Brythonic northern group of Irish, Scottish Gaelic, and Manx.

8. A theme that has long characterized Scottish and Welsh dialogue with the English; see Carruthers and Rawes 2003b, 18.

9. Again, this arrangement alone is not sufficient to suggest an uncentralized order because similar land allocation persisted into medieval times in the open field system (Dodgshon 1975).

10. Current anthropological usage would class *túath* as clans. The *mór túath* ("great *túath*") comprising several *túath* would be tribes.

11. The evidence of several possible uses has led some to question the appropriateness of the term *hillfort*; one archaeologist suggests we should consider them simply as "not-farmsteads" (Hill 1995b, 52), but the defensive nature of these structures appears beyond dispute, even if used for other purposes too, and the term *hillfort* too firmly established to be dislodged (particularly by a negative delineation).

12. A dart-hurling throwing-stick among the Maori, sometimes featuring beautiful carved motifs.

13. See Stead 1997, 44–57 and Cunliffe 1991, 488–91 on weapons.

14. See also Vayda 1960. Accounts of fighting on Fiji convey a similar image (see Clunie 1977, 28).

15. According to Tacitus they were particularly hard on adulterers and loose girls (Mattingly 1967, 117–18).

16. The paying of such compensation continued into the Anglo-Saxon era with wergild.

17. According to Tacitus, among the Germans, "it is numbers [of cattle] that please, numbers that constitute their only, their darling, form of wealth" (Mattingly 1967, 104).

18. See, for example, Rowlands 1980; Ellison 1981; and Barrett and Needham 1988 for a discussion of the idea of "tiers" in the Bronze Age.

19. See, for example, Cunliffe 1981 and Haselgrove 1987.

20. See Karl 2007 for a detailed discussion of comparative terms in Irish, Welsh, and Gaulish.

21. For a readable account of Samoan life see Holmes 1974.

References

Barker, G. 1985. *Prehistoric farming in Europe*. Cambridge: Cambridge University Press.

Barrett, J., and S. Needham. 1988. "Production, circulation and exchange: Problems in the interpretation of Bronze Age bronzework." In *The archaeology of context in the Neolithic and Bronze Age: Recent trends*, ed. J. Barrett and I.A. Kinnes, 127–40. Sheffield, UK: Department of Archaeology and Prehistory.

Bellwood, P. L. 1971. "Fortification and economy in prehistoric New Zealand." *Proceedings of the Prehistoric Society* 37 (1): 56–95.

Best, Elsdon. 1927. *The pa Maori*. Dominion Museum Bulletin, no. 6. Wellington, NZ: Dominion Museum.

Bradley, R., and D. Yates. 2007. "After 'Celtic' fields: The social organisation of Iron Age agriculture." In Haselgrove and Pope 2007, 94–102.

Carruthers, G., and A. Rawes, eds. 2003a. *English romanticism and the Celtic world*. Cambridge: Cambridge University Press.

Carruthers, G., and A. Rawes. 2003b. "Introduction: Romancing the Celts." In Carruthers and Rawes 2003a, 1–19.

Clunie, F. 1977. *Fijian weapons and warfare*. Fiji Museum Bulletin, no. 2. Suva: Fiji Museum.

Crawford, O.G.S. 1927. "Editor's introduction." *Antiquity* 1 (1): 1–4.

Cunliffe, B. 1981. *Coinage and society in Britain and Gaul: Some current problems*. Council for British Archaeology Research Report 38. London: Council for British Archaeology.

Cunliffe, B. 1984. *Danebury: An Iron Age hillfort in Hampshire*. 2 vols. Council for British Archaeology Research Report 52. London: Council for British Archaeology.

Cunliffe, B. 1991. *Iron Age communities in Britain*. London: Routledge.

Darvill, T. 1990. *Prehistoric Britain*. London: Batsford.

Dodgshon, R. A. 1975. "The landholding foundations of the open field system." *The Past and Present Society* 67: 3–29.

Dumont, L. 1975. "Preface to the French edition of E. E. Evans-Pritchard's *The Nuer*." Trans. M. Douglas and J. Douglas. In *Studies in social anthropology: Essays in memory of E. E. Evans-Pritchard by his former Oxford colleagues*, ed. J.H.M. Beattie and R. G. Lienhardt, 328–42. Oxford: Clarendon.

Ellison, A. 1981. "Towards a socio economic model for the Middle Bronze Age in southern England." In *Patterns of the past: Studies in honour of David Clarke*, ed. I. Hodder, G. Isaacs, and G. Hammond, 413–38. Cambridge: Cambridge University Press.

Ellison, A., and P. Drewett. 1971. "Pits and postholes in the British Early Iron Age." *Proceedings of the Prehistoric Society* 37: 183–94.

Evans-Pritchard, E. E. 1940. *The Nuer: A description of the modes of livelihood and political institutions of a Nilotic people*. Oxford: Clarendon.

Firth, R. 1927. "The Maori hill-fort." *Antiquity* 1: 66–78.

Fowler, P. J. 1983. *The farming of prehistoric Britain*. Cambridge: Cambridge University Press.

Frazer, J. 1922. *The golden bough: A study in magic and religion*. Abridged ed. London: Macmillan. (First published in 1890 in 2 vols., with subsequent editions extending to 13 vols.)

Gibson, D. B. 1988. "Agro-pastoralism and regional social organization in early Ireland." In Gibson and Geselowitz 1988, 41–68.

Gibson, D. B., and M. N. Geselowitz, eds. 1988. *Tribe and polity in late prehistoric Europe*. New York: Plenum.

Groube, L. M. 1970. "The origin and development of earthwork fortifications in the Pacific." In *Studies in Oceanic culture history*, ed. R. C. Green and M. Kelly, 1:133–64. Bishop Museum Pacific Anthropological Records, no. 11. Honolulu: Bishop Museum.

Guilbert, G., ed. 1981. *Hill-fort studies: Essays for A. H. A. Hogg*. Leicester, UK: Leicester University Press.

Hanford, S. A., trans. 1967. *Caesar: The conquest of Gaul*. Harmondsworth, UK: Penguin Classics.

Harding, D. W. 2004. *The Iron Age in northern Britain: Celts and Romans, natives and invaders*. London: Routledge.

Harding, Dennis, ed. 1976. *Hillforts: Later prehistoric earthworks in Britain and Ireland*. London: Academic Press.

Haselgrove, C. C. 1987. *Iron Age coinage in South East England: The archaeological context*. British Archaeological Reports British Series 174. Oxford: British Archaeological Reports.

Haselgrove, C. C., and R. Pope, eds. 2007. *The earlier Iron Age in Britain and the near continent*. Oxford: Oxbow Books.

Hawkes, J., and C. Hawkes. 1962. *Prehistoric Britain*. London: Chatto & Windus.

Hill, J. D. 1995a. "The pre-Roman Iron Age in Britain and Ireland (ca. 800 BC to AD 100): An overview." *Journal of World Prehistory* 9: 47–98.

Hill, J. D. 1995b. "How should we study Iron Age societies and hillforts? A contextual study from southern England." In *Different Iron Ages: Studies on the Iron Age in temperate Europe*, ed. J. D. Hill and C. G. Cumberpatch, 45–66. British Archaeological Reports International Series 602. Oxford: British Archaeological Reports.

Holmes, A. 1974. *Samoan village*. New York: Holt, Rinehart and Winston.

James, S. 2007. "A bloodless past: The pacification of early Iron Age Britain." In Haselgrove and Pope 2007, 160–73.

Jesson, M., and D. Hill, eds. 1971. *The Iron Age and its hill-forts*. Southampton, UK: Southampton University.

Jevons, F. B. 1896. *An introduction to the history of religion*. London: Methuen.

Karl, R. 2007. "From head of kin to king of a country. The evolution of early feudal society in Wales." In *Interpretierte Eisenzeiten. Fallstudien, Methoden Theorie. Tagungsbericht der 2. Linzer Gespräche zur interpretativen Eisenzeitarchäologie*, ed. R. Karl and J. Leskovar, 153–85. Studien zur Kulturgeschichte von Oberösterreich 19. Linz, Austria: Oberösterreichisches Landesmuseum.

Kuklick, H. 1991. *The savage within: The social history of British anthropology, 1889–1945*. Cambridge: Cambridge University Press.

Laing, L. 1979. *Celtic Britain*. London: Routledge & Kegan Paul.

Laing, L., and J. Laing. 1995. *Celtic Britain and Ireland: Art and society*. London: Herbert Press.

MacNeill, E. 1924. "Ancient Irish law: The law of status or franchise." *Proceedings of the Royal Irish Academy* 36: 265–316.

Mattingly, H., trans. 1967. *Tacitus on Britain and Germany*. Harmondsworth, UK: Penguin Classics.

Maybury-Lewis, D. 1992. *Millennium: Tribal wisdom and the modern world*. New York: Viking Penguin.

Meinhard, H.H. 1975. "The patrilineal principle in early Teutonic kinship." In *Studies in social anthropology*, ed. J.H.M. Beattie and R.G. Lienhardt, 1–29. Oxford: Clarendon.

Millett, M. 1990. *The Romanization of Britain*. Cambridge: Cambridge University Press.

Murray, M.L., and M.J. Schoeninger. 1988. "Diet, status, and complex social structure in Iron Age Central Europe: Some contributions of bone chemistry." In Gibson and Geselowitz 1988, 155–76.

Norton-Taylor, D. 1974. *The Celts*. Emergence of Man Series. New York: Time Life Books.

Piggott, S. 1965. *Ancient Europe: From the beginnings of agriculture to classical antiquity*. Edinburgh: Edinburgh University Press.

Ralston, I. 1981. "The use of timber in hill-fort defences in France." In Guilbert 1981, 78–103.

Ralston, I., and P. Ashmore. 2007. "The character of Earlier Iron Age societies in Scotland." In Haselgrove and Pope 2007, 229–47.

Rowlands, M. 1980. "Kinship, alliance and exchange in the European Bronze Age." In *The British later Bronze Age*, ed. J. Barrett and R. Bradley, 15–56. British Archaeological Reports British Series 83. Oxford: British Archaeological Reports.

Salzman, P.C. 1999. "Is inequality universal?" *Current Anthropology* 40 (1): 31–61.

Sharples, N. 2007. "Building communities and creating identities in the first millennium BC." In Haselgrove and Pope 2007, 174–84.

Sillitoe, P. 2010. *From land to mouth: The agricultural "economy" of the Wola of the New Guinea Highlands*. New Haven, CT: Yale University Press.

Stead, I.M. 1985 *Celtic art in Britain before the Roman conquest*. London: British Museum.

Te Awekotuku, Ngahuia. 1996. "Maori: People and culture." In *Maori: Art and culture*, ed. D.C. Starzecka, 26–49. London: British Museum.

Vayda, A.P. 1960. *Maori warfare*. Polynesian Society Maori Monograph, no. 2. Wellington, NZ: Polynesian Society.

Wailes, B. 1988. "Some comments on method and interpretation." In Gibson and Geselowitz 1988, 219–28.

Wheeler, M. 1943. *Maiden Castle, Dorset*. Society of Antiquaries Research Report 12. Oxford: Society of Antiquaries.

Space, Place, and Architecture: A Major Meeting Point between Social Archaeology and Anthropology?

Stella Souvatzi

Space and the built forms of it are increasingly recognized as fundamental in social analysis and theoretical discourse across the social sciences. Whether generally, as an integral part of any cultural, social, or ideological aspect of life, or specifically, in terms of the spatial dimension of social action and the materialization of social relationships, they reflect growing interdisciplinary interests, linking not only archaeology and anthropology but also geography, history, philosophy, and sociology. The interdisciplinary value of space lies in space's key role in the processes through which people, at any time, in any culture and any society, construct their relations to each other and their understandings of the world—consequently, in space's central importance for sociocultural theory.

In archaeology, the study of space and architecture has always held a prominent position. Indeed, they both constitute a core class of archaeological data, whereas another core class, material culture, has also always been examined in relation to its positioning in space, whether horizontally, at sites, regions, or landscapes, or vertically, in chronological strata. Archaeologists have long pursued theoretically and methodologically innovative research on space and have incorporated advances and ideas in the other disciplines along the way, not least of which in social anthropology. Despite theoretical differences, there is today a fairly consistent conceptual and analytical framework for space in archaeology, particularly within social archaeology.

In anthropology the spatial dimensions of cultural and social beliefs and practices have always held an interest, but space itself was not recognized as a significant analytical or theoretical concept until the onset of globalization studies and the postmodernist critique in the 1980s. Previous research treated space as a part of "nature" and juxtaposed it to "culture" (Gupta and Ferguson 1992; Hastrup and Olwig 1997; Rodman 2003). As a result, anthropology, the study of culture par excellence, whose "central rite of passage is fieldwork" (Gupta and Ferguson 1992, 6), did not pay attention to space either as a theoretical device that informs the practitioners of *field*work or in terms of the meaning imputed by people to their cultural and physical surroundings. Since the 1990s, however, a new interest in issues of space and place has emerged in anthropology, with renewed coverage, self-reflexive criticisms, and theoretical stimulus, foregrounding rather than backgrounding the spatial dimensions of culture and society. This shift has drawn on research and theory in various disciplines such as geography, urban studies, and sociology, but rarely archaeology. This is surprising, given not only archaeology's long disciplinary experience with space but also the plethora of issues that are currently topical in both disciplines, all of which might apply, in turn, to the subject of space: memory, identity, power, gender, houses, communities, architecture, representation, meaning, social and cultural networks, body and embodiment, boundaries, borderlands and "cultural spatiality," and so on. This lack of reciprocal flow of intellectual knowledge may be understandable in the context of the research agendas of earlier eras and the anxiety to define and "defend" disciplinary boundaries and institutionalization (see Shankland in this volume; also Gosden 1999; Hodder 2005a; Yarrow 2010). But today it is neither understandable nor productive.

This chapter explores, from an archaeological perspective, whether space can provide a meaningful framework for effective interaction between anthropology and archaeology. Can it serve as a conceptual and analytical means for a cross-disciplinary approach to social process and transformation? What are the contrasts and complementarities between the two disciplines on this subject? Do their different methodologies and data sets really separate their respective considerations of human societies, past and present, or could they be seen as complementing each other in practice and as potentially leading to a fuller understanding of social life? In addressing these questions, the chapter presents an up-to-date account of recent developments and topical themes in the archaeology and anthropology of space, evaluating disciplinary contributions and raising issues, consequences, and implications critical to a closer relationship. The last part of the chapter discusses ways that relations between archaeology and anthropology may work out in the future. In keeping with the scope of the 2009 Association of Social Anthropology conference on Archaeological and Anthropological Imaginations: Past, Present and Future (henceforth referred to as "the 2009 ASA conference") and this ensuing volume, the chapter is primarily concerned with what anthropology can learn from archaeology or from areas of archaeological thought it might have not drawn inspiration from as yet. But it also shows the specific ways in which archaeology has already learned from anthropology. The themes discussed in the following represent some of the most prominent and promising directions currently being explored, according to my views, in combination with the results from the panel on space organized for the 2009 ASA conference (henceforth referred to as "the panel").[1]

Contexts of Research and the Current State of Affairs

At present, the major point of similarity between archaeology and anthropology regarding space is their shared view of it as a force shaping social processes, actions, and identities and, thus, as an essential component of social theory. This recognition has, of course, taken various forms over the years and has followed different intellectual histories and theoretical approaches.

In archaeology the earliest and most sustained outside influences come from geography and, to a lesser extent, from the anthropologist Julian Steward's "cultural ecology" (see Blake 2007 for a recent review and further references). Archaeology has borrowed ideas and techniques from geography in order to formulate its own categories and methods of spatial analysis, including notions such as "site," "settlement," and "landscape"; the analytical value of spatial patterning and the quantification of architectural and material distributions across sites, regions, and landscapes; central place theory; site-catchment analysis and, more recently, network analysis; and geographical information systems (GIS) technology as a tool for identifying spatial relationships.

Up until the 1970s archaeological research was conducted mostly at a regional scale and sought to determine environmental conditions in the past in order to reconstruct past landscapes and the impact of the natural environment on human behavior. A fundamental step was the emergence of settlement archaeology in the 1950s and of one of its offspring, household archaeology, in the 1970s. The latter owes much to the general archaeological self-criticism in the 1960s and the introduction of the New Archaeology (soon to become processual archaeology) by Lewis Binford (1962), which was influenced by the distinctively American thesis that archaeology is a form of anthropology. Attention shifted to intra- and intersettlement patterns and to smaller scales of analysis such as "household clusters," activity areas, and dwellings (Flannery and Winter 1976; Wilk and Rathje 1982). Under the influence of systems theory, functionalism, and positivism, which were predominant in the 1960s and 1970s, the objective was the investigation of the causal factors that determine the relationship between social organization and spatial patterning, particularly with respect to economy, in order to formulate explanatory models of sociocultural behavior. Up until the 1980s, landscapes, settlements, and other kinds of space were objects to be measured, analyzed, and compared via powerful statistical methods and distribution maps.

All this time, in anthropology, space and its taxonomies and classifications had a rather submerged presence. Space had more or less been taken for granted as a natural factor governing the set of actions, beliefs, and structures anthropologists have called "culture" and determining cultural differences or, within evolutionist thought, differences in cultural development (Gupta and Ferguson 1992; Hastrup and Olwig 1997). At the same time, it was assumed that spatial territory, society, and culture were strongly linked to each other. True, attempts for more differentiated approaches had appeared already in the early twentieth century, and since the 1950s cultural ecology provided a systematic framework for research concerning the relationship between culture and nature. However, the idea of culture as an objectified entity occupying a discrete space was maintained, and the role of space remained unquestioned. A good example is the study of kinship, a central domain of inquiry in anthropology since its founding and one in which all the major figures of anthropology up until the 1970s made their mark (for reviews, see Carsten 2000; Parkin and Stone 2004). Despite the fact that the analytical vocabulary of the study of kinship always involved notions and terms with clear spatial references such as "residence," "locality," "land," "domestic," and "public," space itself was viewed simply as a neutral container of social and political structures.

The 1980s and particularly the 1990s saw radical changes in the study of space in archaeology and anthropology, resulting from wider epistemological shifts and concerns, influenced by the postmodernist critique. In archaeology, postprocessualism emerged in Britain as a forceful critique of processual archaeology and positivism, advocating that meaning, history, subjectivity, and fluidity in interpretation be taken more into account. Space and human action were reconceptualized as mutually constituting one another in a constant dialectic. In anthropology, the postcolonial critique; self-reflexive discussions on fieldwork and ethnographic practice; the deconstruction of the assumed isomorphism of space, place, and culture; and new perspectives on globalization and locality all proposed "space" as a central notion.

The 1990s were the period of greatest apparent convergence of archaeology and anthropology. The new concept of the "built environment" was commonly employed to describe all products of human building activity, spatial topics proliferated, and the same range of research and theory in other social disciplines influenced anthropological and archaeological interpretations equally. Two broad groups of approaches can be distinguished—"cultural or ideational" and "social"—depending on the principles or aspects they emphasize. Cultural or ideational approaches focus on symbolism and metaphor as cultural phenomena, and a main point they make is that constructed space is inherently meaningful. They draw on a plethora of theoretical perspectives, most notably French structuralism, linguistics, modern philosophy (especially Bachelard 1964), and social and environmental psychology (e.g., Cooper 1974; Eliade 1954; Sanders 1990). Social approaches place the emphasis on the social processes that produce built space and on the dialectical relationship between the socially produced space and the reproduction of social order. Generally drawing on Marxism, they are closely associated with sociologists, geographers, architects, social historians, and political economists (Bourdieu 1977, 1990; Foucault 1975; Giddens 1984; King 1980; Pred 1985). Most influential have been the theories developed by Giddens and Bourdieu, both of which focus on the interaction between social structure and human agency and on the spatial dimension of action as central to an analysis of social practices. Elements of all these perspectives are present in almost all current archaeological and anthropological works. They are discussed in more detail in the following sections.

One would expect that the common focus on the meaningful role of space, along with the common influence by similar theoretical perspectives, would have brought archaeology and anthropology together into an effective dialogue. However, this is not the case. The flow between the two disciplines continues to be one-way. While the archaeology of space, place, and architecture has transformed itself repeatedly over the years, benefiting from ideas of social anthropology along the way, anthropology continues to pay limited attention to archaeological scholarship. Nonetheless, archaeological discussions of space reflect increasing awareness of the fluidity and permeability of analytical domains, as well as of the importance of co-relating the various converging themes and directions. Anthropology has also realized that political, ideological, and sociological factors enter into the use, signification, and understanding of so-called physical space and has reconceptualized cultural and social spaces as based on flows of people and locales. However, space has yet to be fully included in anthropology's interpretative practice. As pointed out by anthropologists (e.g., Kokot 2006, 10), its study exists through a collection of theories and through what anthropologists are attempting to elicit from a variety of categories, terms, and notions. The following discussion draws on the recent development of thought and elaborates on key issues and reasons critical to a closer interaction between archaeology and anthropology.

Multiple Spatial and Social Scales

A critical strength of archaeology is that it has access to multiple scales of space almost at the same time and therefore a great potential to examine social relations at different scales and their interlinkages. In addition, grounded on the spatial and material components of human history, this access extends well beyond the written records to the very first human societies and cultures. Thus, archaeology plays a critical role in documenting the full range of social and cultural variation, as well as in exploring different scales of interpretation.

Houses and Households

The microscale study of space, houses, and daily life is a most important and particularly rich focus of research in both archaeology and anthropology for the past three decades. In archaeology in the 1980s and 1990s there was a stark contrast between American-influenced processual (i.e., functionalist and economic) approaches to "space," "activity area," and houses as material correlates of the household, on the one hand (e.g., most papers in MacEachern, Archer, and Garvin 1989; and in Wilk and Rathje 1982), and British-influenced postprocessual (mostly symbolic and structuralist) approaches to the house as a meaningful entity and to "place" as a more cultural and emotive notion, on the other (e.g., most papers in Parker Pearson and Richards 1994). Recently, however, there is a growing interest in the social analysis of action and the conduct of everyday life, informed by concepts of agency, practice, structuration, and other elements of contemporary social theories. It has resulted in a burgeoning and promising literature on new patterns of social interaction at the small scale of everyday activities and on new questions of ideology and meaning, whether expressed materially or symbolically (e.g., Brumfiel and Robin 2008; Grove and Joyce 1999; Hodder 2005b; Kuijt 2000). There have also been important attempts to refine and unify analysis of the house or the domestic space with analysis of the household as a multidimensional social entity, possibly existing within different spatialities and certainly extending beyond dichotomies such as private/public and domestic/political (e.g., Hendon 2007; Souvatzi 2008b). Such questions show the influence of the social sciences. Feminist, Marxist, and Marxist-feminist scholarship, in particular, contributed considerably to the "deconstruction" of the family, household, or domestic group as a "natural" fact existing outside of the wider circumstances and to their incorporation back into the social and economic environment (e.g., Anderson, Bechhofer, and Gershuny 1994; Bourdieu 1996; Folbre 1986; Hart 1992; Hartmann 1981; Yanagisako 1979).

In anthropology Lévi-Strauss (1983, 1987) first stressed the theoretical and cultural significance of the house as a unit of social structure that integrates and objectifies a number of antagonistic principles. His concept of "house societies" has been taken up by a host of later scholars, who have explored, extended, or attempted to go beyond fields of his theory (e.g., Carsten and Hugh-Jones 1995; Joyce and Gillespie 2000). There have been revealing accounts of how the house can provide a metaphor for ontology, cosmology, landscape, and nonverbal communication (e.g., Blier 1987; Gudeman and Rivera 1990; Hugh-Jones 1995; Waterson 1990); how it interacts with the human body (e.g., Bloch 1995; Carsten 1995); and how it expresses and reproduces gender and kinship relations of power and authority and generally serves to inscribe social distinctions (e.g., Carsten 2004, 35–49; McKinnon 1995, 2000; Waterson 1995). Anthropological works on houses and house societies, however, have perhaps been a bit slow to move fully beyond structuralism or the prevalence of symbolic representation and toward a more actor-oriented approach. With notable exceptions (e.g., Marshall 2000; Pellow 2003; Pine 1996; Waterson 2000), the effect tends to be a rather inactive (and timeless) vision of the house as a rather static assemblage of meanings and metaphors. Gender is still often portrayed as a part of larger dualistic symbolic structures, while extra-domestic spaces and the interlinkages of the house with wider social, economic, and political scales and conditions are much less fully explored.

Four crucial things seem to need further investigation, and they all can be gained from archaeology: (a) "the materiality of the domestic" (Hendon 2007, 275), or how all these social conceptions are realized through the material world; (b) the historical and social construction of domestic space and of the distinctions and identities within and outside it (see next section); (c) the specific ways in which houses interact with each other and with the continually changing wider society within which they exist; and (d) an active vision of the house as a locus where social categories, norms, differences, or inequalities not only are reproduced but can also be contested and reversed. Actually, for conceptual and theoretical inspiration, anthropology can also look to itself and, in particular, to the rich corpus of theory and research on the household as a dynamic social entity constructed on a nexus of social, economic, and ritual everyday practices and relationships, with boundaries that are flexible and sociocultly wider than the more bounded notion of house (see Souvatzi 2008b, 7–20, for a review and references). In this sense households can also be of wider analytical applicability and comparative utility, across not only small-scale or "house societies" but also the rapidly changing postcolonial societies. It is surprising how little impact this discussion seems to have had on the anthropology of houses, certainly less so than on its archaeological counterpart.

Communities

Community is another important theme mutually used by anthropology and archaeology. Both disciplines have rejected earlier functionalist and behavioralist approaches to community as a stable, homogeneous, and territorially discrete collection of people sharing common culture and have reconceptualized it as generally a social entity with flexible boundaries, produced by competing discourses and representations.

In anthropology much of the relevant discussion results from the deconstructivist critique of the isomorphism of space, place, and culture, and the emergence of a bundle of new concepts: deterritorialization; borderlands; diaspora; global, transnational, and translocal spaces; and imagined (as opposed to "natural") communities (see Low and Lawrence-Zúñiga 2003a; Olwig and Hastrup 1997). These new conceptual frameworks attempt to capture the spatial transformations and cultural difference or hybridity produced by the global economy and cultural globalization, emphasizing in particular migration and the movement of people. Space is conceived as fluid and fragmented, and the critical spatial issues are the deterritorialization of culture and community; the increasing interconnectedness of places and people, based on different types of transnational and translocal relations and processes; and the dissolution of the conventional borders and nations. For example, Gupta (1992; also Gupta and Ferguson 1992, 9–13) shows how an assumed common history and the contiguous national borders of Europe are used to create a notion of an imagined transnational community. Ethnographic studies of traditional, small-scale societies have also shown that the space of a community and its perceptions by different interest and identity groups cannot be taken for granted.

The significance of reconceptualizing cultural spaces based on flows of people and locales, as well as of identifying the contradictions of territory, cultural and economic globalization, and modernity, is apparent. It has contributed, among other things, to the breaking down of the static concepts of core and periphery and has already informed archaeological studies, particularly of diasporic communities (see the following). Its potential, however, is tempered by an observed disparity between an overemphasis on deterritorialization and "the pulverization of space in high modernity" (Gupta and Ferguson 1992, 20) on the one hand and the heightened emphasis on the enduring significance of space as a useful analytical concept on the other. Put differently, in all these new approaches "space" enters into the picture in many different ways, but this has not resulted in an analytical theory of space. As anthropologists note, the rising popularity of these notions has not served to increase their analytical sharpness (Kokot 2006, 15), while the relationship between the "imagined community" and place, or how exactly space is *re*territorialized in the contemporary world, remains confusing (Gupta and Ferguson 1992, 20). In addition, the globalization/deterritorialization concept is not as all-encompassing and pervasive as is assumed, and, moreover, it does not allow for a consideration of the articulation of the global and the local scales or the *relational* nature of contemporary processes that take place across space (Low and Lawrence-Zúñiga 2003b, 26).

In archaeology, Yaeger and Canuto (2000, 5) offer exactly such a relational or interactional definition of community as a dynamic, "ever-emergent social institution that generates and is generated by interactions that are structured and synchronised by a set of places and within a particular span of time." Isbell (2000, 250) also points out that "while an 'imagined community' is socially produced in discourse, discourse is not independent of place." Thus, the spatial component of the community retains its significance as the set of physical venues for the repeated, meaningful interaction needed to create and maintain a community, and it is also actively incorporated within the analysis. In this way, even though archaeologists usually recover the static spatial and material remains of communities, they have moved beyond the earlier assumption that communities are equally static and the equation of settlements and regions with communities. Indeed, several archaeological communities have been shown to exist through multiple networks and spatial scales of interaction (e.g., Hare 2000; Yaeger 2000). Similarly, mobility, migration, cultural displacement or discontinuity, borderlands, and, generally, the constant movement of people, goods, and ideas are nothing new either to archaeology or to past societies, as myriad archaeological examples can attest and recent archaeological works on local border and diasporic communities further manifest (e.g., Blake 2007, 243–48; Goldstein 2000; Lilley 2007). They are, in fact, the norm in the history of humankind in any geographical location and any period of time. The only thing that changes in the contemporary world is their scale and rhythm. All this brings again to the fore the issue of scale and the importance of considering the interplay of multiple scales of space and time in the creation and maintenance of a community.

Landscapes

Landscape is yet another theme of the expanding discourse on space and a subject of renewed focus in archaeology and anthropology. In the recent Theoretical Archaeology Group 2010 conference in the United Kingdom, there were at least four sessions explicitly devoted to landscape—from urban to liminal and ritual landscapes—and one session assessing the analytical value of the many current-scape concepts. In anthropology reconceptualizations of landscape started out with the postmodernist critique contesting the very existence of the anthropological "field" as a site of ethnographic observation as well as the meaning of "space" overall. They resulted in a plethora of spatial metaphors—from "ethnoscapes" (Appadurai 1990) and "taskscapes" (Ingold 1993) to "simulacra" and "hyperspace" (Baudrillard 1988; Soja 1989) and "heterotopias" (Foucault 1971) to "locating" or "siting" culture (Low and Lawrence-Zúñiga 2003a; Olwig and Hastrup 1997). Tim Ingold's (1993) understanding of landscape as the number of activities through which people engaged with places as well as the history of those engagements remains one of the few anthropological attempts thus far to look to archaeology for inspiration and to provide a more holistic approach.

In the past twenty years landscape archaeology has explored the multiplicity of ways in which landscape is constructed, conceptualized, and contested in a wide array of geographical and temporal contexts—from the Paleolithic through to the contemporary world—deploying social theory from a range of sources, especially geography, architecture, Marxist thought, phenomenology, and various strands of practice and agency theories (Ashmore 2007; Ashmore and Knapp 1999). Useful research extends from the social and economic dimensions of land use (e.g., Earle 2000; Herrera 2007; Relaki and Catapoti forthcoming) to the range of meanings and sensory experience of landscapes (e.g., Barrett 2009; Tilley 1994), and from a focus on material features and deposits to conceptions of landscapes as records of power relations, social history, and social fragmentation (e.g., Bender 2001; Crumley 1994; Leone, Harmon, and Neuwirth 2005). For example, in his study of the changing landscape of Neolithic and Bronze Age southern Britain, Barrett (1994) suggests that sites of encounters between individuals, linked by paths, served as locales and that the repetition of those encounters and movements over long periods of time led to the development of the monumental Neolithic landscapes characterized by long barrows, enclosures, and cursuses.

All this research can inform anthropologists in many ways and directions, a most important one being the appreciation of the many spatial and temporal scales existing within any kind of landscape. A more concentrated engagement with the materialities of the landscape might also benefit anthropologists—for example, through the location and distribution of material resources; landmarks, monuments, and other symbolic markings; the circulation and long-distance exchange of material culture; and, generally, the material media of ideology and meaning attached to landscape.

Time, History, and Temporality

Space, place-making, and the built environment also incorporate historical, temporal, and transitional processes: continuity and change; shifts in location and type of different sites; disparities and contradictions between cultural ideals or dominant ideologies and actual practice; changing constructions of identities, meanings, and power; and constant interactions between perceptions of space in the short-term and longer-term changes. Issues of conceptualizing and addressing time in relation to space constitute one of the most apparent and greater strengths of archaeology. With the historical depth of its data and its capacity of witnessing the long-term sequence of events, archaeology is very well positioned to account for the dialectical relationship of space and time, histories of spatiality, and the transformation of space to place.

Contrary to what many anthropologists might believe, archaeology is not just obsessed with time, and time for archaeology is not just chronology or even just the long term. Archaeologists have problematized time repeatedly over the years, and there is a growing appreciation, as well as conceptual refinement, of different scales and rhythms of time. The notion of time as an external reality has been criticized as a Western cultural assumption, and, drawing on phenomenological philosophy, particularly Heidegger and Merleau-Ponty, the notion of temporality has recently been proposed as the lived experience of people with the world through both linear and recursive time, a kind of temporal relation to the world manifest at different timescales (Gosden 1994; Thomas 1996; also Bradley 1987; Hodder this volume). The perspective of history as an interacting set of temporal processes combining short-term events, medium-term cycles (or socioeconomic time), and long-term trajectories (or environmental time), advocated by Fernand Braudel (1973) and the *Annales* school, has proved particularly influential on archaeology but has not been taken up uncritically (e.g., Hodder 1987; Knapp 1992). Lastly, the long term is not the only concern of archaeologists, as the ever-growing literature on the microscale study of space and the day-to-day interactions in the shorter term (used in most anthropology) can attest.

Anthropologists have, of course, also problematized time and history. Bloch some time ago, in his study of kinship, reciprocity, and morality, underlined the importance of considering both the long-term and short-term relationships and the degree to which actions are set within longer-term "strategic" frameworks (Bloch 1973). Feuchtwang and Rowlands (2010), in their reevaluation of the long term, discuss ethnographic cases showing different and multiple conceptualizations of time and temporality and suggest a notion of "a history of temporalities" as a common field of inquiry for anthropology, archaeology, and history. According to Ingold (1993), temporality is neither chronology (as opposed to history) nor history (as opposed to chronology) but the unfolding of social life over both time and space. However, in most anthropology of space there is an underlying assumption that architecture fixes and stabilizes social relations—for example, through the repetition of spatial relationships and the representation of the social order. It can also be argued that anthropological research has dealt with social reproduction almost exclusively in the present and the very short term. Filippucci (2010, 70, 72), a social anthropologist, notes that despite the poststructuralist critique in anthropology and the call for a more historical outlook on culture and society, anthropology's take on social memory is characterized by a continuing presentism and functionalism, casting social memory as a construct in, of, and for the present. However, as she points out, "this way of conceptualising memory overlooks the intrinsic temporality of social practices" (p. 70). Indeed, the disconnection of the past from the present collapses the timescale to a state where all actions begin and end simultaneously. It therefore downplays the fact that real-life practices and relationships, and their inscriptions on space, have a variety of timescales and do not just exist outside history.

The current conceptualization of social memory in archaeology, with its focus on materiality and historical process, can serve as an example of what needs further attention in anthropology. Archaeological works have addressed the temporal dimension of social practices and the notions of time and memory in the past, including the "deep" past (e.g., Bradley 2002; Hodder 2006; Joyce 2000; Knapp 2009; Tringham 2000). Objects, buildings, monuments, settlements, and landscapes can all be enmeshed in strategies by which individuals, groups, and communities negotiate the construction of the past. They act as sites for the construction of social memory through the repetition of practices, the construction and use of buildings over time, and the transmission of social knowledge, as well as the transmission of the buildings themselves and of the objects associated with them. Overall, a substantial degree of social memory and symbolic meaning was invested in past sites, linking short-term everyday practices with long-term concepts and memories.

However, this does not mean that built space is simply a source of stability and of a representation of an unchanging past or meaning. It is also a vehicle for change and is itself enmeshed in historical processes. Tilley (1994) proposes a view of landscape as active and as both the medium for and the outcome of action and histories of action. Richards (2004) has suggested that in the monumental architecture of Neolithic Orkney, with its great henge-enclosed stone circles, the interplay between time, place, and architecture effectively fused lines of descent, images of the past, and social relations; brought a physicality to otherwise abstract social categories; and transformed the social world. Watkins (2005) also argues that the burst of architecture in the earliest Neolithic of southwestern Asia constituted "theatres of memory," a powerful frame of symbolic reference at multiple levels, which in turn stimulated significant developments toward a new way of living. A further archaeological inquiry on time relates to the increasing attention to the social dynamics of mobility, site discontinuity, abandonment, or deliberate destruction; the fissioning of communities; and the complex life histories of buildings (e.g., Cameron and Tomka 1993; Chang 2006; Matthews 2006; Peltenburg 1993; Souvatzi 2008b, 98–101, 228–29; Stevanović 1997). These studies have shown that the process of structuring and restructuring space was incessant and that the meanings and social relations associated with buildings, monuments, and landscapes were reconsidered and reinterpreted by each generation.

Another key to understanding the interrelationship of space and time is a view of architecture as process. Reliance on the assumption that architectural order is merely an expression of the social order tends to disregard the fact that the built environment represents the *gradual* and *collective* result of a number of people over spans of time. In her contribution to the panel, Rachel Harkness, an anthropologist, pointed out that the process of architecture and the temporal aspects of the built environment have gone largely unexplored in anthropology. She went on to argue that with its sights turned less toward the symbolic interpretation of given architectural forms, anthropology might have much more to contribute to a study of architecture as something in flux. In the British Neolithic, Barrett (1994) and Richards (2004) have suggested that it is the process of construction, rather than merely the completed form, that is crucial in creating a network of relationships, exchanges, and obligations between different people and at different times. In the Greek Neolithic the emphasis on the creation of a highly structured environment, including large-scale and labor-intensive undertakings such as multiple stone enclosures and large ditches surrounding or dividing settlements, has been interpreted as providing a frame for the continuous negotiation of power relations and social differences, as well as a material mnemonic of those transactions (Souvatzi 2008b, 158–59, 227–29). In small-scale and ethnographic societies, the process of construction can also be understood as the materialization of social institutions, the creation of stable lineages (Edmonds 1999), and the spatial mapping of different group genealogies (Richards 2004), and thus as a form of history. Conceptualized in this way, architecture provides not only a framework for social life but also a framework for human agency and a mechanism for enhancing social interaction.

Toward an Effective Dialogue

Space's many dimensions and levels of analysis give it the potential to be a theoretical and analytical interface of a host of mutually transformative themes, issues, and domains topical in contemporary social archaeology and anthropology, many of which have been presented here. Given also the shared concerns and shared theoretical influences between the two disciplines, space can surely induce complementary and reciprocal engagements from archaeologists and anthropologists, as well as serving to blur rigid disciplinary boundaries.

Anthropology can provide important insights into the different uses and meanings of space in the various contemporary societies and has already prompted archaeologists to rethink certain theories they may have built up concerning past societies. As Thomas (2010, 183) puts it, "Archaeology needs the help of anthropology to stimulate its curiosity" or "to know what to look for," particularly, I would add, on the small, everyday scale. Anthropology can also remind us that perceptions of social space are not automatically validated by time. But there is at least as much for anthropologists to learn from archaeologists. Archaeology has the unique ability to witness remarkable scales of space and time, as well as the long-term sequence of events. It can therefore expand considerably the knowledge of the diversity and multidimensionality of space, both synchronically and diachronically; provide insights into social and spatial practices that may no longer exist; and add a diachronic perspective to cultural and social transformations effected through space.

A main concern should be with issues of social agency and their articulation into a more comprehensive approach to space, spatiality, place-making, and architecture. Anthropology offers diverse theories for conceptualizing cultural spaces and for rethinking the global and the local, territory and deterritorialization. But the important contributions of much of this research have yet to be fully integrated into the analysis of space. Although there have been valuable attempts at theorization (e.g., see Hastrup and Olwig 1997; Low and Lawrence-Zúñiga 2003b), a fully formulated anthropological theory of social space or of culture and space does not seem to exist yet (Kokot 2006, 10). The continuing presence, even though implicit, of structuralism and functionalism in many anthropological works, particularly those on ethnographic societies and on houses, makes it very difficult to conceptualize space as a locus of action and contradiction. At the same time, "the analytic privileging of rupture and instability and focus on discourse and representation under the influence of postmodernism" (Shaw 2002, 9, quoted in Filippucci 2010, 72), particularly in the studies of global, transnational, and translocal spaces, has resulted in an assortment of notions and metaphors, which remain rather exploratory. Anthropology should focus more, I would argue, on the social definition of space and on the relationship between people and space as reciprocal and mutually constituting.

A most crucial requirement for both disciplines to this end is to recognize the importance of a multiscalar approach to both space *and* time that will allow for the interplays between the macro- and microlevels and will explore linkages between a whole range of spatial and temporal relationships. Anthropology has the potential strength to identify a nonlinear temporality (e.g., cyclical, ritual, and mythical time) and its differential impact on human involvement with space. However, it still requires accounts that are historically informed or that effectively acknowledge that space is a locus where the synchronic and the diachronic, the short term and the long term, conjoin or conflict. Archaeology's contribution is particularly crucial to an interpretative theory of social space as a dialectical, historical, and dynamic process. It is essential to realize that action, meaning, and agency, and their inscriptions on space, place, and architecture, do not exist in a historical vacuum. All practices, relationships, and transformations are intrinsically temporal and historically contingent. Cultural diversity and differences, a long-standing concern of anthropology, also are historically constituted. When we reduce them to exogenous factors, or when we view them through a set of dichotomies (as opposed to contradictions), or when we "flatten the past into the present" (Filippucci 2010, 72), we trivialize three key issues: the socially and *historically* specific structure and its interaction with human agency, the importance of relationship over structure, and the dialectics between space and time. Lastly, it should also be clear that there is a difference between choice and acceptance of the wider sociocultural and economic circumstances facing agents, and often between the motives and the effects of action, and therefore that space is constructed by as much as it constructs and reconstructs any social environment.

The relationship between the past and the present has always been a point of debate between anthropologists and archaeologists (e.g., Feuchtwang and Rowlands 2010; Filippucci 2010; Gosden 1999, 167–71; Thomas 2010, 181–83). Here I only wish to express my agreement with the archaeological position that past and present coexist in many ways and on many levels, and there is no gap to be bridged between them (cf. Preucel and Meskell 2007, 10). For example, in anthropology, Filippucci (2010) argues that social memory can cohere around past things even if these are being encountered for the first time. Indeed, all over the world, scenes, spaces, and memories from past cultures were preserved and transmitted over hundreds or thousands of years, materially substantiating the past and offering at the same time an ideal framework for its continuous construction in the present. It is this "afterlife of monuments" (Bradley 1987) and sites that creates a long-term significance of particular places and that, in turn, makes them important themes of the current archaeological and anthropological inquiries into cultural heritage (see the following).

A multiscalar approach to space and time is also crucial for observing and understanding social and cultural variability both synchronically and diachronically and, beyond that, some of the factors that produce it. Archaeological narratives of long-term structural changes usually lack a sense of small-scale variability and its meaning and consequences. But anthropological accounts of the short term also lack a sense of larger spatiotemporal forces. They both need to replace the single focus on one analytical scale with a consideration of the subtlety and variety of social processes on various scales.

In my own work on households in Neolithic Greece (ca. 6800–3300 B.C.E.) (Souvatzi 2008b; also Souvatzi 2008a, forthcoming), I have attempted to move between different scales of space and time in order to examine the entire range of variation in how households organized their daily lives, promoted their goals, and expressed their identities, as well as in how they interacted with each other, with other social institutions, and with the wider social landscape. The spatial, material, symbolic, and social components of practices and relationships indicated that different degrees of variation exist at different spatial and temporal levels, and that the significance of variation depends on context, articulation, and meaning. For instance, with reference to social identity I have found that the material and spatial means through which identities were produced in Neolithic Greece can retain a double meaning of both individual differentiation and collective identification through different manipulation at different scales, contexts, and times. For example, miniature clay house models, anthropomorphic figurines, heads of animals (actual or clay), and fine decorated pottery found in houses were part of domestic rituals, intended to define households as individual groups and to emphasize metaphorically their social and economic importance. However, the same material classes were also found deposited in large communal spaces in central locations within settlements, usually in successive and burnt layers or floors, indicating a repeated practice over considerable spans of time. They apparently represent collective rituals, most likely cycles of ritual and collective discard (if not also deliberate destruction by fire), intended to balance competing positions and identities and to generate and regenerate a dominant ethos of collectivity. Similarly, the considerable architectural uniformity in elements seen from the outside, including highly structured settlement layouts and common construction techniques and orientation of the buildings, suggests the use of architecture for the mediation of collectively accepted principles of identity. It contrasts greatly with a complete lack of conformity in house interiors, which suggests that individual groups promoted their own identities that would have partly counteracted collective standards.

The important implication is that definitions of identity and the meaning ascribed to things and practices change at different scales of space and time, in a process containing the potential for both domination of and resistance to stable forms of social identification. Interestingly, there is no consistent evidence that any of these elements consolidated over time into some stable or single image of identity, focused on the individual or the collective. Identities remained fluid, transient, and susceptible to contestation for thousands of years. Thus, rather than a reified social structure, identity and its creation were a target for achievement and maintenance as well as for transformation.

A final note concerns the nature of the archaeological and anthropological evidence and, in particular, the supposed inability of the archaeological inanimate material traces to stand up to the requirements of a "proper" understanding of sociospatial dynamics, compared to the testimony of animate social beings available in anthropology. Surprisingly, such a comment, echoing Leach's views on the limitations of archaeological data made over thirty years ago (see Thomas 2010, 179–80), was made again by an anthropologist from the panel's audience. It is significant that the response was undertaken by other anthropologists, contributors and attendees alike, rather than by archaeologists. Indeed, the postcolonial critique of anthropology and the reflexive anthropological discussions on fieldwork, ethnographic practice, thick descriptions, and deep understanding have indicated that accounts of social and cultural reality can be as incomplete and absenting of people in anthropology as they may be in archaeology (e.g., see the discussion in Filippucci 2010 and Strathern 2010, 174–75). The construction of otherness in anthropological writing can also be as partial as the archaeological reconstruction of the past; the duration of participant observation is relatively limited, whereas "the idea of an 'informant' [may be] a holdover from a colonialist-era anthropology" (Preucel and Mrozowski 2010b, 9). Besides, as McFayden (2010, 41) argues, social archaeology understands itself as the study of past people, not just of objects in their own right, and there is nothing negative in the ways in which social archaeologists get to know past people.

In short, little is gained by contrasting the validity of our respective data, when we should instead question the validity of our models and approaches. The real challenge lies not in the kinds of archaeological or anthropological evidence but in the kinds of questions we ask of it. Although neither discipline may be able to capture the finer points of the complexity of social reality, past and present, social reality has spatial and material components that can be traced in both the archaeological and anthropological data. It is precisely the materiality, spatiality, temporality, historicity, and specificity of the social production of space and time that create links between place, people, things, and practices and that connect them to key social phenomena. And it is primarily in this way that space can serve as a common frame of reference, a point of dialogue between archaeology and anthropology.

The 2009 ASA Conference Panel on Space, Place and Architecture, and Future Possibilities

The aim of the panel was to bring together anthropologists and archaeologists into a discussion of disciplinary and interdisciplinary views, experiences and case studies on the issue of space, and their implications and consequences. It included eleven papers by anthropologists and archaeologists, as well as one ethnographic film (by Borelli). The contributions addressed key theoretical and analytical issues and covered a wide range of geographical and temporal settings, from the prehistoric Mediterranean to contemporary Africa.

Regarding theory, several papers pointed out that we should not neglect to explore the insights from other disciplines, including the work of the French philosopher Henri Lefebvre on the production of space, whose potential has already been explored in architecture and urban studies (Hadji); geography, particularly on the scale of the city and urban space (Adams); phenomenology in relation to the body and bodily experience among the built environment (Rahmeier); and environmental art theory in understanding the creation of urban space and culture (TenWolde). Prominent themes included the importance of understanding architecture as a process through which people create and re-create world and self (Borelli; Hadji; Harkness; TenWolde); memory, identity, and the process of transformation of space into place (Andrews; Borelli; Donnellan; TenWolde; Vale); embodied space (Rahmeier; Vale); domestic architecture and space (Andrews; Merlo, Rodgers, and Seone; Rahmeier; Vale); urban space and planning, from prehistoric cities to modern urbanization (Adams; Donnellan; Hadji; Harkness; TenWolde); and indigenous understandings of heritage, tradition, and modernization and the creation of multiple histories of space (Borelli; Merlo, Rodgers, and Seone).

In all, several of the diverse approaches to and meanings of space were intriguingly outlined and new avenues for thought and research identified. For example, embodied space, including the material, representational, spatial, and experiential aspects of body space and spatial orientation and movement, is a focal point of research in anthropology and archaeology (e.g., Baxter 2006; Jones 2005; Joyce 2005; Low 2000, 154–79; Munn 2003; see also Duncan 1996 for perspectives from geography). Similarly, urban space and planning, and along with them attention to boundaries, borderlands, and diasporas, are a burgeoning field in both disciplines, as noted earlier.

It is also significant that most contributions were concerned with the appeal of our disciplinary debates and practices to wider public. Indeed, a most promising common direction is emerging from the growing concern over the public impact and social relevance of archaeology and anthropology: the politics of the past and the present with reference to sites, places, landscapes, monuments, and communities, through what is variously called "culture or heritage industry," "public culture," "tourist consumption," and "mass communication" (e.g., see discussion and papers in Preucel and Mrozowski 2010a, 423–617; and in Low and Lawrence-Zúñiga 2003a, 351–407; also Herzfeld's and Meskell's contributions to this volume). It has already led to more sophisticated understandings of the objectification of spaces for the deliberate construction of heritage and the past, as well as of site preservation and representational strategies aimed at promoting and attracting tourism.

Similarly, the reconceptualization of the relation between space and cultural difference offers a new perspective on recent debates surrounding issues of ethics and social justice. It has resulted inter alia in an appreciation of the importance of "multilocality" and "multivocality" (Appadurai 1988; Rodman 2003) and of indigenous concepts of landscape and community and meanings of space. Heterotopian, utopian, and imagined communities; the creation of "authentic" landscapes for tourism and the promotion of certain sites and landscapes; local social movements against spatial changes effected to promote to tourism; and "cultural sites" as loci of conflict are further themes of current inquiry on space in archaeology and anthropology. They can all encourage us to contemplate more effectively the refashioning of space combined with the reordering of reality as well as our participation in it.

In conclusion, archaeology and anthropology have a lot to gain from an effective dialogue. They can work together toward a fuller understanding of different scales of space and time, without compromising their different disciplinary identities, experiences, data, or methodologies. As Strathern (2010, 175) writes, "The kinds of accounts each discipline produces is as fragmentary *as* the other: but not *in relation* to the other." Such interaction promises to yield unique insights not only into space but also into the complexity and variety of social life as a whole. It requires more systematic theoretical self-reflection and a mutual willingness to break down artificial barriers and traditional contrasts and to explore new paths of ideas and interpretation.

Notes

1. The panel was entitled "Space, Place, Architecture: A Major Meeting Point between Social Anthropology and Archaeology?" and was organized by the present

author together with Demetra Papaconstantinou. Contributors came from both anthropology and archaeology and included the following (in alphabetical order): Ellen Adams; Peter Alford Andrews; Caterina Borelli; Lieve Donnellan; Athena Hadji; Rachel Harkness; Stefania Merlo, Mompoloki Rodgers, and Malebogo Seone; Clarissa Rahmeier; Christopher TenWolde; and Ana Vale. I thank them all, as well as the many attendants, for the enthusiasm and lively discussions. The results and implications from the panel are presented at the end of this chapter.

References

Anderson, M., F. Bechhofer, and J. Gershuny. 1994. "Introduction." In *The social and political economy of the household*, ed. M. Anderson, F. Bechhofer, and J. Gershuny, 1–16. Oxford: Oxford University Press.

Appadurai, A. 1988. "Introduction: Place and voice in anthropological theory." *Cultural Anthropology* 3 (1): 16–20.

Appadurai, A. 1990. "Disjunction and difference in the global cultural economy." *Public Culture* 2: 1–24.

Ashmore, W. 2007. "Social archaeologies of landscape." In Meskell and Preucel 2007, 255–71.

Ashmore, W., and B. Knapp, eds. 1999. *Archaeologies of landscape: Contemporary approaches*. Oxford: Blackwell.

Bachelard, G. 1964. *The poetics of space*. New York: Orion.

Barrett, J.C. 1994. *Fragments from antiquity: An archaeology of social life in Britain, 2900–1200 BC*. Oxford: Blackwell.

Barrett, J.C. 2009. "A phenomenology of landscape: A crisis in British landscape archaeology?" *Journal of Social Archaeology* 9 (3): 275–94.

Baudrillard, J. 1988. *Selected writings*, ed. M. Poster. Palo Alto, CA: Stanford University Press.

Baxter, J.E. 2006. "Making space for children in archaeological interpretations." *Archaeological Papers of the American Anthropological Association* 15: 77–88.

Bender, B. 2001. "Landscapes on-the-move." *Journal of Social Archaeology* 1: 75–89.

Binford, L. 1962. "Archaeology as anthropology." *American Antiquity* 28: 217–25.

Blake, E. 2007. "Space, spatiality, and archaeology." In Meskell and Preucel 2007, 230–54.

Blier, S. 1987. *The anatomy of architecture: Ontology and metaphor in Batammaliba architectural expression*. Cambridge: Cambridge University Press.

Bloch, M. 1973. "The long term and the short term: The economic and political significance of the morality of kinship." In *The character of kinship*, ed. J. Goody, 75–87. Cambridge: Cambridge University Press.

Bloch, M. 1995. "The resurrection of the house among the Zafiminary of Madagascar." In Carsten and Hugh-Jones 1995, 69–83.

Bourdieu, P. 1977. *Outline of a theory of practice*. Cambridge: Cambridge University Press.

Bourdieu, P. 1990. *The logic of practice*. Cambridge, UK: Polity.

Bourdieu, P. 1996. "On the family as a realised category." *Theory, Culture and Society* 13: 19–26.

Bradley, R. 1987. "Time regained—the creation of continuity." *Journal of the British Archaeological Association* 140: 1–17.

Bradley, R. 2002. *The past in prehistoric societies*. London: Routledge.

Braudel, F. 1973. *The Mediterranean and the Mediterranean world in the age of Philip II*. London: Collins.

Brumfiel, E., and C. Robin. 2008. "Gender, households and society: An introduction." *Archeological Papers of the American Anthropological Association* 18 (1): 1–16.

Cameron, C., and S. Tomka, eds. 1993. *Abandonment of settlements and regions: Ethnoarchaeological and archaeological approaches*. Cambridge: Cambridge University Press.

Canuto, M.A., and J. Yaeger, eds. 2000. *The archaeology of communities: A New World perspective*. London: Routledge.

Carsten, J. 1995. "The substance of kinship and heat of the hearth: Feeding, personhood, and relatedness among Malays of Pulau Langkawi." *American Ethnologist* 22: 223–41.

Carsten, J. 2000. "Introduction: Cultures of relatedness." In *Cultures of relatedness: New approaches to the study of kinship*, ed. J. Carsten, 1–36. Cambridge: Cambridge University Press.

Carsten, J. 2004. *After kinship*. Cambridge: Cambridge University Press.

Carsten, J., and S. Hugh-Jones, eds. 1995. *About the house: Lévi-Strauss and beyond*. Cambridge: Cambridge University Press.

Chang, C. 2006. "A tribute to Susan Kent's ethnoarchaeological studies on mobility: Ethnoarchaeological and archaeological studies of pastoral nomads in Greece and Kazakhstan." *Archaeological Papers of the American Anthropological Association* 16: 27–36.

Cooper, C. 1974. "The house as symbol of self." In *Designing for human behaviour*, ed. J. Lang, C. Burnett, W. Moleski, and C. Vachon, 130–46. Stroudsberg, PA: Dowden, Hutchinson and Ross.

Crumley, C.L. 1994. "Historical ecology: A multidimensional ecological orientation." In *Historical ecology: Cultural knowledge and changing landscapes*, ed. C.L. Crumley, 1–13. Santa Fe, NM: SAR Press.

Duncan, N., ed. 1996. *BodySpace: Destabilising geographies of gender and sexuality*. London and New York: Routledge.

Earle, T. 2000. "Archaeology, property and prehistory." *Annual Review of Anthropology* 29: 39–60.

Edmonds, M. 1999. *Ancestral geographies of the Neolithic: Landscapes, monuments and memory*. London: Routledge.

Eliade, M. 1954. *The myth of the eternal return: Or cosmos and history*. Princeton, NJ: Princeton University Press.

Feuchtwang, S., and M. Rowlands. 2010. "Re-evaluating the long term: Civilisation and temporalities." In Garrow and Yarrow 2010, 117–36.

Filippucci, P. 2010. "Archaeology and the anthropology of memory: Takes on the recent past." In Garrow and Yarrow 2010, 69–83.

Flannery, K. V., and M. Winter. 1976. "Analysing household activities." In *The early Mesoamerican village*, ed. K. V. Flannery, 34–47. New York: Academic Press.

Folbre, N. 1986. "Hearts and spades: Paradigms of household economics." *World Development* 14: 245–55.

Foucault, M. 1971. *The order of things: An archaeology of the human sciences*. New York: Pantheon Books.

Foucault, M. 1975. *Discipline and punish*. New York: Vintage Books.

Garrow, D., and T. Yarrow, eds. 2010. *Archaeology and anthropology*. Oxford: Oxbow Books.

Giddens, A. 1984. *The constitution of society: Outline of the theory of structuration*. Cambridge, UK: Polity.

Goldstein, P. S. 2000. "Communities without borders: The vertical archipelago and diaspora communities in the southern Andes." In Canuto and Yaeger 2000, 182–209.

Gosden, C. 1994. *Social being and time*. Oxford: Blackwell.

Gosden, C. 1999. *Anthropology and archaeology: A changing relationship*. London: Routledge.

Grove, D. C., and R. A. Joyce, eds. 1999. *Social patterns in the preclassic Mesoamerica*. Washington, DC: Dumbarton Oaks Research Library and Collection.

Gudeman, S., and A. Rivera. 1990. *Conversations in Colombia: The domestic economy in life and text*. Cambridge: Cambridge University Press.

Gupta, A. 1992. "The song of the nonaligned world: Transnational identities and the reinscription of space in late capitalism." *Cultural Anthropology* 7 (1): 63–79.

Gupta, A., and J. Ferguson. 1992. "Beyond 'culture': Space, identity and the politics of difference." *Cultural Anthropology* 7 (1): 6–23.

Hare, T. S. 2000. "Between the household and the empire: Structural relationships within and among Aztec communities and polities." In Canuto and Yaeger 2000, 78–101.

Hart, G. 1992. "Imagined unities: Constructions of the 'household' in economic theory." In *Understanding economic process*, ed. S. Ortiz and S. Lees, 111–29. Monographs in Economic Anthropology 10. Lanham, MD: University Press of America.

Hartmann, H. 1981. "The family as the locus of gender, class, and political struggle: The example of housework." *Signs: Journal of Women in Culture and Society* 6: 366–94.

Hastrup, K., and K.F. Olwig. 1997. "Introduction." In Olwig and Hastrup 1997, 1–15.

Hendon, J.A. 2007. "Living and working at home: The social archaeology of household production and social relations." In Meskell and Preucel 2007, 272–86.

Herrera, A. 2007. "Social landscapes and community identity: The social organisation of space in the north-central Andes." In *Socialising complexity: Approaches to power and interaction in the archaeological record*, ed. S.E. Kohring and S. Wynne-Jones, 161–82. Oxford: Oxbow Books.

Hodder, I. 1987. "The contribution of the long-term." In *Archaeology as long-term history*, ed. I. Hodder, 1–8. Cambridge: Cambridge University Press.

Hodder, I. 2005a. "An archaeology of the four-field approach in anthropology in the United States." In *Unwrapping the sacred bundle: Reflections on the discipline of anthropology*, ed. D.A. Segal and S.J. Yanagisako, 126–40. Durham, NC, and London: Duke University Press.

Hodder, I., ed. 2005b. *Changing materialities at Çatalhöyük: Reports from the 1995–99 seasons*. Cambridge and London: McDonald Institute for Archaeological Research/British Institute of Archaeology at Ankara Monograph.

Hodder, I. 2006. "Memory." In *Çatalhöyük perspectives: Themes from the 1995–99 seasons*, ed. I. Hodder, 183–95. Cambridge and London: McDonald Institute for Archaeological Research/British Institute of Archaeology at Ankara Monograph.

Hugh-Jones, S. 1995. "Inside-out and back-to-front: The androgynous house in Northwest Amazonia." In Carsten and Hugh-Jones 1995, 226–52.

Ingold, T. 1993. "The temporality of the landscape." *World Archaeology* 25 (2): 152–74.

Isbell, W.H. 2000. "What we should be studying: The 'imagined community' and the 'natural community.'" In Canuto and Yaeger 2000, 243–66.

Jones, A. 2005. "Lives in fragments? Personhood and the European Neolithic." *Journal of Social Archaeology* 5 (2): 193–224.

Joyce, R.A. 2000. "Heirlooms and houses: Materiality and social memory." In Joyce and Gillespie 2000, 189–212.

Joyce, R.A. 2005. "Archaeology of the body." *Annual Review of Anthropology* 34 (1): 139–58.

Joyce, R.A., and S.D. Gillespie, eds. 2000. *Beyond kinship: Social and material reproduction in house societies*. Philadelphia: University of Pennsylvania Press.

King, A.D. 1980. "A time for space and a space for time." In *Buildings and society: Essays of the social development of the built environment*, ed. A.D. King, 193–227. London: Routledge.

Knapp, B., ed. 1992. *Archaeology, annales and ethnohistory*. Cambridge: Cambridge University Press.

Knapp, B. 2009. "Monumental architecture, identity and memory." In *Proceedings of the Symposium: Bronze Age Architectural Traditions in the East Mediterranean: Diffusion and Diversity* (Gasteig, Munich, 7–8 May, 2008), 47–59. Weilheim, Germany: Verein zur Förderung der Aufarbeitung der Hellenischen Geschichte.

Kokot, W. 2006. "Culture and space—anthropological approaches." Paper presented at the Swiss Graduate Programme in Ethnology/Anthropology "Key Concepts in Social Anthropology," Basel, October 2006.

Kuijt, I., ed. 2000. *Life in Neolithic farming communities: Social organisation, identity and differentiation.* New York: Kluwer Academic/Plenum.

Leone, M. P., J. M. Harmon, and J. L. Neuwirth. 2005. "Perspective and surveillance in eighteenth-century Maryland Gardens, including William Paca's Garden on Wye island." *Historical Archaeology* 39 (4): 138–58.

Lévi-Strauss, C. 1983. *The way of the masks.* London: Jonathan Cape.

Lévi-Strauss, C. 1987. *Anthropology and myth: Lectures 1951–1982.* Oxford: Blackwell.

Lilley, I. 2007. "Diaspora and identity in archaeology: Moving beyond the black Atlantic." In Meskell and Preucel 2007, 287–312.

Low, S. 2000. *On the plaza: The politics of public space and culture.* Austin: University of Texas Press.

Low, S. M., and D. Lawrence-Zúñiga, eds. 2003a. *The anthropology of space and place: Locating culture.* Oxford and Malden, MA: Blackwell.

Low, S. M., and D. Lawrence-Zúñiga. 2003b. "Locating culture." In Low and Lawrence-Zúñiga 2003a, 1–47.

MacEachern, S., D.J.W. Archer, and R. Garvin, eds. 1989. *Households and communities.* Calgary, Canada: Chacmool.

Marshall, Y. 2000. "Transformations in Nuu-chah-nulth houses." In Joyce and Gillespie 2000, 73–102.

Matthews, W. 2006. "Life-cycle and life-course of buildings." In *Çatalhöyük perspectives: Themes from the 1995–99 seasons*, ed. I. Hodder, 125–49. Cambridge and London: McDonald Institute for Archaeological Research/British Institute of Archaeology at Ankara Monograph.

McFayden, L. 2010. "Spaces that were densely occupied—questioning 'ephemeral' evidence." In Garrow and Yarrow 2010, 40–52.

McKinnon, S. 1995. "Houses and hierarchy: The view from a South Moluccan society." In Carsten and Hugh-Jones 1995, 170–88.

McKinnon, S. 2000. "The Tanimbarese *Tavu*: The ideology of growth and the material configurations of houses and hierarchy in an Indonesian society." In Joyce and Gillespie 2000, 161–76.

Meskell, L., and R. W. Preucel, eds. 2007. *A companion to social archaeology.* Oxford and Malden, MA: Blackwell. (Orig. pub. 2004.)

Munn, N. 2003. "Excluded spaces: The figure in the Australian Aboriginal landscape." In Low and Lawrence-Zúñiga 2003a, 92–109. (Orig. pub. 1996.)

Olwig, K. F., and K. Hastrup, eds. 1997. *Siting culture: The shifting anthropological object*. London: Routledge.

Parker Pearson, M., and C. Richards, eds. 1994. *Architecture and order: Approaches to social space*. London: Routledge.

Parkin, R., and L. Stone, eds. 2004. *Kinship and family: An anthropological reader*. Oxford: Blackwell.

Pellow, D. 2003. "The architecture of female seclusion in west Africa." In Low and Lawrence-Zúñiga 2003a, 160–83.

Peltenburg, E. 1993. "Settlement discontinuity and resistance to complexity in Cyprus, ca. 4500–2500 BC." *Bulletin of the American School of Oriental Research* 292: 9–23.

Pine, F. 1996. "Naming the house and naming the land: Kinship and social groups in highland Poland." *Journal of the Royal Anthropological Institute* 2: 443–59.

Pred, A. 1985. "The social becomes the spatial, the spatial becomes the social: Enclosures, social change and the becoming of places in Skane." In *Spatial relations and spatial structures*, ed. G. Derek and J. Urry, 337–65. New York: St. Martin's.

Preucel, R. W., and L. Meskell. 2007. "Knowledges." In Meskell and Preucel 2007, 3–22.

Preucel, R. W., and S. A. Mrozowski, eds. 2010a. *Contemporary archaeology in theory: The new pragmatism*. Oxford and Malden, MA: Wiley-Blackwell.

Preucel, R. W., and S. A. Mrozowski. 2010b. "The new pragmatism." In Preucel and Mrozowski 2010a, 3–49.

Relaki, M., and D. Catapoti, eds. Forthcoming. *An archaeology of land ownership*. London: Routledge.

Richards, C. 2004. "A choreography of construction: Monuments, mobilisation and social organisation in Neolithic Orkney." In *Explaining social change: Studies in honour of Colin Renfrew*, ed. J. Cherry, C. Scarre, and S. Shennan, 103–13. Cambridge, UK: McDonald Institute for Archaeological Research.

Rodman, M. C. 2003. "Empowering place: Multilocality and multivocality." In Low and Lawrence-Zúñiga 2003a, 204–23. (Orig. pub. 1992.)

Sanders, D. 1990. "Behavioural conventions and archaeology: Methods for the analysis of ancient architecture." In *Domestic architecture and the use of space: An interdisciplinary cross-cultural study*, ed. S. Kent, 43–72. Cambridge: Cambridge University Press.

Shaw, R. 2002. *Memories of the slave trade: Ritual and the historical imagination in Sierra Leone*. Chicago and London: University of Chicago Press.

Soja, E. W. 1989. *Postmodern geographies: The reassertion of space in critical social theory*. London: Verso.

Souvatzi, S. 2008a. "Household dynamics and variability in the Neolithic of Greece: The case for a bottom-up approach to past societies." In *Living well together: Settlement and materiality in the Neolithic of south-east and central Europe*, ed. D. W. Bailey, A. Whittle, and D. Hofmann, 17–27. Oxford: Oxbow Books.

Souvatzi, S. 2008b. *A social archaeology of households in Neolithic Greece: An anthropological approach*. Cambridge and New York: Cambridge University Press.

Souvatzi, S. Forthcoming. "Between the individual and the collective: Household as a social process in Neolithic Greece." In *Household archaeology: New perspectives from the Near East and beyond*, ed. B.J. Parker and C.P. Foster. Winona Lake, IN: Eisenbrauns.

Stevanović, M. 1997. "The age of clay: The social dynamics of house destruction." *Journal of Anthropological Archaeology* 16: 334–95.

Strathern, M. 2010. "Commentary: Boundary objects and asymmetries." In Garrow and Yarrow 2010, 171–78.

Thomas, J. 1996. *Time, culture and identity: An interpretative archaeology*. London: Routledge.

Thomas, J. 2010. "Commentary: Walls and bridges." In Garrow and Yarrow 2010, 179–84.

Tilley, C. 1994. *A phenomenology of landscape: Places, paths and monuments*. Oxford: Berg.

Tringham, R. 2000. "The continuous house: A view from the deep past." In Joyce and Gillespie 2000, 115–34.

Waterson, R. 1990. *The living house: An anthropology of architecture in Southeast Asia*. Oxford: Oxford University Press.

Waterson, R. 1995. "Houses and hierarchies in island Southeast Asia." In Carsten and Hugh-Jones 1995, 47–68.

Waterson, R. 2000. "House, place and memory in Tana Toraja (Indonesia)." In Joyce and Gillespie 2000, 177–88.

Watkins, T. 2005. "Architecture and 'theatres of memory' in the Neolithic of southwest Asia." In *Rethinking materiality: The engagement of mind with the material world*, ed. E. DeMarrais, C. Gosden, and C. Renfrew, 97–106. Cambridge, UK: McDonald Institute for Archaeological Research.

Wilk, R.R., and W.L. Rathje, eds. 1982. "Archaeology of the household: Building a prehistory of domestic life." *American Behavioural Scientist* 25:617–40.

Yaeger, J. 2000. "The social construction of communities in the Classic Maya countryside: Strategies of affiliation in western Belize." In Canuto and Yaeger 2000, 123–42.

Yaeger, J., and M.A. Canuto. 2000. "Introducing an archaeology of communities." In Canuto and Yaeger 2000, 1–15.

Yanagisako, S. 1979. "Family and household: The analysis of domestic groups." *Annual Reviews of Anthropology* 8: 161–205.

Yarrow, T. 2010. "Not knowing as knowledge: Asymmetry between archaeology and anthropology." In Garrow and Yarrow 2010, 13–27.

–11–

Encountering the Past: Unearthing Remnants of Humans in Archaeology and Anthropology

Paola Filippucci, John Harries, Joost Fontein,
and Cara Krmpotich

Introduction

Among the many areas of interest shared by archaeology and anthropology is the study of human bones. This was so from the very organization and inception of these two fields as allied if distinct academic disciplines. Bones and what people did with bones were (and are) thought to reveal much about the very nature and quality of what it is to be human and how we, as humans, inhabit the world. Thus bones were foundational to the constitution of a science of "man." When viewed within a greater ritual context, they are also thought to reveal much about how people inhabit a meaningful world, a world situated between life and death, the seen and the unseen, the past, present, and future.

Although some of the cruder approaches to describing human diversity from the form and capacity of crania have, rightly, fallen out of favor, this shared interest in bones and, in particular, how the living think about, feel about, and interact with bones of the dead persists and continues to animate both anthropological and archaeological scholarship. Despite this shared interest and heritage, however, there has been a comparative lack of conversation between these two disciplines concerning the significance of bone and its social and cultural elaboration. There has been some mutual influence. Anthropological studies of death (Bloch and Parry 1982) and the material articulations and disarticulations of personhood (Strathern 1999) have, in particular, informed archaeological interpretations of funerary assemblages (Fahlander and Oestigaard 2008; Fowler 2001; Graham 2009; McGregor 2008). Social and cultural anthropologists have been less aware of archaeological writings concerning the symbolic efficacy of the materiality of the body. This may reflect what has been described as the "tyranny of the subject" (Miller 2005, 36): a persistent bias against the study of things and stuff in sociocultural anthropology (Buchli 2002). Without their living interlocutors, the material assemblages that are so "vocal" in archaeological research are too often considered mute by anthropologists. In the last decade, a growing body of diverse scholarship on "materiality" and "material culture" has gone some way toward redressing this balance (Buchli 2002; Farquhar and Locke 2007; Miller 2005).

This article is an "anthropological" contribution to what is, as the Association of Social Anthropologists (ASA) conference and this volume attests, an emergent dialogue between archaeology and anthropology, a dialogue in which anthropologists (which the authors all are by training) may do well by being more attentive to what our colleagues in archaeology are doing and writing. This is part of a larger project that seeks to draw together an interdisciplinary network of scholars (including both archaeologists and anthropologists), artists, and activists, interested in some way or another in human bones.[1] Through a series of events, including a panel at the ASA, and correspondences, we have sought to map a common ground to explore and interrogate the affective quality of bones and their various forms of cultural articulation (cf. Krmpotich, Fontein, and Harries 2010). In so doing we have returned again and again to the sensuous presence of bones and, in particular, to their "unearthing" (literal or figurative): those curious and sometimes uneasy moments when, by intention or accident, human remains reemerge, fleetingly or more persistently, to enter social circulation, calling forth emotions, responses, and elaborations.

Unearthing is a particularly useful concept on which to situate an interdisciplinary dialogue concerning human remains for a couple of reasons. Literally, of course, archaeologists are diggers,[2] uncovering the remnants of past lives that lie beneath the surface of the present. More figuratively, we all are in the business of uncovering and bringing into visibility that which is hidden, obscured, or unarticulated. Academics are by no means alone in this. In France, farmers unearth bones of the war dead as they plough their fields (M. Brown 2007; Filippucci 2004). In Zimbabwe, spirit mediums and veterans of the anticolonial struggle unearth graves of their fallen comrades, demanding that state archaeologists follow suit (Fontein 2009). In Spain, organizations devoted to remembrance and reconciliation unearth the remains of the civil war dead (Renshaw 2010). From museum storerooms in North America and the United Kingdom, the Haida unearth the bones of their ancestors (Bell and Collison 2006; Krmpotich 2010). In Newfoundland, some boys playing baseball unearth the skull of a man who becomes, with due attention and scholarship, a Beothuk (Harries 2010). So it goes. The hard, enduring remains of bodies find their way, or are dragged, into visibility and into our public cultures of heritage, commemoration, and reconciliation (Domańska 2005; Ferrándiz 2005; Harrison 2004; Petrović-Šteger 2009; Verdery 1999).

The second reason for focusing on the unearthing of bones is that it puts the emphasis on our sensuous encounter with human remains and the affective qualities of this encounter. These times when bones come into visibility are moments situated in the tension between the inchoate presence of some*thing* and the cultural articulation of that thing as an object and/or subject. Unearthing is not simply an ideational process by which we make "sense" of the past, though it is certainly indivisible from projects that are often animated by, or indeed direct, the unearthing of bones. Unearthing is also a transformative and relational material process of becoming, involving soil, hands, trowels and brushes, and bones (as well as other objects that may be uncovered), through which the flow of human materials with other substances is arrested and channeled, so that human remains are temporarily stabilized into recognizable objects and the work of cultural elaboration can begin. It can involve steel storage cabinets, Coroplast boxes, layers of acid-free tissue, and cotton- or nitrile-gloved hands. It is a process of becoming by which the traces of past lives are reconstituted and come to assert an ambivalent quality of felt presence, which has the capacity to unsettle the here and now, with an indeterminate alterity as the plowing stops or the baseball game is abandoned.

What has struck us is how central this quality of felt presence, indivisible from the materiality of unearthing, is to the practice of archaeology. Of course, it is not only in archaeology that people uncover stuff that unsettles them, that brings about the uncanny feeling of the nearness of past lives, but certainly the authors have heard of, or experienced, enough instances of archaeologists (or forensic anthropologists) having their work temporarily arrested by some material juxtaposition—a piece of hair still clinging to bone, an everyday object among the detritus of violence—to argue that this affective quality of presence, this "force of things" (Bennett 2004), inhabits and animates our academic undertakings, even as it may be marginalized or occluded by them.

This paper, then, sketches the grounds for a theorization of the unearthing of human remains as a relational practice by which we encounter the past in our material engagement with the environment. Such a theorization draws on and engages both anthropological and archaeological scholarship and offers areas in which these traditions of study may enter into a dialogue concerning the affective presence and emotive materiality of bones.

This sketch begins with a consideration of how social and cultural anthropologists and archaeologists have approached the study of human remains and, in particular, the physicality, or materiality, of human remains. We then introduce recent theorizations of the agency of things, the properties of materials, and the affective qualities of our sensuous relationship with things and substances in order to develop an analytic of unearthing that elaborates the notion of the affective presence of bones as being at once insufficient for, and in excess of, their constitution as social objects.

Anthropologists, Archaeologists, and Human Remains

Anthropologists have been interested in practices and beliefs surrounding human remains from the very beginning of the modern discipline, viewing the time of death as a central moment in the life of society, a key rite of passage for the collective as well as for the individual and his or her closest associates (Bloch and Parry 1982; Hertz 1960; Humphreys and King 1981; Huntington and Metcalf 1980). The main focus of the anthropology of death has been on rituals and beliefs, and, starting from the seminal work of Hertz (1960), the manipulation of attitudes toward human remains after death has been studied as profoundly symbolic aspects of behavior, revealing, affirming, or creating core values and beliefs about the nature of society, of personhood, and of time (Battaglia 1990; Bloch 1971; C. Jackson 1977). The parallel, theorized by Hertz, between the treatment of the corpse and the fate of the soul inaugurated an approach to the human body that sees it primarily as a symbolic entity, a metaphor of society (Douglas 1966), and, more recently, an entity "symbolically constructed" by culture, shaped and imagined in relation to culturally variable concepts of personhood (Strathern 1988; Turner 1984). In this perspective, the physicality of "the body" and, specifically, of human remains has been sidelined (cf. Hallam, Hockey, and Howarth 1999). Even approaches that have critiqued a purely symbolic understanding of the body and have sought to combine materiality and representation through theories of "embodiment" (Csordas 1994), the "unbounded person" (Bloch 1988), or "social bodies" (Lambert and McDonald 2009) still tend to focus on the subjective (or intersubjective) apprehension of the physical. However, the materiality of dead bodies, and of bodily substances, while subjectively or intersubjectively apprehended by survivors, also arguably has "object" qualities, insofar as these lack consciousness.

More attention to the object-like physicality of human remains is found in archaeology. Human remains have been a focus of archaeological interest from the very beginnings of the discipline, as key sources of evidence about past people and lifeways (McGuire 1992; Parker Pearson 1999; H. Williams 2003). As Parker Pearson puts it, remains of the dead are central to "the archaeology of life." Buried bodies provide clues about the life of the deceased individual (age, sex, nutritional and disease patterns, and, through the study of attire and burial goods, gender, social status, and other aspects of social and cultural identity) but also, importantly, about the lives of the people who buried them. Accordingly, the analysis of the burial complex as an item of material culture enables archaeologists to reconstruct past rituals and beliefs (Parker Pearson 1999, 3). The study of past mortuary practice in archaeology draws heavily on ethnographic analogy and on social anthropological theorizations about funerary rites, ritual in general, and the body to interpret the material form, location, and contents of ancient burials and monuments as clues to past social orders, hierarchies, and identities (Parker Pearson 1999; Semple and H. Williams 2007; Tarlow 1999; H. Williams 2003).

At the same time, unlike anthropology, archaeology also studies the human remains themselves, in their physical sense, through a specialized branch of the discipline, osteology, that applies to human remains techniques and methods similar to those used to record and study items of material culture: cataloguing, photographing, measuring (Swain 2002). As Sofaer (2006, xiii) notes, osteology classically analyzes human remains from a science-based perspective, focusing on skeletons and other remains as natural, biological objects.[3] The aim of such analyses is to establish the sex and age of the deceased and to derive any available information about disease and nutrition (Chamberlain and Parker Pearson 2001). This approach attends to the physicality of remains, but, for Sofaer, typically this is not fully incorporated into wider archaeological analysis. She argues that once osteological analysis has established sex and age and perhaps disease and nutritional information, the archaeologist moves on toward a "search for social meaning" that leaves the skeletal body behind, using it merely "as a means of underpinning interpretations rather than as a source for generating them" (Sofaer 2006, 2). For Sofaer, archaeological analyses of buried bodies draw on social scientific theorizations of the body that focus on discourse and representation and on the living subject, moving away entirely from the objectivity of the body as a physical entity. She notes that the study of what she calls "archaeological bodies" is dogged by a series of dichotomies: inside (skeletal body)/outside (fleshed body), dead/living, object/subject, science/social science, and ultimately nature/culture (p. 31). Sofaer argues that these polarities should be overcome in order to "deal effectively with the specifically archaeological nature of the body as physically present but lifeless" (p. 41).

The alternative proposed is to study bodies "as material culture." By this Sofaer means, first, that the body, *including* skeletons, should be seen as *physically* shaped and molded by culture, through the mechanical force of habitual action and behavior as well as conscious bodily modifications, and also through cultural patterns of nutrition that in turn can lead to particular types of disease, and so on. Second, she argues that the body in an archaeological setting is material culture because it lacks clear boundaries: (mostly) lacking skin, it may be disaggregated accidentally or on purpose, so that "the point at which the body ends is indistinct, merging with the grave, objects and contexts which surround it" (Sofaer 2006, 49). The grave "envelops the body" and "is itself a form of material culture" so that it is questionable "where the boundary between the person and the material culture is" (p. 50). In this sense the archaeological body is "between nature and culture" (p. 55).

Archaeology in combination with osteology thus teaches anthropologists to take into account the physicality of human remains. Sofaer's work is particularly useful in suggesting that keeping a focus on the material does not mean losing sight of the cultural—as she advocates not splitting the two and uses the term *material culture* to do this. But does Sofaer's idea of the body as material culture fully account for the materiality of buried human remains? Archaeologists especially have begun to express the idea that human remains unsettle scientific practice by triggering responses that are quite unlike those elicited by other material culture, or indeed by nonhuman bones (Fontein 2009, 22–23). For instance, in a recent volume about archaeological encounters with "human mortality" (Downes and Pollard 1999), human osteologists Kirk and Start explore their personal responses to the excavation of several hundred bodies at a burial ground near London, which included fear, sorrow, disturbed sleep, mood swings, and self-doubt about both their ability to finish the job and their own motives in continuing with it. As the same volume's editors put it, "the encounter with the dead for the archaeologist, or [forensic] anthropologist, can shock and disturb" (Downes and Pollard 1999, xii; Kirk and Start 1999). Downes and Pollard also note that human remains mediate "the closest, most immediate contact we have with the past" (p. xii; cf. H. Williams and E. Williams 2007, 48). However, this contact can be almost too immediate, interrupting or hindering the archaeologists' task: "You try not to imagine what it was like, it makes it difficult to do our work," says a forensic specialist working on soldiers' bodies exhumed in 2009 from a mass grave on the former Western Front, adding that "this is easier said than done at times" (P. Jackson 2010). Similarly, for Zimbabwean archaeologists, exhuming war graves in Mozambique can "feel like opening up old wounds" so that "the whole atmosphere is like that of a funeral" (Fontein 2009, 22–23). While not all human remains are associated, as in these cases, with brutal wars, in many diverse contexts human remains can often have an "uncanny" power to evoke the past in a way that unsettles the present, by "revealing what should not be seen" in terms of both that which is buried and also that which is normally unseen in a living human being (Moshenska 2006, cited in H. Williams and E. Williams 2007, 48; cf. Buchli, Lucas, and Cox 2001, 11). Emotional reactions may be triggered by a sense of transgression, both to what's normally classified as human, and normalizing processes of dealing with and containing the transformation of human materials (Fontein 2010), and also to the archaeological premise of "distance" from one's object of study (temporally but also in terms of identity; Buchli, Lucas, and Cox 2001, 10). Whatever the case, it is clear that human remains can trigger emotional responses among archaeologists that override their professional detachment and do not occur toward other sorts of material culture. It is this emotional response that we consider in the rest of this paper, by exploring anthropologically the affective presence of bones.

Theorizing the Affective Presence of Bones

Our theorization of the "affective presence" of human remains, and the disruptive potential and possibilities of unearthing, draws on two comparatively recent and, in many ways closely allied, trends in social and cultural theory. The first is a "return to things" (Domańska 2006; Olsen 2003) and the emphasis on the autonomy, "agency" (Knappett and Malafouris 2008; H. Williams 2004), and/or "properties" (Ingold 2007) of nonhuman actors, "actants" (Latour 1993), things, or materials—be they animals, landscapes, stones, or bones—which proceeds from a broadly phenomenological appreciation of our unfolding and embodied relational being in the world. Although diverse, the different approaches (Ingold 2007; Latour 1993; Miller 2005; Pinney 2005; Tilley 2002) gathered under the rubric of a "return to things" share the desire to overcome conventional distinctions between passive, inanimate objects and active subjects, in order to develop a more nuanced understanding of the relational processes of becoming within which both "objects" and "subjects" are necessarily implicated and emergent. The second is the elaboration of notions of affect, which have been lurking on the margins of philosophy and psychology for some time but have of late found increasing currency within geography (Anderson 2006; McCormack 2010; Thrift 2004), cultural studies (Clough 2007), and, to a lesser extent, anthropology (Navaro-Yashin 2009) and archaeology (Hamilakis and Anagnostopoulos 2009; Harris and Sørensen 2010).

The Autonomy of Materiality

Recent work in social anthropology and archaeology has sought to develop an understanding of materiality that recognizes the relative autonomy of the material world from subjects instead of reducing it to "merely the semiotic representation of some bedrock of social relations" (Miller 2005, 3). In a bid to overcome "the tyranny of the subject" associated with the "linguistic turn" in social anthropology that interpreted material culture through a parallel with text, Daniel Miller (2005, 38) argues for a "dialectics of objectification" in which "the things that people make, make people." The material then becomes central to the constitution of humanity (p. 24), with things not "a mere epiphenomenon of the social" but a central component of it (pp. 12, 31). Archaeologist Chris Tilley meanwhile (2002) suggests that in order to grasp the relative autonomy of material culture from discourse, we can draw on the idea of metaphor. Tilley argues that the linguistic form of words and the material forms of artifacts are "differing modes of communication" that "play complementary roles in social life." Because material culture, like language, is a product of an embodied human mind, things are "solid metaphors objectified in the form of artefacts" (2002, 24). Artifacts, like words, communicate. The autonomy of the material resides in the fact that "artefacts perform active metaphorical work in the world that words cannot," condensing reference through their sensual and tactile qualities and their link with the human body (p. 25).

Pinney challenges both positions as still reducing material objects to social, historical, or cultural contexts of which they are expressive. In order to do justice to the "enfleshed alterity" of the material world, it must be understood as having its own context (2005, 268). For instance, material culture may be seen as part of an aesthetic, figural domain with its own relatively autonomous temporal and formal schedules, which "can constitute history" rather than only being constituted by it (p. 266). For Pinney *materiality* is by definition that "excess, or supplementarity, that can never be encompassed by linguistic-philosophical closure" (p. 266). At the same time he argues that to posit the extreme alterity of objects is to do the same operation of purification (in Latour's sense) that assumes the primacy of the subject as interpreter of the material world: "the more objectively the object appears, the more subjectively the subject arises" (p. 258). Pinney seeks to find a middle ground. He does not claim that material culture is completely unrelated to history and society but also argues that it is not simply its reflection (p. 266). Like Miller, he envisages a dialectic of "subjects making objects making subjects," but in his view this is not smooth but instead rife with disjunctures and fractures. "Objects" are not transcendent but instead make demands that "can never be subsumed to the conventional culture-object space of post-eighteenth century historiography" (p. 269).

Working in a very different vein of analysis, Ingold (2007) too explores the autonomy of the material, although, for him, to talk of materiality or the agency of objects is an unhelpful abstraction that draws attention away from the properties, flows, and transferences of materials and substances. Ingold's perspective illustrates that what matters is not necessarily preconstituted and bounded objects like "the body," bones, stones, or the soil but rather the properties and flows of materials between them. Yet one (perhaps unintended) result of this determination to focus on materials and substances is that inevitably attention is reverted back to what Latour calls "purification": how materials are made to *become* objects, physically but also conceptually, historically, and politically. Beyond overcoming conventional Cartesian dualities, Ingold's emphasis on materials, much like Bill Brown's "thing theory" (2001), points to the complex, and always incomplete, processes of becoming through which both objects and subjects are constantly being (re)constituted, transformed, and reassembled. By extension, there is the suggestion that things, materials, and stuff are always both more and less than the objects and subjects that they constitute, the substantive qualities of which are in excess of, yet imbricated in, their own becoming and unbecoming. This is what Pinney (2005, 270) calls the "alterity (or 'torque') of materiality that can never be assimilated to a disembodied 'linguistic-philosophical closure.'"

The Affective Turn

Allied to recent theorizations on the autonomy of materiality has been a turn to the notion of affect as a way of theorizing processes of relationality and individuation that is not predicated on the modernist distinction between the "in here" of the subject and "out there" of the object. Couzee Venn uses the example of a flock of starlings to open her "rethinking of human relations to the living." She describes a cloud of starlings made up of myriad individuals who give the appearance of a single body, and in this she sees at work "nonconscious, visceral, propriocentric, affective processes connecting bodies" in motion (2010, 130). Following a broadly Spinozian tradition, mostly through the work of Gilles Deleuze, the affective processes that we witness as we watch a cloud of starlings or the ebb and flow of people on city streets are conceptualized as being at once in excess of and anterior to the self-reflexive representational strategies by which we bring various entities into being through acts of purification. These entities include emotions, which are, according to Brian Massumi (2002, 28), "the sociolinguistic fixing of the quality of an experience which from that point onward is defined as personal."

Affect is a process, which is figuratively (and often literally) described on the skin, as the surface between the body (and this includes bodies of all sorts) and the world. In this sense affect is conceptualized as a quality of felt intensity, where this feeling is, in the first instance, not experienced or understood subjectively from within the inner world of the encultured consciousness, nor objectively as a property of some external causal agency, but as a feature of an ongoing process of becoming that is always material and relational. Finding a precursor in Raymond Williams's "structures of feeling," but with an emphasis on the embodied quality of becoming in the world, recent theorizations of affect share a broadly phenomenological or, as Don Ihde would have it, "postphenomenological" approach. The latter, according to Ihde, breaks with the last vestiges of modernist distinction between the subject and object that cling to the grand tradition of phenomenological theorizing and situates phenomenology squarely within "its concrete bodily contexts" and processes of embodiment that are "*both* actional-perceptual and culturally endowed" (Idhe and Brook 2003, 12).

In addressing the unearthing of human remains, notions of affect allow us not only to acknowledge the agency of things, including human remains, but to situate that agency in the very real relational and material processes of becoming and to describe this as an affective process, which has the capacity to create felt intensities, the "demands of objects" described by Pinney (2005), which have an incipient transformative capacity. Key to this is the suggestion, found in the work of Pinney and of Massumi (2000), as well as in Bill Brown's elaboration of thing theory (2001), that affect is both in excess of and insufficient to the "sociolinguistic" strategies by which we can arrest the flow of becoming and constitute various entities, including "the past" and the coemergence of the subject and object. For example, with regards to the quality of colors, Massumi writes that the intensity of blue

> attests to a *self-activity* of experience. When colour is interrogated by language, it displays a self-insistent dynamism that commands itself to the instituted context, into which it breaks and enters, delivering itself to the questioning. This self-delivery or ingressive activity of experience is neither a common property of the language acts that end up expressing it, nor the sole property of any of the language-users involved. The excess of colour slips into language *between* the experimenter and the subject. *It belongs to their joint situation.* More precisely, it *enters* their situation. (2000, 180–81)

What is said of blue may also be said of human remains: that they possess a quality of "self-insistent dynamism" that, even as it "slips into language" to be described according to the cultural disposition of human actors, becoming in fact "human remains" (or "ancestors," specimens, or merely detritus), also possesses an excessive *affective* quality that elides linguistic closure. In this sense, processes of unearthing are not only intentional projects of exhumation and identification but also relational processes of becoming that are animated by the affective materiality of bone and hair and the small everyday objects that lie proximate. It is, in other words, a process by which past lives "break and enter" into the present, as, for example, when we turn a rock over in our hand to discover that it has teeth.

Unearthing Human Remains

Pinney's (2005) bid to theorize the partial autonomy of materiality from the subject worlds of culture and history, Ingold's (2007) insistence on the properties and flows of materials, and the allied theorization of affect are particularly appropriate when considering human remains. While material, human remains do not seem to trigger the same responses that artifacts do. As Sayer (2009, 202) recently put it, human remains tend to "engender a special behaviour" in those who encounter them. This "specialness" of human remains may lie, as Howard Williams (2004) argues, precisely in the fact that they are, in their affective qualities, simultaneously person and object, being neither one nor quite the other.

More precisely, we would argue that before they are subject or object, person or body, human remains are "materials" or things, situated in the tension between vital substance and dead matter, that have the potential to become person or object. The notion of the "thing" has been deployed to denote some sort of nodal point in an onflowing process of becoming, in order to distinguish such "things" from "objects," which assume a fixed and transcendent quality of being. More recently, Ingold considers kites and the flying of kites to describe the difference between thing and object as follows:

> The kite [that] had lain lifeless on the table indoors, now immersed in these generative currents, had come to life. What we had thought to be an object was revealed as what I would call a thing. And the thing about things, if you will, is that far from standing before us as a fait accompli, complete in itself each is a "going on"—or better, a place where several goings on become intertwined. (2009, 6)

The peculiarity of "things," conceived in this sense, is that they do not possess or reveal meaning. In this respect, as Bill Brown argues, they are distinct from objects. "We look through objects," he writes, "because they are the codes by which our interpretive attention makes them meaningful, because there is a discourse of objectivity which allows us to use them as facts" (2001, 4). Things, however, do not possess this transparency that allows us to look through them toward whatever is behind or beyond them. As "objects in process" (Domańska 2006, 181) (like a kite in the wind), or materials in movement, "things" do not "mean," for such meaning assumes a discrimination between subject and object; rather, they are felt as shifting qualities of intensity within the fabric of material becoming (like the tug on the string perhaps).

In considering human remains as "things," therefore, we are arguing that such a consideration begins with a nodal point in processes of material becoming, unearthing in this case, by which certain qualities of felt presence are registered. What is peculiar about human remains (though one does not wish to overstate this) is precisely that this felt presence is peculiarly difficult to resolve into meaning. In other words, as Howard Williams (2004) suggests, bits of bodies are materials and things that are not so easily stabilized to become objects or subjects, although much work and effort is often exerted to achieve this transformation. The other peculiar thing about human remains is that they seem to possess a spectral quality that elides the normative distinctions between dead and alive, past and present temporalities, in that they are not simply present as things but in this presence also suggest an absence, a some*thing* else that they are but also are not (Davis 2005; Derrida 1994; Wylie 2007). In this sense they evoke the past and constitute an ambivalent material trace of past being. The question is, if we begin our consideration with human remains as things and materials rather than objects, how may we understand this "evocation" of the past, the spectral sense of some*thing* that has come before, which haunts the thing at hand?

The Affective Presence (and Absence) of the Past

The specific way in which human remains evoke the past is stressed by Paul Williams, commenting on the display of human remains in "memorial museums" commemorating atrocities. Williams argues that such remains are often exhibited as evidence that an atrocity has occurred (2007, 46) but that

> while bones are vitally primary and *literally* the person in question, they struggle to communicate much about life. . . . A focus on bodies appears to test the idealized memorial-remembrance experience, which is based on an empathetic projection of one's self onto the object of contemplation. While "it could have been me" is a fantastical projection in relation to any historical circumstance (made possible by the safe knowledge that it was not), is it really possible to produce such a split ego that we imagine ourselves among the dead? (p. 40)

This contrasts with personal belongings and artifacts, which, for Williams, aid memory in the sense of identification or empathy with past people, especially if there is a sense that they are "all that remains" of an individual or a life (p. 31; cf. Swain 2002, 99).

What is interesting in Williams's comment is the idea that human remains at once literally *are* the past or from the past—and as such can, for instance, act as evidence that a certain event has occurred—and yet they have extreme difficulty, in the absence of highly specialized knowledge practices such as forensic science, or indeed divination, in "saying" anything specific about past life or lives, as opposed to past death or past loss. They tend to trigger empathetic understanding or identification with moments of death or loss, rather than lives lived. While both are material, human remains, unlike artifacts, cannot be easily "read" in a symbolic sense.

Swain makes a similar distinction, though less emphatically, noting that in the context of archaeological museums "skeletons have the capacity to be used as symbols for past individuals, but more commonly other objects are used" (2002, 99). In contrast to Swain, we argue that human remains are often used as symbols in museum contexts, though perhaps not as symbols of individuals but rather of composite, idealized persons, much like the composite, constructed ethnographic "characters" that ethnologists constructed and used in the past (Reed-Danahay 2001). Similarly, human remains can become symbols much like natural history specimens come to stand for their species more generally; they are sought for their averageness, for their ability to represent all individuals. Associated artifacts (however loose that association is) trick us into thinking we know "that person" (or character) beyond their averageness or their typicality. Such artifacts allow us to ascribe imagined preferences, emotional states, and homologous responses to life. The obvious exception that may prove the rule here are human remains that have been turned into artifacts—the sacred relics of saints, for example (Geary 1986), or indeed potent body parts used for occult purposes, such as Kalilose witch guns in western Zambia (Gewald 2010), which may or may not be symbolic of particular individuals but gain their potency exactly not from representing past lives but from being remnants of them.

In this context, Tilley's (2002, 23–24) use of the idea of metaphor in striving to understand material culture above and beyond a parallel with text—to grasp its otherness from words—may be applicable to artifacts as products, like language, of an embodied human mind, but it is less useful for human remains. Human remains, while material, are not (necessarily) the products of an embodied human mind: they "are," or were, an embodied human. Although human bodies or parts thereof can be metaphors of or stand for other things, after death their materiality, while potent, is not necessarily seen as communicative. Human remains in and of themselves are often not very "readable"; they require significant technical, professional, or ritual specialization and indeed elaboration to be read. Therefore, instead of metaphor, metonymy may be a more useful figure for thinking about the particular materiality of human remains.

Runia discusses metonymy as a trope for the relationship between the past and the present. His discussion is especially provocative when considering human remains. Metonymy, he says, is denotative rather than connotative (2006, 15). A classic example is the "part for the whole" type of metonymy, which also exemplifies the fact that metonymy is the trope of "presence in absence," in the sense that the part both is and is not the whole (p. 6). This is suggestive in terms of human remains because they literally are parts for the whole: body parts of a whole body, inanimate parts of a once-living being. If objects or artifacts connote a human being, remains may be said to denote him/her. So also it may be said of human remains that they evoke the presence of a human but also simultaneously his or her absence, insofar as they both are and are not him or her; they are evidence of both life and death.

Runia (2006) also writes that what characterizes metonymy is that it willfully transposes a word or a concept from one context to another in which it is inappropriate: for instance, the crown stands for the king, so one may say "the Crown has decided to act." But the crown is not the king; to say that "it" acts is to mix contexts, placing an inanimate object into the context of action, in which it does not belong. Runia transposes this reasoning to the temporal plane and beyond the linguistic context, using metonym to model the link between past and present. For him the prototypes of this are fossils or relics, instances of the "part for the whole" type of metonym (p. 16), crossing temporal contexts. His point is that these things do not just cross but also link temporal contexts. They stand for something in the past, and so they present (rather than represent) the past and are denotative more than connotative of a past reality or event, juxtaposing it to the here and now (p. 17). As such, they act as "holes through which the past discharges into the present" (p. 16); they transfer presence more than meaning (p. 17). They are also "introverted," not fully belonging to/engaging with the context they occur in (p. 18). They operate as things out of place, not giving meaning but evoking presence and calling for meaning: "whereas metaphor 'gives' meaning, metonymy insinuates that there is an urgent *need* for meaning" (p. 19). Monuments for Runia are more hybrid examples of the same thing: they say something (connotation, metaphor) about something they stand for (denotation, metonymy). The denotative aspect is greatest in the case of modern monuments about events that are hard to represent, such as the Holocaust or the Vietnam War: monuments are less interpretations of the event than repositories for something that has haunted the present ever since that event occurred (p. 17). People respond to their disturbing presence by interacting with them (e.g., through commemorations) and eventually incorporating them into the existing context until they become platitudes (the way monuments may eventually cease to be noticed, or become clichés). On occasion, however, the thing denoted is too "powerful" and so resists or disables any attempt at incorporation; yet nonetheless it is present, even as this presence has no meaning, and so it can "infect" the context and "transform it 'in its own image'" (p. 18).

These ideas are productive templates for thinking about human remains and the responses they elicit. As indicated, people can feel afraid, disturbed, or unsettled as a result of encounters with human remains. The remains generate confusion and uncanny, hard-to-classify emotions. In this sense they may be said to "infect the context" in which they occur or appear and transform it in their own image: unreadable, they produce unreadable emotions. In this sense, then, the process of unearthing can be considered as a transformation in the "affective atmosphere" (Anderson 2009)—quite literally so, as in the case of the excavation of Soviet mass graves (Paperno 2001). Giving evidence before the Committee on Un-American Activities Dr. Malinin, who performed autopsies on the nameless corpses, was shown photographs and asked to authenticate these as images of the exhumed bodies. He replied by saying "yes," but then he added, "But these photographs cannot begin to portray the screams, the stench in the air, and the emotion which permeated the air as the relatives of these innocent victims went from body to body undertaking to identify their loved ones" (Paperno 2001, 96).

As this passage indicates, human remains also elicit responses that could be described as being "incorporated" into the context. In the air thick with the stench of decay and the inarticulate emotions of the bereaved, the work of identification and reclamation begins. This is the work of naming and, in naming, transforming things into subjects. Kirk and Start (1999) report that archaeologists working on the London cemetery site tended to give a name to each body they excavated. The same is done by anatomy students with bodies they work on in dissection classes (M. Spear, pers. comm.). As is well known, naming is a crucial means of incorporation into social networks and contexts (Bodenhorn and vom Bruck 2006). This includes fictional names, as in the cases mentioned, but also the considerable efforts made to identify a person whose remains have been unearthed; a process that is central, for instance, to the work of archaeologists excavating soldiers' remains on the Western Front (like the forensic scientist cited earlier; see also M. Brown 2007; Price 2008). In this case, naming brings with it the promise of reconnecting the remains to an actual social network, the kin of the deceased, to whom the remains should be returned for burial as seen in the case of Fromelles (*BBC News* 2010) and elsewhere (see M. Brown 2007, 56). A similar urgency to identify named persons from remains animates archaeological excavations of Zimbabwean war graves (Fontein 2009), even if in some cases the named identity of remains has even driven excavation processes, such as the forensic exhumations of victims of postcolonial violence in Matabeleland described by Eppel (2001), or the events described by Cox (2005) and Shoko (2006) in the Mount Darwin area in the north, where relatives, war veterans and mediums possessed by the restless dead recovered their "own" bones from mass graves.

Whether or not a person is identified, a common response to human remains in such contexts is less "it could have been me" (cf. P. Williams 2007) than "it could have been my relative" (cf. M. Brown 2007, 56; M. Brown and Osgood 2009). Instead of identification, what is triggered is a feeling of recognition, and consequently of care and responsibility—kinship in the sense of inclusive care rather than exclusionary pedigree. Similarly, human remains from more distant times can be presented and perceived as "ancestors" or sometimes, with a significant phrase, "adopted ancestors" (H. Williams and E. Williams 2007, 48, 53), strangers one wants to take into one's own circle of care and memory. Such adoption may differ from the construction of nationalist kinship in the celebration of forefathers (cf. Verdery 1999) common to the "distinctively modern complex for commemoration of the sacrifice of life in the cause of the nation-state" (Werbner 1998, 72)—heroic figures whose remains inspire adoration and exclusivity, rather than evoking frailty, nurturance, and dependence—although this distinction often blurs, as, for example, in Zimbabwe, where all ancestors (family, "royal," or national) can inspire adoration and exclusivity, even as they make demands for atonement, nurturance, and return. To some extent all commemoration implicitly responds to the requirement to "feed" the dead (Rowlands 1999, 144) or "finish the work of the dead" (Kuchler 1999, 55), and such responses express a desire for ethical engagement, also suggested by the very ambiguous term *respect* that recurs in accounts of how archaeologists and anthropologists (should) relate to human remains (see M. Brown 2007; Krmpotich, Fontein, and Harries 2010; Sayer 2009, 202; Swain 2002, 97).

Conclusion

The distinction between metaphor and metonym is useful for our consideration of why "unearthing" or encountering human remains is often a profoundly different kind of experience and process from unearthing or encountering other kinds of things. If initially human remains appear poignant because they seem more obviously "human" than other material objects and artifacts, then at second glance this poignancy does not easily or clearly make them more communicative as metaphors or objectifications of human beings or of past lives lived. Because they "are" or were human beings, bones and bodily remains can signal presence more than meaning; they denote more than they connote.

This excessive metonymic quality of human remains, over and above their metaphorical capacity, does not make them fundamentally different from or opposed to nonhuman remnants of the past but rather points to the autonomous and excessive affectivity, or "torque" of materiality, of all materials and things; the abundant potentiality or alterity of thingness that is inevitably imbricated in and yet beyond the relational processes and flows of becoming through which all objects and subjects emerge, and which must be arrested and stabilized for entities such as the past, "the body," a person, or an artifact to be constituted. What then appears to make human remains different from, and yet exemplary of, other things is their resistance to processes of "purification" and stabilization. In this view the problem of bones and human materials is that their excessive metonymic qualities defy, perhaps much more than other things, efforts to turn them into meaningful metaphors. As a result, they can be subject to huge and often highly specialized efforts and dramatic overdeterminations into particular types of subjects/objects, such as ancestors, victims, heroes, or specimens—processes that are often unusually problematic, politicized, and contested.

Because human remains point readily to the insufficiency of symbolization/metaphorization and the deficiency of "sociolinguistic closure," the excessive potentiality of their thingness points easily and often problematically to other potential becomings and other possibilities, and indeed to other temporalities. In Pinney's (2005) terms we could say that human remains challenge "contemporaneity," manifesting and embodying "the intransigence of the object" or materiality's partial disconnection from the historical/cultural context. Partially resistant to interpretation and thus hard to connect to the historical/cultural context, human remains may make evident the heterogeneity of time. Difficult to contextualize, human remains may "contain their own prior context" (Strathern 1988, 33, on objects for the people of Mount Hagen, New Guinea, cited in Pinney 2005, 268), "making demands" on culture and history, and are therefore paradigmatic of materiality as "excess, or supplementarity, that can never be encompassed by linguistic-philosophical closure" (Pinney 2005, 266). At the same time, following Pinney, human remains should not be considered "pure" objectness: Their materiality is dialectically linked with the subject, though not smoothly (as in mutual creation, or as in objects manifesting a cultural or historical context). Instead, they are part of a dialectical relationship marked by "disjunctures and fractures" in which objects make "implacable demands" (Adorno 1978, 40, cited in Pinney 2005, 269). It is therefore perhaps the peculiarly fractured nature of their becoming that makes people strive to contextualize and encompass human remains through notions and ethics of kinship and naming, care, recognition, and respect. Perhaps by these means remains are encompassed "as alterity," rather than fully subsumed or comprehended as signs, a necessarily fraught and incomplete process. As we unearth or encounter human remains, then, they "unearth" and reveal "our consistent inability to accept the alterity of the world as alterity" and our ultimately insatiable desire "to see it instead as a comprehensible sign" (Docherty 1996, 157, cited in Pinney 2005, 266).

Notes

1. The "Bones Collective" research network (http://www.san.ed.ac.uk/research/bones_collective) organized a series of research seminars and workshops in 2008/9 including the panel at the Association of Social Anthropologists (ASA) conference 2009. This article and a special issue of the *Journal of Material Culture* (December 2010) derive from these events. We would like to thank everyone involved in these events for their spirited and critical contributions to our ongoing conversations.

2. The notion that digging is central to the work of archaeologists, and that archaeologists are by extension "diggers," albeit of a trained and disciplined kind, finds expression in, among other things, the existence of the "diggers forum," the name given to a virtual chat room of the Institute of Archaeologists (http://www.archaeologists.net/groups/diggers).

3. Physical anthropology presents a bridge between anthropology and archaeology, being nominally a practice of anthropology but methodologically more akin to archaeology. Ales Hrdlicka, perhaps the most prominent early physical anthropologist, unearthed—if not always properly excavated—human remains to aid his inquiry into racial typologies and indigenous societies in the Americas, as well as prehistoric migration patterns (see, for example, Hrdlicka 1913, 1919, 1944).

References

Adorno, T. 1978. *Minima moralia: Reflections from damaged life*, trans. E.F.N. Jephcott. London: Verso.

Anderson, B. 2006. "Becoming and being hopeful: Towards a theory of affect." *Environment and Planning D: Society and Space* 24 (5): 739–54.

Anderson, B. 2009. "Affective atmospheres." *Emotion, Space and Society* 2: 77–81.

Battaglia, D. 1990. *On the bones of the serpent: Person, memory and mortality in Sabarl Island society*. Chicago: University of Chicago Press.

BBC News. 2010. "Fromelles soldiers to be reburied." January 29. Available online: http://news.bbc.co.uk/1/hi/magazine/8473444.stm.

Bell, L., and V. Collison. 2006. "The return of our ancestors, the rebirth of ourselves." In *Raven travelling: Two centuries of Haida art*, ed. D. Augaitis, N. Collison, R. Davidson, P. McNair, M. Jones, and B. Reid, 140–45. Vancouver, BC: Vancouver Art Gallery, Douglas & McIntyre.

Bennett, J. 2004. "The force of things: Steps toward an ecology of matter." *Political Theory* 32 (3): 347–72.

Bloch, M. 1971. *Placing the dead: Tombs, ancestral villages and kinship organization in Madagascar*. London and New York: Seminar Press.

Bloch, M. 1988. "Death and the concept of the person." In *On the meaning of death*, ed. S. Cederroth, C. Corlin, and J. Lindstrom, 11–31. Uppsala, Sweden: Amqvist & Wiksell International.

Bloch, M., and J. Parry, eds. 1982. *Death and the regeneration of life*. Cambridge: Cambridge University Press.

Bodenhorn, B., and G. vom Bruck, eds. 2006. *The anthropology of names and naming*. Cambridge: Cambridge University Press.

Brown, B. 2001. "Thing theory." *Critical Enquiry* 28 (1): 1–22.

Brown, M. 2007. "The fallen, the front and the finding: Archaeology, human remains and the Great War." *Archaeological Review from Cambridge* 22 (2): 53–68.

Brown, M., and R. Osgood. 2009. *Digging up plugstreet*. Yeovil, UK: Haynes.

Buchli, V. 2002. "Introduction." In *The material culture reader*, ed. V. Buchli, 1–22. London: Berg.

Buchli, V., G. Lucas, and M. Cox. 2001. *Archaeologies of the contemporary past*. New York: Routledge.

Chamberlain, T., and M. Parker Pearson. 2001. *Earthly remains: The history and science of preserved human bodies*. London: British Museum.

Clough, P. 2007. "Introduction." In *The affective turn: Theorising the social*, ed. P. Clough and J. Halley, 1–33. Durham, NC, and London: Duke University Press.

Cox, J.L. 2005. "The land crisis in Zimbabwe: A case of religious intolerance?" *Fieldwork in Religion* 1 (1): 35–48.

Csordas, T. 1994. *Embodiment and experience*. Cambridge: Cambridge University Press.

Davis, C. 2005. "État present: Hauntology, spectres and phantoms." *French Studies* 59 (3): 373–79.

Derrida, J. 1994. *Spectres of Marx: The state of the debt, the work of mourning and new international*. London: Routledge.

Docherty, T. 1996. *Alterities: Criticism, history, representation*. Oxford: Clarendon.

Domańska, E. 2005. "Towards the archaeontology of the dead body." *Rethinking History* 9 (4): 389–413.

Domańska, E. 2006. "The return to things." *Archaeologia Polona* 44: 171–85.

Douglas, M. 1966. *Purity and danger*. London: Routledge and Kegan Paul.

Downes, J., and T. Pollard, eds. 1999. *The loved body's corruption: Archaeological contributions to the study of human mortality*. Glasgow: Cruithne Press.

Eppel, S. 2001. "Healing the dead to transform the living: Exhumation and reburial in Zimbabwe." Availabe online: http://www.icrc.org/themissi.nsf/32db2800384 e72adc12569dd00505ac6/72889407ac24b246c1256b04004739f6/$FILE/healing %20the%20dead-%20calif%20conf%202001.rtf.

Fahlander, F., and T. Oestigaard, eds. 2008. *The materiality of death: Bodies, burial, beliefs*. Oxford: Archaeopress.

Farquhar, J., and M. Locke. 2007. "Introduction." In *Reading the anthropology of material life*, ed. J. Farquhar and M. Locke, 1–16. Durham, NC, and London: Duke University Press.

Ferrándiz, F. 2005. "The return of civil war ghosts: The ethnography exhumations in contemporary Spain." *Anthropology Today* 22 (3): 7–12.

Filippucci, P. 2004. "Memory and marginality: Remembrance and the Great War in Argonne (France)." In *Memory, politics and religion: The past meets the present in Europe*, ed. F. Pine, D. Kaneff, and H. Haukanes, 35–37. Münster, Germany: LIT.

Fontein, J. 2009. "The politics of the dead: Living heritage, bones and commemoration in Zimbabwe." *ASAOnline* 1/2. Available online: http://www.theasa.org/ downloads/asaonline/pdf/asaonline0102.pdf.

Fontein, J. 2010. "Between tortured bodies and resurfacing bones: The politics of the dead in Zimbabwe." *Journal of Material Culture* 15 (4): 423–48.

Fowler, C. 2001. "Personhood and social relations in the British Neolithic with a study from the Isle of Man." *Journal of Material Culture* 6 (2): 137–63.

Geary, P. 1986. "Sacred commodities: The circulation of medieval relics." In *The social life of things: Commodities in cultural perspective*, ed. A. Appadurai, 169–91. Cambridge: Cambridge University Press.

Gewald, J.-B. 2010. "From Kaliloze to Karavina: The historical and current use and context of 'Kaliloze witch guns' in western Zambia." BAB Working Paper no. 3. Available online: http://www.baslerafrika.ch/upload/files/WP_2010_3_Gewald.pdf.

Graham, E.-J. 2009. "Becoming persons, becoming ancestors. Personhood memory and the corpse in Roman rituals of social remembrance." *Archaeological Dialogues* 16 (1): 51–74.

Hallam, E., J. Hockey, and G. Howarth. 1999. *Beyond the body: Death and social identity*. London: Routledge.

Hamilakis, Y., and A. Anagnostopoulos. 2009. "What is archaeological ethnography?" *Public Archaeology* 8 (2–3): 65–87.

Harries, J. 2010. "Of bleeding skulls and the postcolonial uncanny: Bones and the presence of Nonosabasut and Demasduit." *Journal of Material Culture* 15 (4): 403–21.

Harris, O., and T. Sørensen. 2010. "Rethinking emotion and material culture." *Archaeological Dialogues* 17 (2): 145–63.

Harrison, S. 2004. "Skull trophies of the Pacific War: Transgressive objects of remembrance." *Journal of the Royal Anthropological Institute* 12: 817–36.

Hertz, R. 1960. *Death and the right hand*. London: Cohen and West. (Orig. published 1905)

Hrdlicka, A. 1913. *Remains in eastern Asia of the race that peopled America*. Washington, DC: Smithsonian Institution.

Hrdlicka, A. 1919. *Physical anthropology: Its scope and its aims; its history and present status in the United States*. Philadelphia: Wistar Institute of Anatomy and Biology.

Hrdlicka, A. 1944. *The anthropology of Kodiak Island*. Philadelphia: Wistar Institute of Anatomy and Biology.

Humphreys, S. C., and H. King, eds. 1981. *Mortality and immortality: The anthropology and archaeology of death*. London: Academic Press.

Huntington, R., and P. Metcalf. 1980. *Celebrations of death: The anthropology of mortuary ritual*. Cambridge: Cambridge University Press.

Ihde, D., and S. Brook. 2003. *Postphenomenology—again*. Aarhus, Denmark: University of Aarhus.

Ingold, T. 2007. "Materials against materiality." *Archaeological Dialogues* 14 (1): 1–16.

Jackson, C. O. 1977. "American attitudes to death." *Journal of American Studies* 11: 297–312.

Jackson, P. 2010. "The lost soldiers of Fromelles." *BBC News*, January 29. Available online: http://news.bbc.co.uk/1/hi/scotland/8485734.stm.

Kirk, L., and L. Start. 1999. "Death and the undertakers." In Downes and Pollard 1999, 200–208.

Knappett, C., and L. Malafouris, eds. 2008. *Material agency: Towards a non-anthropocentric approach*. New York: Springer.

Krmpotich, C. 2010. "Remembering and repatriation: The production of kinship, memory and respect." *Journal of Material Culture* 15 (2): 157–79.

Krmpotich, C., J. Fontein, and J. Harries. 2010. "The substance of bones: The emotive materiality and affective presence of human remains." *Journal of Material Culture* 15 (4): 371–84.

Küchler, S. 1999. "The place of memory." In *The art of forgetting*, ed. A. Forty and S. Küchler. Oxford: Berg.

Lambert, H., and M. McDonald. 2009. *Social bodies*. Oxford: Berghahn Books.

Latour, B. 1993. *We have never been modern*. Cambridge, MA: Harvard University Press.

Massumi, B. 2000. "Too-blue: Colour-patch for an expanded empiricism." *Cultural Studies* 14 (2): 177–226.

McCormack, D. 2010. "Remotely sensing affective afterlives: The spectral geographies of material remains." *Annals of the Association of American Geographers* 100 (3): 640–54.

McGregor, G. 2008. "Elemental bodies: The nature of transformation practices during the late third and second millennium BC in Scotland." *World Archaeology* 40 (2): 268–80.

McGuire, R.H. 1992. *Death, society and ideology in a Hohokam community*. Boulder, CO: Westview.

Miller, D. 2005. "Materiality: An introduction." In *Materiality*, ed. D. Miller, 1–50. Durham, NC, and London: Duke University Press.

Moshenska, G. 2006. "The archaeological uncanny." *Public Archaeology* 5: 91–99.

Navaro-Yashin, Y. 2009. "Affective space, melancholic objects: Ruination and the production of anthropological knowledge." *Journal of the Royal Anthropological Institute* 15: 1–18.

Olsen, B. 2003. "Material culture after text: Re-membering things." *Norwegian Archaeological Review* 36 (2): 87–104.

Paperno, I. 2001. "Exhuming the bodies of Soviet terror." *Representations* 75: 89–118.

Parker Pearson, M. 1999. *The archaeology of death and burial*. College Station: Texas A&M University Press.

Petrović-Šteger, M. 2009. "Atomising conflict—accommodating human remains." In Lambert and McDonald 2009, 47–76.

Pinney, C. 2005. "Things happen: Or, from which moment does that object come?" In *Materiality*, ed. D. Miller, 256–72. Durham, NC, and London: Duke University Press.

Price, J. 2008. "The Devonshires held this trench, they hold it still: Sacred landscapes of the Great War." In *Landscapes of clearance: Archaeological and anthropological perspectives*, ed. A. Gazin-Schwartz and A.P. Smith, 180–89. Walnut Creek, CA: Left Coast Press.

Reed-Danahay, D. 2001. "Autobiography, intimacy and ethnography." In *Handbook of ethnography*, ed. P. Atkinson et al., 407–25. London: Sage.

Renshaw, L. 2010. "Scientific and affective identification of Republican civilian victims from the Spanish Civil War." *Journal of Material Culture* 15 (4): 449–63.

Rowlands, M. 1999. "Remembering to forget: Sublimation as sacrifice in war memorials." In *The art of forgetting*, ed. A. Forty and S. Kuchler, 129–45. Oxford: Berg.

Runia, E. 2006. "Presence." *History and Theory* 45: 1–29.

Sayer, D. 2009. "Is there a crisis facing British burial archaeology?" *Antiquity* 83: 199–205.

Semple, S., and H. Williams, eds. 2007. *Early medieval mortuary practices: Anglo-Saxon studies in archaeology and history*. Oxford: Oxford University Press.

Shoko, T. 2006. "'My bones shall rise again': War veterans, spirits and land reform in Zimbabwe." African Studies Centre Working Paper, no. 68. Leiden: African Studies Centre.

Sofaer, J. 2006. *The body as material culture: A theoretical osteoarchaeology*. Cambridge: Cambridge University Press.

Strathern, M. 1988. *The gender of the gift*. Stanford, CA: Stanford University Press.

Strathern, M. 1990. "Artefacts of history: Events and the interpretation of images." In *Culture, history and the Pacific*, ed. J. Siikla, 25–44. Helsinki: Transactions of the Finish Anthropological Society.

Strathern, M. 1999. *Property, substance and effect: Anthropological essays on persons and things*. London: Athlone.

Swain, H. 2002. "The ethics of displaying human remains from British archaeological sites." *Public Archaeology* 2: 95–100.

Tarlow, S. 1999. *Bereavement and commemoration*. Oxford: Blackwell.

Thrift, N. 2004. "Intensities of feeling: Towards a spatial politics of affect." *Geografiska Annaler Series B* 86 (1): 57–78.

Tilley, C. 2002. "Metaphor, materiality and interpretation." In *The material culture reader*, ed. V. Buchli, 23–26. Oxford: Berg.

Turner, B. 1984. *The body and society*. Oxford: Basil Blackwell.

Venn, C. 2010. "Individuation, relationality, affect: Rethinking the human in relation to living." *Body and Society* 16 (1): 129–61.

Verdery, K. 1999. *The political lives of dead bodies*. Ithaca, NY, and London: Cornell University Press.

Werbner, R. 1998. *Memory and postcolony: African anthropology and the critique of power*. London: Zed Books.

Williams, H. 2003. *Archaeologies of remembrance*. New York: Kluwer Academic/Plenum.

Williams, H. 2004. "Death warmed up: The agency of bodies and bones in early Anglo-Saxon cremation rites." *Journal of Material Culture* 9 (3): 263–91.

Williams, H., and E. Williams. 2007. "Digging for the dead: Archaeological practice as mortuary commemoration." *Public Archaeology* 6 (1): 47–63.

Williams, P. 2007. *Memorial museums: The global rush to commemorate atrocities*. Oxford and New York: Berg.

Wylie, J. 2007. "The spectral geographies of W. G. Sebald." *Cultural Geographies* 14 (2): 171–88.

Archaeology, Anthropology, and Material Things

Julian Thomas

Introduction: Two Complementary Departments

According to Vere Gordon Childe, archaeology and anthropology represent "two complementary departments of the science of man" (1946, 243). Certainly, the two disciplines came of age in the nineteenth century, bound together by colonialism and universal evolutionism (Gosden 1999, 27). At that time they not only shared an outlook but were also distinguished by overlapping pools of practitioners (Adams 1998, 1; Bowden 1991, 46). Yet the eclipse of the cultural evolutionary project set the two communities on different trajectories, at least in the British context. Archaeology's absorption with classification, and social anthropology's concern with function, clearly reflected differing disciplinary realities (Childe 1946, 251; Radcliffe-Brown 1935, 598). However, the desire for a conversation between the "complementary departments" appears to have declined during the twentieth century. In the United States the lodging of Americanist archaeology within university departments of archaeology, the hegemony of Boasian particularism, and the timely emergence of the neo-evolutionism of Leslie White and Julian Steward maintained the connection until the end of the millennium. Only then, with cultural anthropologists seeking to redefine their objectives in the postcolonial era, was there a call for separation. Ironically, this came from archaeologists who considered themselves to be "four-field anthropologists," dismayed at what they understood to be a retreat from issues of diversity, generalization, long-term process, and materiality on the part of their colleagues (Gillespie, Joyce, and Nichols 2003, 155).

The sporadic interchanges that have taken place between archaeologists and anthropologists over the past century have often been governed by a perceived asymmetry between the two (Yarrow 2010, 14). Lacking direct access to the people whom it studied, confronted with evidence that was fragmentary and incomplete, yet daunted by the diversity of human societies, archaeology sometimes looked on anthropology with envy (Gosden 1999, 7). The use of ethnographic analogy, whether as a means of inspiring new interpretations of archaeological materials, or of testing and contesting existing explanations, was often conceived as a means of coping with this lack of contact with living human beings (Ascher 1961; Bonnichsen 1973, 277). The broader the familiarity that archaeologists had with existing human groups, the better their chance of comprehending their own evidence. However, there was some concern that social anthropologists might not always collect information on technology, the manufacture of artifacts, the collection of raw materials, the construction of dwellings, subsistence practices, and the disposal of waste materials. In other words, there was a level of dissatisfaction with a perceived failure on the part of anthropologists to address the material world. As a consequence, archaeologists began to undertake ethnographic research of their own, under the rubric of ethnoarchaeology. The intention was to acquire information in the present that could directly illuminate the traces of the past (Lane 2006, 405; Stiles 1977, 88). In some cases, this imperative was transformed into an "artifact physics," which sought to remove the acts and impacts that create the archaeological record from their social context, creating unambiguous links between static traces in the present and dynamic happenings in the past (Binford 1983, 417). In this form, ethnoarchaeology became part of a "science of the archaeological record" that also drew on the results of experimental archaeology in order to establish causal connections between acts and outcomes. More recently, the ethical problems involved in ethnoarchaeology have begun to be recognized. There is undoubtedly something troubling about studying people in an instrumentalist fashion, not as a means of understanding their own cultural world, or contemporary predicament, but as a means to the end of understanding other people entirely (Fewster 2001). At the same time, the use of analogy has shifted subtly, becoming increasingly connected with the need to disrupt and delegitimate our assumptions and prejudices about the past. For some, it can be taken as read that the past will have been different from the present (Spriggs 2008, 542), although it is arguable that we will always need some prompting in addressing the precise ways in which it was different. The task of circumventing our own preconceptions is unending.

Some of these issues were addressed thirty years ago by Sir Edmund Leach, in a paper originally presented at a conference discussing the relationship between archaeology and anthropology (Leach 1977). Leach contended that the two disciplines were fundamentally incompatible, because one was concerned with lifeless things, while the other dealt with conceptual and verbal categories (1977, 166). While artifacts might reflect cognitive ordering, the relationship between ideas and objects was not sufficiently straightforward for the one to be "read off" from the other. It is apparent that, in classic structuralist fashion, Leach was presuming not simply that thoughts in the mind are separate from actions and objects in the world but that they logically precede them. Artifacts made by human beings are "representations of ideas" (Leach 1977, 167). So concepts are generated in language and imposed onto tangible reality. As Leach puts it, "the things that men make are 'projections', 'externalisations' of their inner selves, and I would suppose that this had always been the case" (1977, 168). For Leach, archaeologists were at an inherent disadvantage, for while anthropologists observe social practice, archaeologists see only its residues. Curiously, he seems not to have reflected that his own pursuit of the cultural grammars and rules hidden behind social life was every bit as inferential as archaeological interpretation. Yet being both a structuralist and a universalist, Leach foresaw the possible emergence of a structuralist archaeology. He argued that since all human beings think in the same way, the preoccupations of Paleolithic mammoth-hunters will have been very similar to our own: they will have been concerned with boundaries and entrances, with culture and nature, with their own bodies and their orifices (Leach 1977, 170). His principal misgiving was not concerned with the distance between past and present, but that any methodology for connecting ideas with objects would be untenable in the absence of verbal exegesis on the part of the artisan. For many archaeologists, however, the past remains worthy of study precisely because many prehistoric societies have no direct analogues in the present, while even in more recent periods material things tell us different things about people than their utterances and writing do. It seems highly unlikely that all aspects of culture will lead us back to a single, uniform generative structure.

Objects, Subjects, and Presences

In the years since Leach's intervention, the categorical separation between the disciplines has been compromised to some extent. Social anthropology has undergone two distinct phases of renewed interest in physical things. The first of these gave rise to an entire subdiscipline of material culture studies, by applying the conceptual apparatus of cultural critique to the production and consumption of objects and artifacts (Miller 1985, 1998). The second, still emerging, involves a kind of enlightened empiricism, in which an attempt is made to break down the distinction between the world of things experienced and that of theorized explanations. This shift from epistemology to ontology arrives at a point far removed from Leach's universal structuralism, emphasizing not that people apprehend the world through different cognitive schemas but that they actually inhabit worlds that are put together differently (Henare, Holbraad, and Wastell 2007, 8). At the same time, various forms of social archaeology have developed, explicitly concerned with questions of symbolism, meaning, structure, and personhood (Fowler 2004; Hodder 1982). While archaeology may still see itself as confronted with the problems of missing human beings and a static record of action, there is growing acceptance that anthropologists also deal with evidence that is fragmentary and imperfect (Lucas 2010, 30; Yarrow 2010, 22). Despite this, it is arguable that the potential synergy between the subjects is still held back by deeply ingrained elements of Cartesian rationalism, which encourage us to misapprehend both people and things. Because we almost instinctively identify persons and things as autonomous and context-free we neglect their conditionality (Edwards 2005). Our problem is that in the contemporary West, the dominant understanding of the world is as composed of independent entities, which can be represented in, and processed by, human minds. The world is thus rendered meaningful by mental processes.

At a very basic level, this scheme informs the commonsense expectations that archaeologists and anthropologists have of their disciplinary practice. Archaeologists lament their inability to "recover" human beings in the way that they recover artifacts, while anthropologists apparently encounter human beings in the same way that one achieves copresence with any other kind of entity, although admittedly this copresence generally involves face-to-face dialogue. Yet it can be suggested that whatever makes us human is not restricted to having a physical body of a particular kind, which is bounded or sutured by its skin and occupies a particular locus in space. Putting this another way, human beings are not "present" in the way that mere objects are (Heidegger 1996, 348). These problems are compounded by the distinction that we routinely make between active creatures and passive materials, which manifests itself in archaeology in the form of the opposition between dynamic past societies and their static archaeological record. As Tim Ingold (2007, 17) has pointed out, there are problems with the view that agency is a kind of force at the disposal of human beings, who use it in order to render inert matter animate. In a way that recalls the Aristotelian cosmology of the Renaissance, Ingold proposes that things are *in life*, in the sense of being engaged in the generative flux of materials. This effectively challenges the notion that the relationship between subjects and objects is one of straightforward cause and effect.

Both archaeologists and anthropologists routinely discuss the way that human being is extended over space and time, often through the medium of material things. A good example is Keith Ray's discussion of the groups of artifacts dated from the eleventh century and later from Igbo Ukwu in Nigeria. Ray (1987, 70) demonstrates how titled men were "presenced" in contexts of ritual and dedication through the appearance of their elaborate metal-tipped staffs, which evoked their implied relationships with supernatural beings. Similarly, Nancy Munn (1977, 1986) has shown how the circulation of objects such as Gawan canoes can be employed to extend what she calls "inter-subjective time-space," which is to say enduring social relationships between the self and others at a greater or lesser distance. I want to take Munn's observations not in the weak sense that the onward path of an exchange good promotes the fame or renown of its owner or maker but in the strong sense that the spatial reach of a person's being is extended, in their capacity as the condition of the possibility of the artifact. In Heideggerian terms, it is the having-been-there of the person that is revealed in the artifact as an abiding presence (Malpas 2006, 14). This, then, is a process of implication at a distance.

In a similar way, it is the absent presence of people who are no longer alive that archaeology legitimately concerns itself with. For, just as human beings are not *there* in the same way as mere objects, so their absence amounts to more than just nonoccurrence. We might say that what distinguishes archaeological remains is not their mere age but the way that their existence implies the having-been-there of past people (Heidegger 1996, 349). The forms, distribution, and traces of wear on ancient artifacts, and the configuration of spaces and architecture, explicitly refer to the former existence of people who have now vanished (Thomas 2007b, 17). This is why archaeological sites and finds have a haunted or uncanny quality: they continually point outside and beyond themselves to persons who are no longer there. As a number of authors have pointed out, archaeology often takes the form of a reoccupation of a site, in which one's actions in excavating features, and even one's bodily postures and movements, reiterate the unconsidered practices of past people, perhaps achieving an unusual kind of proximity to them (Edgeworth 2010, 59). The point that needs to be emphasized is that there is all the difference in the world between seeking out something that is not there and attending to an absent presence. To make inferential statements about the acts of past people on the basis of material traces that they have left behind is not the same as an act of pure imagination, although it may be just as creative. In this sense, archaeologists are just as much concerned with human presences as anthropologists are, although they achieve this in a rather different way, and arguably one that remains to be more thoroughly understood.

From Objectification to Conditionality

Turning from archaeological approaches to persons to anthropological approaches to things, it is notable that the principal theoretical framework within material culture studies concerns itself with the process of *objectification*. While this approach often resists the simple view that artifacts are the material embodiment of a preexisting idea, it nonetheless retains the notion of a dialectical movement between a subject and an object (Tilley 2006, 60). Although ideas, values, and social relations are understood as being brought into being in the same process that creates both material things and human subjects, it is arguable that any notion of objectification demands a distinction between an inner world of mind and an outer world of materials, even if this is one that emerges through a world-historical process. Indeed, Danny Miller's discussion of Hegel turns on the idea that the human subject externalizes some part of itself, which then stands opposed to it, before being consumed and reabsorbed. It is, in other words, grounded on the subject–object duality (Miller 1987, 20). The progressive differentiation of the object world and the elaboration of consciousness and reason are linked in a dynamic movement that gradually separates human beings from nature. Indeed, the argument conforms to some extent with the Enlightenment view that the use of independent reason, in which deliberation precedes action, is both the hallmark of higher creatures and the means by which human beings transform their own conditions of existence. As Karl Marx put it:

> A spider conducts operations that resemble those of the weaver, and a bee puts to shame many an architect in the construction of her cells. But what distinguishes the

worst architect from the best of bees is this, that the architect raises his structure in imagination before he erects it in reality. At the end of every labour-process we get a result that already existed in the imagination of the labourer at its commencement. (1970, 178)

This is what has come to be described as a "productionist metaphysics," which implies that meaning and significance are removed from the realm of things and concentrated in a cognitive domain. As a result, objectification studies generally identify the mind as the source of intelligibility and form, which are imposed onto inert materials (Cheah 1996, 109). Thus, for instance, Miller (1987, 57) describes the way in which the cultural order may be naturalized by mapping it onto the landscape and presents this as a form of objectification. Evidently, this cultural order must have some immaterial existence before the process of inscription takes place, and the conclusion must be that it inhabits an ethereal world of thought.

Wherever we revert to the model of an inner and an outer world, matter is relegated to the status of a substrate onto which form is imposed. And where thought and substance constitute separate realms, it is inevitable that the distinguishing characteristic of material things comes to be their representability within the mind. But an alternative approach is to understand material things as emerging out of the maker's engagement with materials, instead of conforming to any conceptual blueprint. This argument has been very effectively made by others (e.g., Heidegger 1993, 353; Ingold 2007) and encourages us to think not in terms of the relationship between matter and form but instead that between forces and materials. People do not act on the material world from a position of exteriority; they follow materials through a world in which they are themselves embedded (Ingold 2010, 96). These points are well taken, but for the purposes of this contribution I will concentrate on the way that materials are *discovered* through the process of making. In the modern West, materials for construction or manufacture are exhaustively characterized according to their thermal, tensile, and load-bearing properties; spatial dimensions; grain size; texture; and color. But this way of describing materials does not actually convey the way that we encounter them: we do not experience a series of separate kinds of sense data and force them together to create an rounded understanding of how things are. On the contrary, the isolation of the attributes of a substance or an object is a process of disaggregation, which is derived from a more holistic and less analytical understanding acquired in the course of everyday life (Vycinas 1969, 240). This listing of the qualities of materials is closely linked to standardization. Yet this is a very unusual situation, and for most of human history people will have become aware of what materials are like in an implicit way, in the course of making a pot out of clay, or carving a bowl out of wood. As well as being inexplicit and possibly not capable of being verbalized, this knowledge of materials is only a fragment of what might potentially be learned. So human practices reveal qualities of materials as they work them into forms, but much more remains occluded.

What we can take from this is the way that things can potentially disclose their own conditions of possibility: the circumstances to which they are indebted—in this case, the practices of making enable the capacities of a material to come forward, at an intuitive level. But, equally, material things can be the points of access for wider webs of conditionality. Vincent Vycinas (1969, 260) gives the example of the way that a loaf of bread, in its taste, color, and texture, speaks to us about the soil that that the grain was grown in and the weather conditions under which it ripened. We become aware of these connections that spin outward from the bread through breaking, smelling, and eating it: it informs us in an inconspicuous way. Similarly, we gather an understanding of tools and artifacts through using them, within a set of practices governed by a social context, and also from when they fail to do what we require of them, demanding that we attend to them in a more deliberative manner. Using a scythe to cut grass, we can learn something of the fashioning of the wooden handle, and the tree that it was cut from, and the casting of the metal blade, without having to ask explicit questions. But when the blade grows dull and needs to be sharpened, a different kind of knowledge is generated. By contrast, modern mass-produced artifacts often tell us rather less about the conditions that underlie them. Edwards (2005, 460) suggests that this is characteristic of a society organized for efficiency and productiveness: the objects that we use from day to day efface their own circumstances of making, and as a consequence they do not intrude on or disrupt the smooth and seamless progress of a life that does not encourage its own evaluation. In a sense, we might want to argue that what Marx has to say about the alienation of commodities under capitalism, and the way that the relationship between the object and its creator becomes obliterated, is only a subset of the way that the implicit relationality of things has been eroded in modernity.

The key point here is that the conditions and connections that stand behind any material thing are always-already there, awaiting discovery. Yet our expectations are colored by modern design practices, which involve isolating a series of abstract requirements that an artifact has to fulfill. These are generally cast as problems that need to be solved. This is a very unusual form of making, in which explicit problems are matched with devised attributes, and these are effectively bolted onto the thing. What all of this serves to obscure is that just as humans are not fleshly objects but dispersed presences, so things are "gatherings" of conditions; as Bruno Latour puts it, composites of energies, materials, and relations. Latour (2004, 236) goes on to say that material things are as much matters of concern as matters of fact. Glossing this, we could argue that it is the way that things *matter* to us that opens up their networks of conditionality. So, for instance, in building a house, we acquire an inconspicuous familiarity with the character of soil and subsoil, the direction and force of the wind, the proximity of water, the direction of the sunlight, the aesthetic qualities and workability of wood and stone, cob and thatch. As Heidegger would have it, things assemble a world for us, so long as we do not impose our abstract requirements on things, ordering and regimenting them for the sake of it. By implication, we enjoy a closer relationship with those things that allow us into their conditionality and open up a world to us.

What archaeology and anthropology share is that they are both attempts to achieve some kind of familiarity with worlds other than our own, even within our own immediate surroundings. It may be that the task of understanding the practices and meanings of other people will always be an incomplete one (Geertz 1983, 70). But whether we begin with people and their utterances, or with material things, what we are attempting to do is to explore the relational background, composed of conditions of possibility, which secures the intelligibility of entities and actions. In other words, our task is one of trying to make explicit what would be implicit to the inhabitants of other worlds. Obviously, this is achieved in rather different ways depending on whether it is undertaken through verbal testimony and participant observation, or by attending to the constitutive conditions of artifacts and architecture. But it is imperative to recognize that the distinction is not between an anthropology that deals with human beings who are physically there and an archaeology that is concerned with absence. Rather, we are simply addressing different modes of human presence and its dispersal.

Equally, it may be mistaken to imagine that archaeology is more distant from the human beings that it studies because of the temporal distance that separates us from particular past epochs. Artifacts recovered from an archaeological site refer to absent persons, and this absence is what constitutes their historicity (Heidegger 1996, 349). But they do not become progressively more historical as time goes on, just as the people themselves do not become more absent as the evidence becomes more ancient. We might want to argue that people from the Upper Paleolithic are more culturally distant from us and that it is consequentially more difficult to approach their world than that of, say, the ancient Romans. But it is surely an error to imagine that there is a direct "read-across" between chronology and human proximity. Irrespective of period, there are episodes of human life that are represented in the archaeological record in such a way as to afford some degree of access to a past horizon. Burials, hearths, knapping clusters, and kill sites document intimate moments of human presence with some degree of immediacy. Nonetheless, this kind of evidence is fraught with the danger of imposing ourselves on the past in a narcissistic fashion. When the archaeological record confronts us with traces that appear immediately accessible, the temptation is always to imagine that we can achieve some kind of empathy with very distant people. One alternative is to adopt a more "contemplative" approach, which seeks to acknowledge the difference of the past by letting it be itself (Karlsson 1998, 242). Just as in our dealings with objects and materials in the present, there will always be some aspects of the evidence that remain occluded.

Architecture in the Stonehenge Landscape

Hopefully, a brief example will serve to demonstrate the kind of approach to material things that has been advocated in this paper. Since 2004, the author has been involved in a field investigation of the prehistoric archaeology of Salisbury Plain, together with colleagues from five different U.K. universities, under the rubric of the Stonehenge Riverside Project (Parker Pearson et al. 2006). Much of the excavation work conducted by the project has been concentrated on the Late Neolithic (3000–2400 B.C.E.) monumental complex of Durrington Walls and Woodhenge, which has been demonstrated to have been connected by means of a pair of avenues and the River Avon to Stonehenge itself, three kilometers to the southwest. So, effectively, Stonehenge and Durrington represent a single, integrated structure, unified by a pattern of movement that involved passage over or through the river itself (Parker Pearson et al. 2009). At the eastern entrance of the great henge enclosure of Durrington Walls, my colleague Mike Parker Pearson has revealed a settlement of small houses of wattle-and-daub construction and with central hearths, which predate the bank and ditch of the monument (Parker Pearson 2007, 129). These appear to have been constructed and used over a relatively short period of time, which possibly coincided with construction at Stonehenge, and indicate episodes when large numbers of people were gathered in the vicinity of the monumental complex. The houses were clustered around the metaled avenue that connected the massive southern timber circle with the river. Small numbers of houses like those at the eastern entrance are found in various parts of Britain in the middle of the third millennium B.C.E., associated with Grooved Ware pottery. However, the only settlements anywhere near as large as that at Durrington are in the Orkney Islands, where essentially similar houses were rendered in stone (C. Richards 2005, 7).

In the western part of the interior of Durrington Walls, a geophysical survey revealed a series of small penannular enclosures arranged around a terrace overlooking the dry valley containing the southern timber circle (Thomas 2007a, 152). Contrary to expectations, when excavated, two of these were shown to contain small buildings very similar to those at the eastern entrance. However, each was surrounded by a timber palisade, as well as an enclosure ditch, and one was hidden behind a facade of enormous posts, which may have carried heavy lintels, the timber equivalent of the arrangement at Stonehenge (Figure 12.1). In contrast with the rather filthy houses at the eastern entrance, these more isolated structures had been kept very clean, with animal bones and pottery sherds apparently tidied up and buried in pits. Even the postholes and stakeholes of the buildings had not trapped loose fragments from the surface. One important contrast with the eastern entrance houses was the presence of four large postholes, presumably representing roof supports, surrounding the hearth at the center of each building. The evidence from these structures could be read as indicating that these were the dwellings of important or unusual people, or that they were cult houses or shrines, which nonetheless shared aspects of their construction with houses.

Finally, in the area immediately to the south of Durrington and Woodhenge, where a number of Early Bronze Age mortuary mounds were later constructed, Joshua Pollard excavated a series of large timber structures (Pollard 1995; Pollard and Robinson 2007). Each of these was composed of four enormous postholes, with

Figure 12.1 One of the Late Neolithic buildings inside the western enclosures at Durrington Walls (reconstruction by Aaron Watson).

an entrance marked by a pair of pits, which in some cases broke a surrounding palisade (Figure 12.2). Although these structures were clearly not roofed, their architectural similarities with the buildings in the western enclosures are obvious, although they emphasize some features of the latter and omit others. Revealingly, they also resemble the structure inside the nearby Coneybury Hill henge monument, the northern timber circle at Durrington, and the first phase of the southern timber circle that formed the enduring focus of the entire Durrington Walls complex and that arguably provides the wooden counterpart of the stone settings at Stonehenge (J. Richards 1990, 134; Wainwright and Longworth 1971, 23).

Given these similarities, it is obviously tempting to suggest that this whole architectural tradition was underlain by some form of structural grammar or cosmological order. But we can suggest instead that the creation of increasingly elaborate spatial forms involved a series of creative improvisations on the familiar theme of the domestic dwelling. Existing skills and know-how were drawn on in order to create spaces in which the sacred, the spirits, or the ancestors might manifest themselves. Conceivably, the structures south of Woodhenge were deliberately intended to recall those most durable elements of the western enclosures buildings that would have survived after they had fallen into disrepair: the four central roof supports and the surrounding palisade. On a colossal scale, these structures re-created an already ancient and decrepit house of the spirits. At a time when larger social groups were being consolidated in order to undertake projects such as the construction of Stonehenge, the notion of the household community and its sedimented history was being mobilized in order to provide a metaphor for sociality in general (Thomas 2010). Indeed, it is possible to argue that Stonehenge itself emerged from this same background of

Figure 12.2   One of the timber structures excavated by the Stonehenge Riverside Project to the south of Woodhenge. Photo: David Robinson.

habitual practices of working materials and familiar inhabited spaces, rather than suddenly appearing out of nothing, the resplendent idea of a Neolithic genius, or realizing the blueprint of some displaced Mycenaean architect (Pollard 2009).

Conclusion

Archaeology and anthropology both attend to human presences, although they do so in different ways, not least because they are concerned with very different modes in which those presences manifest themselves. Material things, and particularly arti-facts, are not mute and isolated entities but point to absent presences, which adhere to them in a variety of ways. While we can learn much from studying them in an ana-lytical fashion, we can also follow the network of connections in which they are im-plicated. This insight suggests that sociality extends through the material world and that objects are not merely the products or outcomes of activities and relationships between people that are otherwise metaphysical. Human beings and made things are the conditions of each other's possibility, and our shared task is to explore the condi-tionality of social life in the past and the present.

References

Adams, W. Y. 1998. *The philosophical roots of anthropology*. Stanford, CA: Center for the Study of Language and Information (CSLI).

Ascher, R. 1961. "Analogy in archaeological interpretation." *Southwestern Journal of Anthropology* 17: 317–25.

Binford, L. R. 1983. "Middle-range research and the role of actualistic studies." In *Working at archaeology*, by L. R. Binford, 411–22. New York: Academic.

Bonnichsen, R. 1973. "Millie's Camp: An experiment in archaeology." *World Archaeology* 4: 277–91.

Bowden, M. 1991. *General Pitt-Rivers*. Cambridge: Cambridge University Press.

Cheah, P. 1996. "Mattering." *Diacritics* 26: 108–39.

Childe, V. G. 1946. "Archaeology and anthropology." *Southwestern Journal of Anthropology* 2: 243–51.

Edgeworth, M. 2010. "On the boundary: New perspectives from ethnography and archaeology." In Garrow and Yarrow 2010, 53–68.

Edwards, J. C. 2005. "The thinging of the thing: The ethic of conditionality in Heidegger's later work." In *A companion to Heidegger*, ed. H. Dreyfus and M. Wrathall, 456–67. Oxford: Blackwell.

Fewster, K. 2001. "The responsibilities of ethnoarchaeologists." In *The responsibilities of archaeologists: Archaeology and ethics*, ed. M. Pluciennik, 65–73. Oxford: British Archaeological Reports s981.

Fowler, C. 2004. *The archaeology of personhood: An anthropological approach*. London: Routledge.

Garrow, D., and T. Yarrow, eds. 2010. *Archaeology and anthropology: Understanding similarity, exploring difference*. Oxford: Oxbow Books.

Geertz, C. 1983. " 'From the native's point of view': On the nature of anthropological understanding." In *Local knowledge: Further essays in interpretive anthropology*, by C. Geertz, 55–70. New York: Basic Books.

Gillespie, S. D., R. A. Joyce, and D. L. Nichols. 2003. "Archaeology is anthropology." In *Archaeology is anthropology*, ed. S. D. Gillespie and D. L. Nichols, 155–69. Arlington, VA: American Anthropological Association.

Gosden, C. 1999. *Anthropology and archaeology: A changing relationship*. London: Routledge.

Heidegger, M. 1993. "Building, dwelling, thinking." In *Martin Heidegger: Basic writings*, ed. D. F. Krell, 343–63. London: Routledge.

Heidegger, M. 1996. *Being and time*, trans. J. Stambaugh. Albany: State University of New York Press.

Henare, A., M. Holbraad, and S. Wastell. 2007. "Thinking through things." In *Thinking through things*, ed. A. Henare, M. Holbraad, and S. Wastell, 1–31. London: Routledge.

Hodder, I. R., ed. 1982. *Symbolic and structural archaeology.* Cambridge: Cambridge University Press.

Ingold, T. 2007. "Materials against materiality." *Archaeological Dialogues* 14: 1–16.

Ingold, T. 2010. "The textility of making." *Cambridge Journal of Economics* 34: 91–102.

Karlsson, H. 1998. *Re-thinking archaeology.* Gothenburg, Sweden: Gothenburg University.

Lane, P. 2006. "Present to past: Ethnoarchaeology." In *Handbook of material culture*, ed. C. Tilley, W. Keane, S. Küchler, M. Rowlands, and P. Spyer, 402–24. London: Sage.

Larsson, M., and M. Parker Pearson, eds. 2007. *From Stonehenge to the Baltic.* Oxford: British Archaeological Reports s1692.

Latour, B. 2004. "Why has critique run out of steam? Matters of fact and matters of interest." *Critical Inquiry* 30: 225–48.

Leach, E. 1977. "A view from the bridge." In *Archaeology and anthropology: Areas of mutual interest*, ed. M. Spriggs, 161–76. Oxford: British Archaeological Reports s19.

Lucas, G. 2010. "Triangulating absence: Exploring the fault-lines between archaeology and anthropology." In Garrow and Yarrow 2010, 28–39.

Malpas, J. 2006. *Heidegger's topology: Being, place, world.* Cambridge, MA: MIT Press.

Marx, K. 1970. *Capital.* Vol. 1. London: Lawrence and Wishart.

Miller, D. 1985. *Artefacts as categories: A study of ceramic variability in central India.* Cambridge: Cambridge University Press.

Miller, D. 1987. *Material culture and mass consumption.* Oxford: Blackwell.

Miller, D., ed. 1998. *Material cultures: Why some things matter.* London: University College London Press.

Munn, N. 1977. "The spatiotemporal transformations of Gawa canoes." *Journal de la Société des Océanistes* 54: 39–51.

Munn, N. 1986. *The fame of Gawa: A symbolic study of value transformation in a Massim (Papua New Guinea) society.* Durham, NC: Duke University Press.

Parker Pearson, M. 2007. "The Stonehenge Riverside Project: Excavations at the east entrance of Durrington Walls." In Larsson and Parker Pearson 2007, 125–44.

Parker Pearson, M., A. Chamberlain, M. Jay, P. Marshall, J. Pollard, C. Richards, J. Thomas, C. Tilley, and K. Welham. 2009. "Who was buried at Stonehenge?" *Antiquity* 83: 23–39.

Parker Pearson, M., J. Pollard, C. Richards, J. Thomas, C. Tilley, and K. Welham. 2006. "Stonehenge, its river and its landscape: Unravelling the mysteries of a prehistoric sacred place." *Archäologischer Anzeiger* 2006: 237–58.

Pollard, J. 1995. "The Durrington 68 timber circle: A forgotten Late Neolithic monument." *Wiltshire Archaeological and Natural History Magazine* 88: 122–25.

Pollard, J. 2009. "The materialisation of religious structures in the time of Stonehenge." *Material Religion* 5: 332–53.

Pollard, J., and D. Robinson. 2007. "A return to Woodhenge: The results and implications of the 2006 excavations." In Larsson and Parker Pearson 2007, 159–68.

Radcliffe-Brown, A. R. 1935. "On the concept of function in social science." *American Anthropologist* 37: 394–402.

Ray, K. 1987. "Material metaphor, social interaction and historical reconstructions: Exploring patterns of association and symbolism in the Igbo-Ukwu corpus." In *The archaeology of contextual meanings*, ed. I. Hodder, 66–77. Cambridge: Cambridge University Press.

Richards, C. C. 2005 *Dwelling among the monuments: The Neolithic village of Barnhouse, Maeshowe Passage Grave and surrounding monuments at Stenness, Orkney*. Cambridge, UK: McDonald Institute.

Richards, J. 1990. *The Stonehenge environs project*. London: English Heritage.

Spriggs, M. 2008. "Ethnographic parallels and the denial of history." *World Archaeology* 40: 538–52.

Stiles, D. 1977. "Ethnoarchaeology: A discussion of methods and applications." *Man* 12:87–103.

Thomas, J. S. 2007a. "The internal features at Durrington Walls: Investigations in the Southern Circle and Western Enclosures, 2005–6." In Larsson and Parker Pearson 2007, 145–58.

Thomas, J. S. 2007b. "The trouble with material culture." *Journal of Iberian Archaeology* 9/10: 11–23.

Thomas, J. S. 2010. "The return of the Rinyo-Clacton Folk? The cultural significance of the Grooved Ware complex in Later Neolithic Britain." *Cambridge Archaeological Journal* 20: 1–15.

Tilley, C. Y. 2006. "Objectification." In *Handbook of material culture*, ed. C. Y. Tilley, W. Keane, S. Kuechler, M. Rowlands, and P. Spyer, 60–73. London: Sage.

Vycinas, V. 1969. *Earth and gods: An introduction to the philosophy of Martin Heidegger*. The Hague: Martinus Nijhoff.

Wainwright, G. J., and I. Longworth. 1971. *Durrington Walls: Excavations 1966–1968*. London: Society of Antiquaries.

Yarrow, T. 2010. "Not knowing as knowing: Asymmetry between archaeology and anthropology." In Garrow and Yarrow 2010, 13–27.

Index

Aberdeen University, 85, 89

Africa, 4, 24, 25, 26, 43, 135, 137–41, 158, 160, 188

Agadjanian, A., 23

Agamben, G., 86–7

Alevis, 7, 10

Allaby, R., 66

Allen, N., 27

American Anthropological Association (AAA), 33

Anatolia, 4, 6, 7, 11, 22

Appadurai, A., 123, 181, 189

archaeology
    and ethnography, 65–76, 133–44, 219–32 passim
    and nationalism, 42–4
    and things, 119–32 passim
    history of, 1–14
    in North America, 133–35

archaeometry, 9, 14, 67, 74
    Journal of, 68

architecture, sacred, 91–132

Arendt, H., 70

Askew, K., 24

Asia, 23, 25, 54, 140, 146, 183

Aşıklı Höyük (excavations at), 69, 70

Association of Social Anthropologists (ASA), 5, 31, 33, 77, 88, 141, 173, 188–90, 212

Atalay, S., 69, 72

Athens, 2, 6, 8, 50, 56

Australia, 136, 140

Australian aborigines, 162

Avebury (excavations at), 134

Baha'is, 91–132

Balkans, the, 2, 6, 7, 8, 23

Bangkok, 46–61

Barnard, A., 27

Bartu, A., 72

Bektashis, 2, 7

Bender, B., 25, 181

Bernal, M., 44

Binford, L., 120, 175, 220

Bloch, M., 70, 73, 178, 182, 197, 199, 200

Boas, F., 219

bones, 11, 69, 128, 197–218, 227

Brand, S., 78–9

Britain, 1–15, 44, 67, 113, 133, 134, 145–68 passim, 176, 181, 227

British School at Athens, 2–3, 6–8

Bronze Age, 25, 30, 146, 168, 181, 227

Brown, B., 204, 206

Brown, K., 51

Buchli, V., 134, 197, 198, 202

Byzantium, 51, 53

Caesar, Julius, 52, 60, 148–61 passim

Cambridge University, 2, 6, 19, 31, 32, 38, 59, 133

Campbell. S., 10

Carr, E., 32

Çatalhöyük (excavations at), 10, 65–75

cattle, 69, 109, 138, 156, 158, 159

Caucasus, 23

Chapman, J., 5, 126

Childe, G., 9, 25, 26, 31, 32, 70, 219

China, 43

Christianity, 3, 6, 23, 32, 36, 52, 91, 97, 98, 102–3

Clark, G., 42

Cosmides, L., 82

Crete, 10, 50

culture, anthropological analysis of, 120

Cunliffe, B., 146, 148, 149, 153, 155, 162, 167, 168

Dale, G., 32

Darwin, C., 27, 31, 81–5